LB
1044.87
.T43
2002

Teaching & learning online
751091000312567

D0144106

Edited by **John Stephenson**

Teaching & Learning Online

Pedagogies for New Technologies

WITHDRAWN

NORTH ARKANSAS COLLEGE LIBRARY
1515 Pioneer Drive
Harrison, AR 72601

KOGAN
PAGE

PRO
LB
1044.87
.T43
2002

First published in 2001
Reprinted in 2002

Apart from any fair dealing for the purposes of research or private study, or criticism or review, as permitted under the Copyright, Designs and Patents Act, 1988, this publication may only be reproduced, stored or transmitted, in any form or by any means, with the prior permission in writing of the publishers, or in the case of reprographic reproduction in accordance with the terms and licences issued by the CLA. Enquiries concerning reproduction outside those terms should be sent to the publishers at the undermentioned addresses:

Kogan Page Limited
120 Pentonville Road
London
N1 9JN
UK

Stylus Publishing
22883 Quicksilver Drive
Sterling
VA 20166-2012
USA

© John Stephenson and named authors, 2001

The right of John Stephenson and the named authors to be identified as the authors of this work has been asserted by them in accordance with the Copyright, Designs and Patents Act 1988.

British Library Cataloguing in Publication Data

A CIP record for this book is available from the British Library.

ISBN 0 7494 3511 9

Typeset by Saxon Graphics Ltd, Derby
Printed and bound in Great Britain by Biddles Ltd, *www.biddles.co.uk*

Contents

Notes on contributors

Shirley Alexander is Professor of Learning Technologies at the University of Technology, Sydney where she is Director of the Institute for Interactive Media and Learning. Her activities are underpinned by research in student learning and focus on the appropriate use of new media technologies in higher education.

Kyriaki Anagnostopoulou is Learning Technologies Advisor in the Centre for Learning Development at Middlesex University. Her role encompasses collaborative initiatives aimed at promoting and supporting the pedagogically effective uptake of learning technologies.

Curtis J Bonk is Associate Professor in Educational Psychology as well as Instructional Systems Technology at Indiana University (IU) where he has received many teaching awards. He is a member of the Center for Research on Learning and Technology at IU and has published widely regarding online teaching and learning.

David Boud is Professor of Adult Education at the University of Technology, Sydney. He has wide experience of innovative approaches to teaching and assessment and has written extensively on work-based, experiential and autonomous learning.

Marion Coomey is a professor at Ryerson Polytechnic University in Toronto, Canada. She teaches courses in writing and production for radio and television journalists. Her doctoral research project (at Middlesex University) examines the effects of collaborative online learning on journalism students worldwide.

Richard Davis is a professor at California State University at Chico. He earned his doctorate in marketing. He has specialized in small business management and marketing research.

David Dickinson has a senior advisory role in the computer industry with interests in curriculum research. He provides advice and consultancy in the UK, mainland Europe and the United States. He has been a school misfit, engineer and teacher in an inner city environment.

Allan Ellis is an associate professor in the School of Social and Workplace Development at Southern Cross University in northern New South Wales, Australia. He teaches postgraduate courses in Adult Learning and Educational Technology and researches into networked learning technologies. He is the Founder and Chair of the AusWeb conference series.

Martin Good is Chairman of Cambridge Training and Development Ltd (CTAD), which has been developing educational resources for 20 years. Cambridge Training and Development specializes in adults with literacy and numeracy problems, and the development of professionals to help them with their learning.

Noriko Hara is currently a postdoctoral research fellow in the School of Information and Library Science in the University of North Carolina. Her research agenda includes communities of practice, online learning and science communication. She also designs, develops and evaluates educational Web sites.

Stewart Hase is a psychologist and a senior lecturer in the School of Social and Workplace Development at Southern Cross University in northern New South Wales, Australia, with an interest in work-based learning and using education to develop more adaptable citizens.

Barry Jackson is Director of Learning Development at Middlesex University, where he is responsible for leading the development and implementation of the university's strategy for improving learning and teaching. The strategy includes the development of pedagogically appropriate online learning for students.

Jamie Kirkley has taught online since 1997 and is completing her dissertation on student collaboration in an online problem-based learning unit at Indiana University. She manages the development of the Learning to Teach with Technology Studio, a Web-based professional development system for K-12 teachers.

Sisko Mällinen is a senior lecturer at Lahti Polytechnic, Finland, with 20 years of teaching experience. She has spent the last two years developing online education and is currently a postgraduate student at the University of Tampere, Finland (Licenciate/PhD degree in Education).

Robin Mason is Professor of Educational Technology within the Institute of Educational Technology at the UK Open University. She is Director of the Masters Programme in Open and Distance Education, a global Web-based programme of courses about the theory and practice of distributed learning.

Terry Mayes is Head of Learning and Educational Development at Glasgow Caledonian University. Previously, he was a lecturer in cognitive psychology at the University of Strathclyde, Research Manager of the Scottish Human-

Computer Interaction Centre and Director of Research in the Institute for Computer-Based Learning at Heriot-Watt University.

Maya Milankovic-Atkinson is Programme Leader for the Middlesex University MSc Business Information Technology Distance Learning. She worked in ICL Ltd for three years as systems engineer, followed by 17 years in higher education with interests in curriculum development and innovation.

Alan Murphy is Director of Curriculum, Learning and Quality in the School of Computing Science at Middlesex University. He instigated the distance-learning programmes in the Global Campus project and was responsible for developing the ideas of local Learning Resource Centres.

Ron Oliver lectures in communications and multimedia at Edith Cowan University in Western Australia. He has broad experience in the design, development and evaluation of multimedia and computer-based learning materials. His current activities involve the development and evaluation of effective online learning environments.

Vanessa Paz Dennen is an assistant professor of Educational Technology at San Diego State University. She has been researching online instruction and teaching online since 1997, and works with other faculty in designing learning activities and promoting online collaboration among learners in their Web-based courses.

Steve Pollock works at the BBC. He was Head of Learning Support, the department responsible for successful educational campaigns such as Computers Don't Bite and Webwise. He was advisor to the University for Industry on the future of learning through broadcasting and learning online.

Chris Sadler is the Academic Development Manager for the Global Campus project at Middlesex University. He has lectured in computer science for 17 years and has been a software development manager for five.

Dennis Schlais is a professor at California State University at Chico. He earned his doctorate in finance. His extended areas of study are simulations and active learning with Web-based pedagogy.

Keith Shaw is an independent consultant in e-learning and technology-based training. He began developing computer-based learning material in 1972 while teaching in schools and universities. In 1982, he founded a company to develop technology-delivered training solutions, which he managed for 15 years.

David Squire acts as a new media and learning consultant for the BBC. He set up desq in 1998, and now works with broadcasters and educators to bridge the gap between education and new media.

John Stephenson is Professor and Head of the International Centre for Learner Managed Learning at Middlesex University and advisor to the UK University for Industry on pedagogical aspects of online work-based learning. He was previously Director of Higher Education for Capability.

Valerie Stewart is an industrial psychologist with a background in science and psycholinguistics. She specializes in mapping personality and cognition and has put Kelly's repertory grid onto an interactive platform. She has been a visiting professor at the University of Cape Town and is the author of eight books.

Jef van den Branden is Educational Director of EuroPACE and LINOV (Leuven Institute for Innovative Learning). He is currently involved in EUNITE (European Universities Network for IT in Education). He has studied educational technology at K U Leuven, Belgium.

Quentin Whitlock is joint Managing Director of Dean Interactive Ltd and a partner in Dean Associates. He has been involved in training technology for many years in both the business and academic fields with a particular interest in technology-based and interactive multimedia.

Mark Woodman is Professor of Information Technology at Middlesex University where he initiated the development of the University's Global Campus materials. He has over 20 years experience of distance education and won awards at the Open University from the British Computer Society and the Design Council.

Introduction

Scope

For the purposes of this book, 'teaching and learning online' refers to electronic means of distributing and engaging with learning — typically via the Internet and related electronic media services. It does not attempt to cover the much longer tradition of educational television and radio or the use of telephone-supported distance learning. It includes broadcasting in so far as it is part of the overall Internet scenario. Throughout the book we refer to 'online learning' as shorthand for the full process of teaching and learning online on the assumption that all teaching activity is aimed at learning. It is not assumed by any of the authors that online learning will exist entirely without interaction between teachers and learners or between learners and learners. Neither is it assumed that it will replace existing schooling or campus-based learning, although it might significantly affect how formal teaching is organized. However, it is assumed that online learning will meet the needs of many for whom conventional education is inappropriate or unavailable, supplement the range of learning opportunities for those currently in educational institutions, change the relationships between teacher and learner and significantly enhance the reach of learning throughout the community.

The trend to 'online anything'

It is not difficult to see why governments, educational administrators and companies are enthusiastic about exploiting the potential of the Internet and Web-based online learning. Online learning offers the prospect of direct delivery of learning to existing learners, and to groups traditionally excluded by personal circumstances from institutional learning, coupled with assumed economies of scale. There is also the bonus – especially for governments and companies – that the use of online learning will generally promote greater proficiency in information technology (IT) skills with assumed spinoffs in personal employability and corporate competitiveness. Many teachers are attracted by the scope the medium offers for experimentation with the design of materials and, for a growing number of potential learners, online *anything* is becoming a preferred way of communicating with friends, accessing entertainment, surfing for information, banking and electronic purchasing. Computer usage in the First World is rising rapidly, echoing previous technical innovations such as television and video recorders. In the United Kingdom, for instance, computer warehouses are already regular features of retail parks and prime-time television advertising campaigns.

The trend to 'online anything' is powerful and difficult to resist. Education is part of that trend. But does it really amount to anything other than doing what was previously done but doing it faster, on a greater scale and for more people? Economies of scale and wider access are, of course, desirable in themselves, but does the medium add value to the learning experience? Is there anything about the medium that suggests that a new educational pedagogy is emerging – one that has something positive to offer teachers and learners alike? If it is not a new paradigm of learning, does online learning make existing approaches more effective?

Many commentators have observed that much online learning appears to have been developed because it was possible, technically, to do so and without explicit reference to any pedagogical principles. This has produced some interesting and stimulating learning materials but in the main it has produced much of what could best be described as electronic page turning. Moreover, there is little systematic research evidence on which to judge the overall effectiveness of the medium. The medium itself is too young for any satisfactory evaluative longitudinal study to have been completed and is still evolving rapidly. Nevertheless, the drive towards 'online anything' is persuading institutions, companies and governments to invest heavily in the new medium confident that the benefits will justify the costs.

An expert seminar

After more than a decade of rapid development, most of it since 1997, what have we learnt about the new medium? What works and what does not work? With this in mind, the International Centre for Learner Managed Learning (ICLML) at Middlesex University, London, United Kingdom invited a number of people with substantial expertise or experience of different aspects of online learning to come together to share their experience and to formulate, if possible, guidance or advice for dissemination amongst those seeking to develop the medium further. To our surprise, people came from Australia, Belgium, Canada, Finland, Italy and the United States, as well as from across the United Kingdom. Still more satisfying was the fact that we were able to attract a mix of specialists, including academics, programme managers, materials designers and commercial producers.

The book

Participants were asked to circulate a paper to all participants beforehand and to rewrite their paper following the issues raised in the seminar. This book is a selection of some of the items to emerge from this process. The chapters have been arranged into six parts according to their general theme. Each author addresses the issue of online pedagogy from a different starting point. Part 1 begins with the academics whose main interest is the pedagogy itself. Part 2 contains two items focused on the growing volume of case study research and evaluations of particular systems, each of which draws on the research evidence in formulating observations on pedagogical issues. Part 3 presents the experience of practitioners with substantial experience of running online courses, and who are also able to discuss the pedagogical aspects of their work. Part 4 contains reports from practitioners describing the challenges of introducing online learning into traditional institutional environments. Part 5 presents the views of commercial designers and producers who have the job of converting educators' aspirations into practical and commercial reality, often without direct guidance on the pedagogical issues involved. The final section, Part 6, is more future orientated. It contains a review of the emerging knowledge society and some of the new technical breakthroughs in broadcasting systems and software design that are certain to have an impact on the scope and style of online learning in the immediate future. The book concludes with an endpiece composed by the editor after reviewing the full content of the seminar papers, looking for pointers on the pedagogical way forward.

The continuing debate

Details of the original ICLML seminar are posted on the ICLML Web site (http://www.iclml.mdx.ac.uk/TLonline). The site contains extracts from some of the debate at the seminar as well as comments submitted by visitors to the site. Readers of this book are invited to visit the site and contribute online to the debate on online teaching and learning.

Part 1

From theory to practice:
the academics

The main focus of the items in Part 1 is pedagogical, not operational, although each chapter is grounded in some practical experience of online learning. The authors review the challenges and opportunities of online learning from their own distinctive pedagogical perspectives. Alexander and Boud take an *experiential* view of learning, arguing that online learning is, in itself, a misnomer. It is more appropriate to see online learning as a tool or support for learning that will substantially take place offline. Mayes presents a strong case for a *constructivist* view of education and sees ways in which well-constructed online learning can sustain such an approach. Hase and Ellis argue that learning as a whole should be much more *learner managed* even than conventional distance learning. They further argue that online learning has the capacity, if used appropriately, to help bring it about. The authors of all three items share the view that, without careful structuring, online learning is likely to replicate the pedagogical stance of its designers and users.

1

Learners still learn from experience when online

Shirley Alexander and David Boud
University of Technology, Australia

Editor's introduction

Alexander and Boud argue that much of the potential for online learning is being lost because too much of the pedagogy of online learning has been transferred unreflectively from didactic traditional teaching where the computer substitutes for the teacher and textbook as conveyor of information. A more productive approach is to regard online learning as an example of learning from experience using a new medium and access to new resources. The authors draw on work about how learners learn from complex experience and show how these ideas can be used to conceptualize opportunities and constraints in online learning. Five propositions about learning from experience are illustrated with examples of how online learning can be used to facilitate rich experiences beyond those available in other media.

Over the last two decades there has been a steady rollout of new information technologies such as multimedia-capable computers, the ever-increasing power of which is accompanied by a reduced cost. More recently, the rapid growth of the Internet has resulted in enthusiastic claims for technology's ability to provide high-quality education for all. This combination of factors has created a climate in which investors and entrepreneurs have identified online learning as a major market area of the future. In many cases the predictions for growth are accompanied by claims that the technologies will lead to 'revolutions in learning' and those revolutions are often attributed to the particular information and communication technologies (ICT) themselves.

The rise of the new technologies has coincided with a crisis of confidence in traditional education and increasing demands for higher and continuing education that have not been able to be adequately met by institutions constrained by years of public sector financial stringency and regulation. Information and communication technology has been looked to as providing solutions to a wide variety of problems.

The use of ICT in learning

There is no doubt that the physical environment has a surprisingly powerful influence on teaching. The lecture theatre makes possible certain forms of large-group presentation; the overhead projector makes possible the presentation of text and images to all those in the room, and the networked computer makes access possible to a vast range of digitized information. The environment makes some activities possible and constrains others but it does not change the fundamental processes of human learning. Students still need to actively engage with what is to be learnt; they still have to have ways of expressing their understanding if they are to be confident that they have learnt and they need to feel that what they are doing is worthwhile.

However, in the most basic sense, the online learning environment is just another physical environment: more complex than some others, but a new space for teaching and learning. Technology itself does not improve learning (Alexander and McKenzie, 1998). Its use makes possible some kinds of activity (such as one-to-one communication with many different people) and limits others (such as spontaneous spoken conversation). Until recently it has been seen by many educational practitioners as an alien environment in which those with an interest in teaching and learning in non-digitized environments (that is, most teachers and educational developers) are somehow deskilled and rendered unable to contribute effectively to the discussions about the new medium. With some notable exceptions, developments have often been driven by those wanting to explore the limits of technology rather than understanding how it influences learning.

Acceptance of the online environment as just another space for learning does not deny its potential to reconceptualize what is possible in teaching and learning. We observe that it has generally failed to do this so far. Online learning has been far more successful in eliminating the limitations of time and space for learning transactions with origins in face-to-face and text-to-text encounters.

In this chapter we argue that greater acknowledgement should be given to the fact that most of what we know about teaching and learning is applicable in all learning environments, including online. We further argue that, given the nature of the medium, it is particularly productive to view online learning as examples of students' learning from experience. The ideas on which we draw are represented in two previous projects. The first is collaboration between the second author and a group of educators who were interested in making sense of how we learn from complex experience. This resulted in the books *Using Experience for Learning* (Boud, Cohen and Walker, 1993) and *Working with Experience: Animating learning* (Boud and Miller, 1996). The second is an evaluation study undertaken by the first author in which she was commissioned to undertake a national study on how the use of information technologies in universities benefits student learning. The subsequent report *An Evaluation of Information Technology Projects for University Learning* (Alexander and McKenzie, 1998) was the first study that investigated how the large number of projects supported by an Australian government funding agency were or were not contributing to learning.

Our interests lay in the ways in which learners approach learning tasks, the conceptions they have about what they are doing and the factors that influence learning in complex environments. We intend to draw upon what we know about learning from experience to illuminate some of the issues involved in online learning and to suggest that it is helpful to conceptualize online learning as a process of students learning from experience. We start with some observations about early uses of online learning and proceed to examine more recent ideas.

Opportunities for online learning

Much of the early use of the Internet in teaching has been to automate existing practices in a way that appears 'up-to-date' but which is essentially a more time-consuming and expensive way of reproducing existing (and often ineffective) practices. The reproduction of lecture notes on a Web site, for example, when coupled with an automated version of multiple choice questions to test the students' ability to memorize the material, has been a popular early method of 'teaching online'.

E-lectures

The teaching strategy that has been used for centuries is lecturing – an expert telling groups of students what they should know. Attempts to describe the learning that results from the teacher's actions have resulted in descriptions of the very different reactions and responses that students have (see, for example, Ramsden, 1992).

Some lecturers have attempted to break down this one-way method of communication by using various techniques such as buzz-groups so that students have an opportunity to discuss and compare their understandings with others but, by and large, students spend most of their time listening and writing notes. The effectiveness of this technique has been reported as not being as great as many obviously assume given the popularity of this technique (Bligh, 2000).

The news about lectures is not all bad, however. They can have an impact in stimulating and motivating student interest in a subject. A teacher's personal enthusiasm for a subject can be transmitted through non-verbal behaviours such as eye contact with students, voice projection, body language and story telling. Students can be stimulated by seeing and hearing a person talking about what excites him or her, and provoked by observing an expert showing or demonstrating alternative ways of thinking about problems. This physical presence of the lecturer who uses a variety of communication strategies conveys to students that what they are learning is not something that is disembodied, but something that is humanized. Lecturers who rarely, if ever, use these techniques invariably receive poor feedback from students.

Despite what we know about effective and ineffective lecturing, much of what is passed off as 'online learning' or 'e-learning' is little more than lectures that are delivered online in the form of text, audio and/or video. E-lectures have been described by Harasim *et al* (1995: 125) as a way of 'providing a crucial concept or technique that students need to be able to apply to a problem or discussion'. In the case of text and audio-delivered lectures, gone are many of the motivational aspects of the teacher's physical presence as described above and their ability to respond to the cues presented by a live audience. There is, however, some potential added value in online learning such as that described by Paulsen (1995) who notes the particular advantage of providing the opportunity for guest experts from around the globe to contribute to a class by posting excerpts of articles, statements and so on.

Despite their potential for stimulation, lectures and their electronic form (e-lectures) are clearly regarded as a way for students to be exposed to a body of information. The over-emphasis of knowledge transmission characteristic of the conventional lecture-based courses is often reproduced in new media. As has been noted above, the delivery of information *per se* does not promote the kind of learning outcomes that constitute a university education where independent thought, reflection and abstraction are valued. It is critical, therefore, for learning designers to provide activities to facilitate students' engaging with and making sense of that content. These complementary activities should provide opportunities for students to find a bridge between what they already know, and that which they have read, heard or seen in the e-lecture. Students need opportunities to reflect on the ways in which their individual understanding aligns with that of the lecturers, and the ways in which it is different. Without such activities, learners may attempt to simply memorize information contained in the lecture so they can reproduce it in examinations or other assessment activities but be unable to use it.

The activities should also provide opportunities for students to actively construct their own understanding of the subject matter. We know that learning is never a passive act. It involves active construction and reconstruction of ideas and experience, usually through a range of carefully designed activities by a teacher who not only has expert knowledge of the content area, but also knows about the ways in which students come to understand that content (Laurillard, 1993). Designing these activities is one of the most important roles undertaken by teachers. To abrogate that role to the student, as occurs when e-lectures are used in isolation from other activities, is to deny the important professional role of the teacher and place a greater burden on individual learners than they are able to carry.

Finally, the complementary activities should promote the social construction of understanding. E-lectures, in isolation of other activities, do not facilitate the important discussion in which the learners' own experiences are interpreted and tested against those of others, resulting in the construction and reconstruction of ideas and meaning.

Learning from experience

Before proceeding to look at what we regard as more productive uses of online learning, we will consider what is known about learning from experience. Learning from experience is neither a special activity nor one that needs to be facilitated by others. It is what human beings do all the time throughout their lives. It can be useful, therefore, to examine formal teaching and learning activities from the perspective of what we know about learning from experience. This enables us both to see some of the ways in which this understanding has been ignored and how learning events can be redesigned to make them more effective experiences for those involved.

The earlier study identified five propositions about learning from experience that have informed a vast array of rich educational practice in the non-digitized world (Boud, Cohen and Walker, 1993). These are:

- *Experience is the foundation of, and the stimulus for, learning.* All learning builds on what has gone before. A new experience is understood in terms of what is already known. The desire to learn emerges from the experience of the learner, either arising from an existing commitment or from the challenge of a new situation.
- *Learners actively construct their own experience.* Learning is never a passive

act. It involves active construction and reconstruction of ideas and experience. Only the trivial or the fragmentary can be learnt by rote and even then there can be considerable expenditure of effort on the part of the learner. Learning can be enjoyable and engaging, but only when the learner is substantially involved.

- *Learning is a holistic process.* Learning, even of academic subjects, is never solely a cognitive endeavour. It involves the emotions and the will. A focus on one to the exclusion of others creates a partial and impoverished experience. Satisfaction derives from engaging as a whole person.

- *Learning is socially and culturally constructed.* Learning does not occur in isolation. Peers influence it, by social and cultural expectations and by what is accepted by the community as legitimate outcomes. In order to learn we all need interventions from outside ourselves whether these are the direct influence of others or their indirect influence transmitted through learning resources.

- *Learning is influenced by the socio-emotional context in which it occurs.* Learning does not occur in isolation and it is not a purely intellectual enterprise even when dealing with academic subjects. The extent to which we can sustain learning over time is a function of the emotional and personal support we can gain from others. The extent to which we are motivated to learn depends as much on the context of learning as it does on intrinsic interest in the object of study.

Realizing the potential of interactivity

In contrast to the automation of transmission modes of learning, characteristic of e-lectures, other practitioners have seen the Internet not as a tool primarily for the dissemination of content (the automation of books, papers and so forth) but as one to facilitate communication between students, and between students and their teachers. The emergence of online learning strategies such as computer conferencing, including online debates and role-play/simulations, foregrounds communication between people as a critical component of learning that is afforded by the use of the Internet. These and other online teaching and learning strategies will be examined below from the experiential learning perspective.

In the next section we review a number of activities that 'afford' behaviours that generate learning. These build on the idea developed by Laurillard *et al* (1999) that it is not sufficient for multimedia learning resources to permit a range of uses, some of which might be highly efficacious. Affordances for learning must be explicitly designed into resources to ensure that they are used in ways that prompt the kinds of learning for which they were created. The notion of affordances is the analogue of what skilled and experienced teachers do to engage learners in those aspects of the curriculum that will have the most impact on their learning. We review the design features of activities that encourage students to build on what they already know, to actively construct and reconstruct their ideas and experience through reflection and interaction with peers so that they use and extend the information transmitted in the e-lectures. These activities include a range of activities that are collectively referred to as *computer conferences*.

Computer conferencing

Hiltz (1995: 101) defines a class conference as 'an exchange of ideas and information'. Harasim *et al* (1995: 19) refer to computer conferencing as being 'based on the concept that software facilities can be built into the computer to allow groups to coordinate and organize the material in a manner appropriate to their communication objective'. The range of activities within the paradigm of the computer conference range from small- or large-group online discussions, online debates, and role-play/simulations.

The learning that results from a computer conference depends much more on the skills of the moderator rather than, as is often implied, on the number of features present in the particular conferencing software tool used. Many authors (for example Mason, 1991; Salmon, 2000; Harasim *et al*, 1995) have emphasized the critical role of the moderator in organizing the conferences and in affording online socialization and networking amongst the conference participants, at the same time as they maintain their critical intellectual role. We seek here to add to that discussion, by articulating the important role of the moderator in designing and facilitating learning activities that assist learners to learn from experience. We believe that the key features of online learning which enhance learning from experience include the following:

- establishment of a climate for learning that values the learner;
- active engagement with problems and challenges;
- interactivity and responsiveness;
- simulation of rich environments;
- peer discussion.

Some of the best examples of online learning draw their inspiration from face-to-face experiential learning events and take the notion of learning from experience into new dimensions. Good examples of this include online debates and the use of simulations and role-plays for learning.

Online debates

In online debates, students typically form groups of six, half of whom take the affirmative, and the other half the negative side of a debate. The teacher puts forward a topic such as 'the life and death of Princess Diana was a distraction from more important things'. Each team has access to a private shared workspace in which they put together their opening statements, rebuttals and closing statements. Each of these documents must be posted to the conferencing system by pre-specified dates, and each piece of work is allocated a word limit to correspond to the time limit of a traditional debate. Teams are graded on the quality of their arguments and responses.

Our interest is in the ways in which learners approach these activities. What conceptions do they have about what they are doing and what factors influence their learning in this complex environment? What are the design features of online debates that encourage students to engage in the kinds of activities that encourage learning from experience?

The design features of an online debate to afford learning from experience include the ideas that:

- Learners' participation in a debate requires an active role as they reflect on their own understanding and experiences to develop an individual meaning of the debate topic and of the particular side of the debate the individual's group has been assigned.

- Where learners find that the side of the debate they have been assigned is at odds with their own perspective, the act of formulating and articulating a counterargument challenges them to reflect on commonalities and differences and may in fact result in a transformation of their own view.

- Group work affords the possibility of learners' sharing of their individual perspectives, often causing individuals to reconstruct their own understanding in the light of other interpretations.

- Preparation (and subsequent posting) of a group's opening statements exposes and challenges individual assumptions as the group of learners works toward a shared understanding and meaning of the topic.

- Reading the opposing group's arguments causes reflection and reconstruction of both individual and group understandings.

- Posting of statements of rebuttal is a public record of a group's understanding and hence provides an engaging and motivational context for the activity.

Despite the best intentions of the teacher, learners may experience online debates in different ways as the first author found when using an online debate to promote understanding about online learning of a group of adult educators. The adult educators were interviewed by a visiting colleague about their experiences of the online debate and reported the following:

- Some of the learners had no prior experience of debates, did not under-stand the genre of debate, and spent more time worrying about what they should do than in thinking through their own perspective on the topic.

- One learner had major technical difficulties in connecting to the Internet and was not able to participate in the online group discussion.

- In one group there was little or no sharing of understanding and meaning – rather, the tasks were divided up such that one learner collected the relevant information, another formulated the argument, and another did the typing and conversion of the documents to HTML.

- Some students reported feeling uncomfortable with the genre of debate as they were loathe to criticize the arguments of others.

- The constraint of meeting deadlines for posting of rebuttals resulted in some students not having the time to reflect upon the arguments and hence not having time to reconstruct their own understandings.

Hence, some of the very features that were designed as affordances of learning from experience, in fact became disruptions to learning. Subsequent iterations of the online debate design have continued to evolve to minimize the disruptions and maximize the learning opportunities. This illustrates an important point. What may be regarded as affordances by the course designer need to be tested empirically to ensure that they actually have the desired intent. Without this they cannot be regarded as affordances.

Role-plays and simulations

Role-plays and simulations provide opportunities for students to enact their theoretical knowledge in a close-to-real-world situation. Students work alone or in groups to assume the role of a person who is significant in the particular situation. They need to understand how the person whose role they are playing thinks and acts so they can respond in character to the simulated scenario.

The design features of role-play/simulations to afford learning from expe-rience include the ideas that:

- Learners become immersed in as authentic an experience as is possible and this context provides the stimulus for learning.
- Learners use a variety of sources to collect information on which to construct an individual perspective on the character/role they are playing, and then reconstruct it during meetings with other group members where individual perspectives are challenged and influenced by those of others as events unfold. There is genuine interaction between students who communicate matters to each other in role.
- Learners build on their own understanding of the topic by acting out their role and constantly rebuilding that understanding after receiving feedback on their actions.
- Learners continually reflect on their goals, the actions they took and the feedback they received as a result of their actions.

One example of this strategy is the Middle East politics simulation reported by Vincent and Shepherd (1998) and Alexander and McKenzie (1998). As noted in the former, the aims of the simulations were to:

- introduce students to the facts of Middle East politics;
- give them experience with the complexities of negotiation and decision making in 'real' political systems;
- improve their skills in using computer technology and the Internet as tools for the workplace.

Students were located in institutions in different countries. They were formed into small groups of between two and four students. Each group was assigned the role of a unique character or identity, of a person (or organization) that might be involved in a Middle Eastern situation. The group studies the person in order to understand their character's culture, political agenda and connections: what influences their thinking and speech, what decisions they are likely to make or to support, as well as who their enemies and supporters are likely to be. The role-play had three distinct phases – preparation of the role profile, the simulation exercise and a post-simulation conference.

Groups were formed locally, so most students met face-to-face to discuss and prepare their role profile. The online role play provided the focus for learning, but much of the students' learning took place offline in a variety of settings.

After approximately two weeks the role profiles were placed on the Web for perusal by other groups. The moderator then released a 'scenario' – a hypothetical situation that may occur in the Middle East. Each group used e-mail to respond to the various issues involved in each scenario in a way that advanced the status of the character they were playing.

This role-play took place over a period of three weeks, and concluded with a live international teleconference at which the various characters met in real time to discuss the issues that developed through their negotiations around the given scenario. As reported by Vincent and Shepherd (1998), debriefing takes the form of group preparation of a final report in which they reflect on their approach to the scenario, and on what they have learnt about Middle East politics, international relations and diplomacy from the simulation.

In practice, however, not all groups function in a way which promotes the kind of active learning described above. As noted in Alexander and McKenzie (1998: 79) some groups reported difficulties in reaching compromises, and others recognized the need for more diplomacy within the group. An uneven workload was reported by other groups, signifying a less-than-ideal socio-emotional context for learning. Clearly, support of group processes is an important role for the moderator of activities such as this one.

Students reported a high degree of engagement and motivation during the simulation. One student, for example, set his alarm at several time periods during the night so he could see what was happening. Another reported that her entire family became engaged in the daily activities with family dinner conversations revolving around what happened in the Middle East today, and several reported the simulation as having 'taken over their lives'. There was evidence of the kind of systems thinking the moderator was trying to encourage. One student described his approach to the simulations as:

> you have to be careful what you decide, what effects it's going to have upon the region and you have to know what's happening in other parts – like if you're on the border and there are problems or conflicts or whatever...
> (Alexander and McKenzie, 1998: 75)

We have included this example, not only because it is a good example of the use of online learning that exemplifies the propositions about learning from experience identified earlier. It is also a contemporary example of a face-to-face simulation that the second author experienced over 25 years before and that had such a powerful effect on him that it has influenced the way in which he has viewed international conflicts ever since.

The power of role-play and simulation translates to the online medium, but it permits new dimensions to be explored in ways that were impractical in a face-to-face workshop. These include:

• Involvement of students from different countries in a common activity online meant that their cultural practices could be examined as part of the experience.

- The simulation could take place at times that suited participants rather than all being present at an intensive weekend. Because it was extended over time the simulation was 'slowed down' thus permitting those running the activity more opportunity to intervene to deal with problems as they arose.
- The text-based nature of the simulation provides a high degree of anonymity for students, where the sense of ego is different from that of face-to-face encounters.

Conclusions

In a short chapter it is only possible to touch upon the range of possible online learning activities. We believe that it can be fruitful to examine each from the point of view of how they prompt learning and the extent to which the propositions about learning from experience are exemplified in them. New ideas, such as that of affordances, are being developed to assist in interrogating programs using new media from a learning perspective, and these in turn can prove useful in examining learning opportunities in conventional settings.

The irony of taking a learning-centred perspective on these new opportunities is that this focuses us strongly on what the teacher/educational designer needs to do to maximize students' learning from experience. This focus on what the teacher is doing to enable learning may be seen to be contrary to current rhetoric surrounding student-centred learning, which focuses on what students do to the exclusion of what the teacher is doing. There is a vital role for pedagogy that is in danger of being neglected in the rush to make all things possible in the open environment of the Internet.

Learning does not occur in isolation and it is not a purely intellectual enterprise even when dealing with academic subjects. The extent to which we can sustain learning over time is a function of the emotional and personal support we can gain from others. The extent to which we are motivated to learn depends as much on the context of learning as it does on intrinsic interest in the object of study. Providing an opportunity for students is only part of the real challenge – an experience without feedback and reflection is a somewhat empty experience.

References

Alexander, S and McKenzie, J (1998) *An Evaluation of Information Technology Projects for University Learning*, Committee for University Teaching and Staff Development and the Department of Employment, Education, Training and Youth Affairs, Canberra

Bligh, D A (2000) *What's the Use of Lectures?*, Jossey-Bass, San Francisco.

Boud, D, Cohen, R and Walker, D (1993) Understanding learning from experience, in Boud, D, Cohen, R and Walker, D (eds) *Using Experience for Learning*, SRHE and Open University Press, Buckingham, pp 1–17.

Boud, D and Miller, N (1996) *Working with Experience: Animating learning*, Routledge, London.

Freeman, M (1998) Videoconferencing: a solution to the multi campus large classes problem?, *British Journal of Educational Technology*, **29** (3), pp 197–210.

Harasim, L, Hiltz, S R, Teles, L and Turoff, M (1995) *Learning Networks: A field guide to teaching and learning online*, The MIT Press, Cambridge, MA.

Hiltz, S R (1995) *The Virtual Classroom: Learning without limits via computer networks*, Ablex Publishing Corporation, Norwood, NJ.

Laurillard, D (1993) *Rethinking University Teaching: A framework for the effective use of educational technology*, Kogan Page, London.

Laurillard, D, Stratfold, M, Luckin, R, Plowman, L and Taylor, J (1999) Affordances for learning in a non-linear narrative medium, *Journal of Interactive Media in Education*, http://www-jime.open.ac.uk/99/laurillard/

Mason, R (1991) *Moderating Educational Computer Conferencing*, http://www.emoderators.com/papers/mason.html

Paulsen, M F (1995) *The Online Report on Pedagogical Techniques for Computer-Mediated Communication*, http://www.hs.nki.no/ morten/cmcped.htm

Ramsden, P (1992) *Learning to Teach in Higher Education*, Routledge, London.

Salmon, G (2000) *E-Moderating: The key to teaching and learning online*, Kogan Page, London.

Vincent, A and Shepherd, J (1998) Experiences in teaching Middle East politics via Internet-based role-play simulations, *Journal of Interactive Media in Education*, **98** (11), http://www-jime.open.ac.uk/98/11

2

Learning technology and learning relationships

Terry Mayes
Glasgow Caledonian University, UK

Editor's introduction

In this chapter, Mayes argues that before adopting any new educational technology we should first clarify the pedagogical basis on which we wish to proceed. The emerging pedagogical consensus, he argues, is around constructivism – collaborative learning, authentic tasks, reflection and dialogue – and the promotion of identities and learning communities. The most effective educational way of using online technology, therefore, is to focus on supporting the learner's involvement in collaboration, authentic tasks, reflection and dialogue, and to do so in a way which addresses issues of identity and community. Mayes explores these concepts in some depth, describes three levels of courseware and reports on a systematic review of student experiences of their use.

Pedagogy for online learning

Do we need a new pedagogy for online learning? There are many claims being made for the effectiveness of online learning, and these need to be subject to critical scrutiny. Some of these claims refer to advantages over classroom-based teaching that can result from the use of learning technology. On the validity of some of the claimed advantages for online learning will rest the future of new forms of educational provision.

Some of the discussions about online learning have been accompanied by a subtle shift in the language used to describe education and training. Increasingly, education is described in terms of the 'delivery of materials', or even as the delivery of *learning*. This shift in emphasis may be seen as a by-product of the powerful new capabilities for accessing, structuring and presenting information. These capabilities – for example the capability to create virtual worlds for exploration – are so compelling that it is easy to regard them as providing powerful new educational paradigms. In fact, the tendency for new technologies to be seen as heralding a revolution in educational methods and then consistently failing to make an impact, has often been noted (Mayes, 1995). The evidence from the past is clear: new technologies, however effective in other fields, don't inevitably lead to major change in education.

It is arguable that real change in the way education is provided, especially to learners who may not previously have had the opportunity to benefit – as in the example of the development of the Open University – need not be driven by technologies at all, nor even by new pedagogies. Rather it depends on developing novel forms of organizational processes and structures while carefully *maintaining* and *enhancing* the pedagogical principles that remain fundamental to almost all forms of learning. This still leaves opportunity for large-scale change in the way education and training are organized – where and when learning occurs, how resources can be accessed, how learning can be assessed – but at the centre there are some activities that still *must* occur. By this view it is not new pedagogies that we need, but new ways of providing existing pedagogy efficiently and flexibly. This may provide the real challenge for online learning. It is the challenge of how to offer the pedagogical experience equivalent to that of an individual tutorial with a knowledgeable, sympathetic and well-equipped teacher to large numbers of learners in geographically dispersed and socially diverse settings.

In a recent overview of the theoretical underpinnings of student-centred learning environments, Jonassen and Land (2000) remark that never before has there been so much agreement about the pedagogical fundamentals. The shared theoretical assumptions are those of constructivism, and they result from two distinct shifts of emphasis. First, there has been a shift from a representational view of learning in which an acquisition metaphor guided design (Anderson *et al*, 1987) to a constructivist or constructionist view in which learning is primarily developed through activity (Papert, 1990). A second shift has been away from a focus on the individual, towards a new emphasis on social contexts for learning (Glaser, 1990).

This convergence at the theoretical level seems to be paralleled by a separate and very different convergence at the policy level. While the pedagogical view is based on collaborative learning, authentic tasks, reflection and dialogue, the language of e-learning policy making seems to describe a world in which there is accreditation of smaller and smaller 'bites of learning' gained from 'learning packages' delivered online to the desk at home or in the workplace. The latter view places much less emphasis on contact with tutors, and the importance of individual feedback. This view, of course, is based on the anticipated cost benefits of dispensing with the need for conventional (and expensive) educational structures, and is motivated, at least in part, by a genuine desire to bring the benefits of advanced education to new classes of learners. We should be wary of positioning these two approaches against each other. While the organizational or management approach can be criticized for failing to take sufficient account of pedagogical theory, which in the end drives the whole enterprise, so the pedagogues fail to show how the methods on which the constructivist approach is based will be widely accessible and cost effective. One aim of the present chapter is to argue for the design of learning environments that would not only support the modern pedagogical consensus but would also be scalable.

One aim of the constructivist approach is to design learning tasks that are authentic to the work and social contexts in which the skills or knowledge are normally embedded. This has led to the design of what are sometimes called 'practice fields' (Barab and Duffy, 2000). Examples of practice fields are to be found in problem-based learning (Savery and Duffy, 1996), anchored instruction (Cognition and Technology Group at Vanderbilt – CTGV, 1990, 1993) and cognitive apprenticeship (Collins, Brown and Newman, 1989). In each of these methods the emphasis is on the relationship between the nature of the learning task in educational or training environments, and its characteristics when situated in real use.

Another aspect of the acknowledgement that learning must be related to real-world tasks and situations, however, is the influence of a wider social context. Here the concept of a community of practice is introduced. With it comes an emphasis on the individual's relationship with a group of people rather than the relationship of the activity itself to the wider practice, even though it is the practice itself that identifies the community. This provides a different perspective on what is 'situated'. For Lave (1997), and Wenger (1998), it is not just the meaning to be attached to an activity that is derived from a community of practice: the individual's *identity* is shaped by the relationship. Lave and Wenger's perspective, however, emphasizes the stable and long-term nature of communities of practice. In the view of Fowler and Mayes (1999) this restricts the potential usefulness of the idea for the design of learning environments, where short-term and more fragile groups may nevertheless exert a powerful influence on the motivation to learn. Indeed, evidence on the shaping of social identification (Turner, 1991) seems to demonstrate that potent social identities can be created through membership of temporary groups. Indeed, the way in which learners' identities are formed and maintained in educational settings is an important issue for further research.

A framework for the design of learning technology

Conceptualization, constructionism and dialogue

The conceptual framework that we have adopted for approaching the pedagogy of online learning is one that attempts to map a broad account of learning directly onto the design of supportive technology (Mayes and Fowler, 1999). The main value of this analysis is to emphasize where in the learning cycle the support most needs to be directed. The framework describes what, in the pedagogical consensus, are the three main elements of a learning process – conceptualization, construction and dialogue. It also incorporates the idea of a learning cycle – acknowledging that learning is not a one-off process (a view unfortunately encouraged by the nature of our assessment methods) but that it involves continuous revisiting and tuning of concepts and skills. The three components can be thought of as stages – although not necessarily ordered in the way traditional stage models of learning have suggested (see, for example, Fitts and Posner, 1967) – but, rather, emphasizing the processes or modes of learning that, according to the pedagogical consensus, all successful learning must involve.

Conceptualization is the process of coming to an initial understanding through contact with, and exploration of, a new exposition of some kind. *Construction* involves some activity in which the new understanding is brought to bear on a problem, and feedback about performance will be gained. The third, consolidating stage involves the full integration of the new understanding with the learner's general framework of knowledge (if we are considering the learning of a motor skill, we would use a different terminology here but the same principles would apply). This is the stage at which aspects of expertise begin to appear, the learner beginning to use the new understanding, or to practice the new skill, in the context of real application. Initially we referred to this as the *dialogue* stage, emphasizing here the importance of discussion and reflection as the new understanding becomes applied to something. However, because dialogue seems central to the whole cycle it seems more appropriate to regard dialogue as the force that moves the learner through each of the stages. It is in the dialogue that the main opportunity for teaching occurs – where the learners' attention can be redirected, misconceptions corrected, new questions posed, and answers given to the learners' individual questions. This is what has traditionally been thought of as the stuff of tutorials – centred on the individual learner's growing understanding. It needs to occur in each of the modes of learning described above.

A more general term for the third stage might be *application*. Recently, Chris Fowler and I have suggested using the term *identification* (Fowler and

Mayes, 1999), which, as we will see below, emphasizes the relevance of the motivational and social dimension. This third stage can also be viewed as a process of externalizing the learning. This is not only learning 'what' and 'how', but also 'when'. Here is where a new layer of expertise in *when to use* the underlying skill or knowledge develops. This is the musical expression of the violinist, the 'road sense' of the driver, the 'people skills' of the manager. Few processing resources are now required to enact the performance of a skill, or to retrieve the information associated with a concept, so attentional power can be focused on the context in which it is being used or performed. I now favour adopting the term *contextualization* for this mode of learning. In the contextualization mode we see those aspects of apprenticeship and peer learning that set the social context for learning coming into play. Here, too, we see scope for an expression of individual differences. Since the emphasis now will be on real-world learning, the *use* of the knowledge or skill acquired through a long period of construction, achieving those goals that will have motivated the learner to reach this stage will take on renewed relevance.

Primary, secondary and tertiary courseware

With this framework in mind let us now consider the role of learning technology. The most straightforward role is to present the subject matter. Advances in digital media have made this an exciting business but we must not fall into the trap of thinking that multimedia presentations, even those which permit the learners to immerse themselves in virtual worlds, are actually teaching. What is being learnt from any presentation of information depends far more on what the learner already knows than on the extrinsic properties of the presentation. However, to the extent that what we have called *primary courseware* allows new concepts to be created and explored then it can directly support conceptualization. This is now a familiar and highly effective use of technology, directly enhancing understanding. But this kind of courseware is generally used in adjunct mode, supplementing classroom teaching. It cannot satisfy the need for activity, feedback and dialogue.

Secondary courseware, on the other hand, refers to any use of software in the designing and performance of tasks. One form of this will comprise descriptions, instructions and materials for the learning tasks themselves. The term also refers to the task-support environment. However, our concept of secondary courseware is wider than specialist software designed specifically to support the structuring of material. It would involve any use of the computer to produce output when the task is primarily for learning. Integrated together, primary and secondary courseware provides both information and tools for learners to develop concepts and to test their adequacy by using the concepts – in the writing of an essay, say, or by producing data from an experiment in a virtual laboratory, or by designing something. Primary courseware by itself is not sufficient. The point of identifying a class of software other than that which conveys subject matter is to underline the constructivist's belief in the crucial role of tasks in online learning. However, for learning to occur the system must allow feedback about the learners' performance on these tasks. The key question is the extent to which this can be accomplished through self-assessment, or automated through the indexing of performance, or provided through 'canned' answers to antici-pated questions, or even achieved through the methods of intelligent tutoring. Secondary courseware will provide the practice fields in Barab and Duffy's terminology. To extend this metaphor – if feedback can be built into the practice routine in some way then it is not necessary to have a coach permanently present and, in our terms, the required dialogue can be contained within the courseware. Some of the new online universities are attempting to achieve just this solution, which tackles head on the key problem – that individual tutors for every student are too expensive.

The third stage in our learning cycle refers to ways in which the new learner makes use of newly acquired knowledge. As we have emphasized above, dialogue with tutors and peer learners is the main determinant of learning in this contextualizing mode, where feedback is crucial. The feedback necessary for contextualization will differ from that required for construction – more to do with relevance and interpretation than the 'yes, that works' kind of feedback, and therefore more likely to involve discussion and extended discourse. *Tertiary courseware*, in the sense the term is used here, includes all the resources that support dialogue. This should not only involve the tools that support direct one-to-one synchronous discussion, or the structuring of discussion around threads in conferencing environments, or even the database of frequently-asked questions that are compiled from previous dialogues, but it should offer the new learner access to what Cumming (1993) has referred to as the 'discussion layer'.

The 'discussion layer' concept requires a new kind of courseware that captures the essence of being part of a community of learners, providing access to the questions, comments and dialogues of previous learners. One thing that online learning can offer that has never before been possible in classroom education is the possibility of recording all the individual dialogues that take place between tutors and students, or between peer learners. In principle it ought to be possible to capture these, structure them in some kind of database, and make them available to new learners. Since this would potentially require much less development effort to compile than to author conventional multimedia courseware, then this kind of approach might offer a genuinely cost-effective solution. The question is whether access to tertiary courseware of this kind can offer at least part of the classroom experience, where much learning occurs as a consequence of simply observing other learners struggling with the same material, and of simply overhearing other learners attempting to articulate their insights and misconceptions. To describe this kind of learning we have borrowed Bandura's term, *vicarious* learning (Bandura, 1986).

The vicarious learner

My colleagues and I in the 'vicarious learner' project mounted trials of the tertiary courseware approach in courses in two collaborating universities. A novel Web-based learning environment was constructed (novel at that time), involving an SGML-based integration of primary and secondary courseware, with special software capturing a dialogue component. Data included extensive online usage logs, specially designed questionnaires, and video-taped interviews with a sample of the learners.

From these trials, we developed our notion of *task-directed discussions* (TDDs), based on games used to elicit dialogue in teaching foreign languages. Students were engaged as subjects to participate in these TDDs, which were captured on video. Over 20 hours of video were then digitized, structured and made accessible in a database of tertiary courseware, which was used in an extensive evaluation experiment. A set of 11 TDDs was devised. The idea was to focus attention onto an explicit and shared set of concepts that have been derived from the primary material (here, over 100 concepts). Thus the primary material remains the target for the discussion but the form and scope of each discussion is controlled through defined manipulations of the concepts. A follow-up experiment was carried out in which 37 subjects each undertook 10 hours of learning over five days, during which they were exposed to various conditions of use of the multimedia system, called Dissemination. The system gave all subjects access to primary courseware but half the subjects had additional access to the database of TDD-derived discussions.

Our overall conclusions from this work can be summarized as follows:

- In current HE contexts, spontaneous dialogue suitable for 're-use' is rare, and even in online teaching and learning environments it is hard to capture. This conclusion follows from our initial expectation that we would capture mainly questions from students about the subject matter, with explanations and clarifications from tutors. In general the students that we studied were reluctant to pose questions of this kind. Most spontaneous questions were seeking clarification of the learning tasks and the assessments.

- The direct and short-term effects on learning of using tertiary courseware in the particular implementation we studied are complex and prone to individual differences in its use. Nevertheless, learners who made most use of tertiary courseware showed the highest short-term learning gains.

- Being given access to the dialogues of previous learners has significant effects on the way in which peer discussion subsequently proceeds. New learners will model aspects of their dialogues around the nature of the example dialogues they have accessed.

- Students rate the experience of learning through this kind of courseware as beneficial and enjoyable.

- Overall, access to the dialogues of previous learners encourages a modelling of what it takes to be a successful member of a community of learners and a means of more effective immersion into the language and practice of students' chosen areas. This finding leads us back to the importance of participation in a community of practice.

Communities and relationships

In his book *Communities of Practice*, Wenger (1998) articulates a point around which we can integrate the ideas presented in this chapter, namely, that issues of education should be addressed first and foremost in terms of identities and modes of belonging, and only secondarily in terms of skills and information. This view encourages us to consider pedagogy for online learning not just in terms of techniques for supporting the construction of knowledge but more generally in terms of their effects on the formation of identities. For Wenger, knowledge is a matter of competence in a valued enterprise. The value is given by social participation – in particular, by being an active participant in the practices of social communities, and by constructing an *identity* in relation to each community. Participating in a community – it may be a project team, say, or a member of a professional group – is both a kind of action and a form of belonging. Wenger's approach accounts for both aspects of situated learning: meaning is given both to the situated activities themselves and to the process of social identification that drives the learners' activity.

For Wenger, participation is not the same thing as collaboration. It goes beyond direct engagement in specific activities, and is 'not something we turn on and off'. Wenger's conceptualization of communities of practice gives us a way of defining personal meaning in a way that is not just circular. However, it is not a description of learning *per se*, or of how people learn together. It provides a very high level design heuristic and in that sense it tells us where we should start looking for design principles that address the key question of motivation.

In the context of our isolated distance learning student, the most salient community of practice is the wider group of learners with whom the current student wishes to identify. There may eventually be a community of practitioners in an activity or occupation beyond the world of education or training, but in that community the learner's current educational activity may not yet be regarded as legitimate peripheral participation. Barab and Duffy (2000) discuss some of the recent attempts that have been made to design learning environments and tasks, which help to create communities of *learners*. Clearly, the Lave and Wenger approach may be more readily applicable to the design of online learning if the practice in question is that of a community of students, or at least a wider community of learners, or, wider still, of scholars and thinkers.

Fowler and Mayes (1999) have discussed a rather different approach, but one that also attempts to capture the essence of the idea that learning environments should be designed around a recognition of the importance of the learner's personal identification with others. This approach takes the notion of a *learning relationship* as central, rather than a community of practice. Our experience of communities is mediated through individual relationships. In an initial attempt to study their nature we have distinguished between explorative, formative and comparative learning relationships, and characteristics of these have been studied in a project observing 16-year-olds attending schools in three different European countries (the United Kingdom, Finland and Portugal). One goal of our research is to look at the way that learning relationships influence the development of a learning career.

Conclusion

The framework for a pedagogy of online learning offered here attempts to derive principles for the design of learning technology from a constructivist account of learning. In so doing the need to support dialogue, both to provide feedback on task performance in 'practice fields', and to help to develop personal identity in a community of learners, is emphasized. One approach is described that aims to exploit the potential of online learning to record the learning experiences and dialogues of some learners to support the vicarious learning of others. The overall value of this approach seems less to do with conceptual learning, and more to do with modelling the role and language of a learner. The study of individual learning relationships may offer further insight into the social basis of the motivation to learn and may point to new ways to exploit vicarious learning. This needs to be designed on a large enough scale for it to offer at least a partial solution to the fundamental problem in online learning: too few tutors and too many learners.

Acknowledgements

I am very pleased to acknowledge the contributions made to the ideas discussed here by colleagues with whom I have collaborated over several years. I would especially like to thank Chris Fowler, John Lee, Finbar Dineen, Jean McKendree, Jim Gallacher and Christina Knussen.

References

Anderson, J R, Boyle, C F, Farrell, R and Reiser, B J (1987) Cognitive principles in the design of computer tutors, in *Modeling Cognition*, ed P Morris, Wiley, New York.

Bandura, A (1986) *Social Foundations of Thought and Action*, Prentice-Hall, Englewood Cliffs, NJ.

Barab, S A and Duffy, T M (2000) From practice fields to communities of practice, in *Theoretical Foundations of Learning Environments*, eds D H Jonassen and S M Land, Lawrence Erlbaum, Mahwah, NJ.

Cognition and Technology Group at Vanderbilt (CTGV) (1990) Anchored instruction and its relation to situated cognition, *Educational Researcher*, **19**, pp 2–10.

Collins, A, Brown, J S and Newman, S E (1989) Cognitive Apprenticeship: Teaching the craft of reading, writing and mathematics, in *Knowing and Learning: Essays in honour of Robert Glaser*, ed L B Renswick, Erlbaum, Hillsdale, NJ.

CTGV (1993) Anchored instruction and situated cognition revisited, *Educational Technology*, **33**, pp 52–70.

Cumming, G (1993) A perspective on learning for intelligent educational systems, *Journal of Computer Assisted Learning*, **9**, 229–38.

Fitts, P M and Posner, M I (1967) *Human Performance*, Brooks-Cole, Belmont CA.

Fowler, C J H and Mayes, J T (1999) Learning Relationships: from theory to design, *Association for Learning Technology Journal* (ALT-J), **7** (3), pp 6–16.

Glaser, R (1990) The re-emergence of learning theory within instructional research, *American Psychologist*, **45** (1), 29–39.

Jonassen, D H and Land, S M (eds) (2000) *Theoretical Foundations of Learning Environments*, Lawrence Erlbaum, Mahwah, NJ.

Lave, J (1997) The culture of acquisition and the practice of understanding, in *Situated Cognition: Social, semiotic and psychological perspectives*, eds D Kirshner and J A Whitson, Lawrence Erlbaum, Mahwah, NJ.

Lave, J and Wenger, E (1991) *Situated Learning: Legitimate peripheral participation*, Cambridge University Press, Cambridge.

Mayes, J T (1995) Learning Technologies and Groundhog Day, in *Hypermedia at work: Practice and theory in Higher Education*, eds W Strang, V B Simpson and D Slater, University of Kent Press, Canterbury.

Mayes, J T and Fowler, C J H (1999) Learning technology and usability: a framework for understanding courseware, *Interacting with Computers*, **11**, pp 485–97.

Papert, S (1990) An introduction to the fifth anniversary collection, in *Constructionist Learning*, ed I Harel, MIT Media Laboratory, Cambridge, MA.

Savery, J and Duffy, T M (1996) Problem-based learning: an instructional model and its constructivist framework, in *Constructivist Learning Environments: Case studies in instructional design*, ed B Wilson, Educational Technology Publications, Englewood Cliffs, NJ.

Turner, J C (1991) *Social Influence*, Open University Press, Milton Keynes.

Wenger, E (1998) *Communities of Practice: Learning, meaning and identity*, Cambridge University Press, Cambridge.

3

Problems with online learning are systemic, not technical

Stewart Hase and Allan Ellis
Southern Cross University, Australia

Editor's introduction

Hase and Ellis argue that the real issue should be about moving from teacher-controlled to learner-controlled learning, not about moving from traditional to online learning. The latter provides opportunities for the former, but only if specifically planned. They explore the issue of aligning all stakeholders into a common expectation of the online experience.

This chapter explores two major issues relating to learner-managed learning arising from the experience of developing and delivering an online undergraduate degree at Southern Cross University in New South Wales. The degree had already been delivered for a number of years by both face-to-face and print-based distance education. The online project involved complete redevelopment of subjects to make best use of the emerging technology. It was not a case of mounting existing study guides and teaching materials on the Web. Rather it has been a time of rapid and continuing learning that still involves all stakeholders coming to terms with pedagogical and system challenges. It is within this context that this chapter examines some potentially useful learning for the programme's ongoing development.

A journey in distance education

Our view is that pedagogy and, to a lesser extent, andragogy are limited approaches to education. This position has been argued more fully elsewhere (Hase and Kenyon, 2000) and is further supported by the extensive literature about lifelong learning, learner-managed learning and capability.

Nevertheless, the headlong rush to deliver educational programmes online seems to be underpinned by three principal factors: economics, fascination with technology and pedagogy. Which of these is the primary incentive is unclear. One receives the impression that the desire to access a global marketplace and not be left behind the competition is ahead of the capacity to understand and exploit any possible pedagogical advantages that online learning might have. Several commentators have noted, for example, that there is a gap between our understanding of how people can best learn online and the design of courses (for example, Foley and Schuck, 1998).

This gap between technological and pedagogical change has occurred before in the history of distance education in Australia. When distance education was first embraced, albeit reluctantly, by the higher education sector in the early 1970s, our understanding of how people might learn at a distance using print-based learning materials was severely limited. The compulsory residential school was used as a way of exposing students to traditional face-to-face lectures and tutorials. It was as if fully distance programmes were not quite acceptable without at least a small face-to-face component.

Learning how to provide courses by distance education was assisted by pioneers such as Knowles (1970) and Rowntree (1974). Instruction using study guides and books of readings became the norm for distance education learners. The dominant educational principle was self-directed learning and instructional design became a science that aimed to increase the potential for adult learning. More recently we have seen this translated into 'flexible delivery' and 'distributed learning', although what these terms mean in relation to pedagogical approach remains unclear.

As Hase and Kenyon (2000) note, self-directed learning is certainly a worthy concept but it falls short both theoretically and practically as a means of establishing a learner-focused approach to learning. We found most distance education programmes were highly teacher-directed, dominated by pedagogical rather than andragogical approaches. In fact it appears that distance education, as it has been practised, is no more likely to be student centred or heutagogical (Hase and Kenyon, 2000) than a lecturer in a crowded lecture theatre using slides with all the 'bells and whistles'.

One of the major pedagogical themes underpinning the current enthusiasm for online learning appears to be social constructivism (Fisher, Phelps and Ellis, 2000; Palloff and Pratt, 1999). Interactive learning environments increase the control of the learner over learning although this seems to have more to do with increasing motivation through self-directedness, than increasing the level and scope of learners' control over their own learning (McLoughlin and Oliver, 1995). The advantages of being able to communicate and collaborate quickly and easily with other learners and lecturers through chat rooms, e-mail and Web-based conferencing, online learning are notions of the need for self-directed learning, access to vast amounts of information, the capacity for increasing experiential learning, and ease of access.

It is with this background that we entered the era of online learning and set out to learn ourselves what it all means. As might be expected, we are left with more questions than answers.

Pedagogical issues

In terms of Coomey and Stephenson's online paradigm grid (see Chapter 4), people may need to spend time in each quadrant depending on their needs. However, it is our view that the current challenge for educational providers, and universities in particular, is how to make the paradigm shift away from teacher-centred to Coomey and Stephenson's SE quadrant (learner control of open-ended strategic learning), which involves heutogogical approaches to learning. Never before has the opportunity been so ripe to make this shift given the technology currently available to us and the clamour for citizens with new and appropriate capabilities including the capacity for self-managed learning.

As the literature suggests, the dominant theme underpinning the approach to online delivery is constructivist, but what are the realities for key activities such as interaction, access to materials and assessment?

Interaction

With print-based distance learning, interaction between learners and lecturer is usually confined to the teleconference. Learners may call the lecturer independently but these calls are usually confined to requests for extensions of time or queries about marked assignments. Web-based learning shells provide the opportunity for 'synchronous' or 'asynchronous interaction', and encourage the use of e-mail and chat rooms. This is seen as an opportunity for learners to discuss important issues, engage in problem solving, learn from others, clarify, and air their views.

There are, however, some challenges to be overcome before learners and lecturers alike can maximize the full communication potential of online learning. Learners find this difficult not least because of its novelty. It is important, in the first instance, that the technology is free of problems in order to avoid discouragement and even panic, particularly when approaching assignment deadlines. The response is often to drop out of the online version of the course and ask for the print-based version. This has the further effect of undermining confidence in being an independent learner.

As most learners and lecturers understand, communicating well in writing is a complex skill. Sending e-mails and using chat rooms is yet another skill to be learnt, which is different from writing assignments or reports. Chatting to people on the Web is disembodied communication and you can never quite be sure of how what you are writing may be construed. Most experienced users of e-mail know to keep e-mail messages short and to be careful about pressing the 'enter' key when writing something contentious. To become an effective online learner requires the command of this new skill. There may also be a need to moderate lists and chat rooms to ensure that the ever-present prankster does not offend others and that the site is not abused in other ways.

Another issue is how learners are stimulated to become involved in discussions. The preferred approaches so far have tended to be teacher centred. The lecturer may provide prompts at various stages and thereby encourage discussion. This is very time consuming for the lecturer and dependent on a high degree of effort in an already-busy schedule. Other approaches involve focusing an assignment task around a discussion or making it a condition of receiving a passing grade. Managing online discussion is an important area of skill development for educators.

This coercion of students is analogous to the effort of the teacher in a classroom setting and is simply a transfer of those skills to an electronic means. However, some of the problems associated with interaction may be associated with the design of learning materials and this is discussed further below.

Access to data

Another guiding principle supporting the development of online learning programmes is easy access to learning materials. A very important skill for any independent learner is to know where to get information. Thus knowing how to use the Internet, where the best information can be found, and electronic access to the library's databases is critical. Interestingly, however, some databases only provide abstracts and the learner cannot easily access full text articles without having to order them in print form and books ordered online still need to be posted. Thus lecturers find the need not only to prescribe but also provide many resources in the same way that they provided books of readings in the past. Similarly, they also find the need to prescribe Web sites and list the addresses as part of the course materials.

This situation is clearly problematic in the development of independent learners who need to be encouraged to do their own searching rather than being directed to what the lecturer perceives to be important. Given that many learners feel that they should write 'what the lecturer wants' it is likely that many will not search widely or well when there is the very real opportunity to do so.

Assessments

Online chat rooms and e-mail provide an excellent opportunity for learners to negotiate assessment items with the lecturer and peers, and to do something other than develop competency to write essays. A couple of subject developers took advantage of this and were able to hand over some control of assessment to the learner. The overall design of learning materials depends entirely on the particular understanding that the lecturer has about how people learn. Those with a teacher-directed focus tend to use strategies such as providing commentary, organizing learning week by week, providing activities to be done sequentially, and mounting slide presentations. More learner-managed approaches involve:

- negotiation of course objectives and assessment;
- the use of assessment rather than course content as the focus for learning;
- summaries of major concepts and learner freedom to pursue topics of interest;
- formative assessment;
- creative questioning that covers a broad rather than a narrow field of interest;
- the capacity to free learners to search for learning resources, with guidance as appropriate, rather than supplying all learning materials;
- team approaches to assessment;
- the use of real life applications of learning.

Online learning offers a wonderful opportunity to provide learning experiences that not only develop competency but also aspects of capability such as independent learning skills, self-efficacy, creativity, working in teams, and using competences in novel as well as familiar circumstances (Hase, Cairns and Malloch, 1998; Stephenson and Weil, 1992). Making best use of this opportunity requires careful consideration of:

- curriculum design that develops these characteristics of capability and is flexible enough to cater for the individual learner's current capability;
- a shift in thinking by lecturers and instructional designers towards more learner-centred approaches to course development;
- greater flexibility in assessment that goes beyond teaching people how to write assignments;

- incorporating but going beyond constructivist approaches; and
- how to enhance the potential for learner creativity.

Alignment

The second major issue that arose out of our experience in online learning is what we have chosen to call alignment. In this case we are concerned with the problem of aligning the expectations of learners, lecturers and administrators in the development of innovative approaches to learning.

The various elements that underpin the successful delivery of education programmes from an educational institution vary depending upon the mode of delivery. Various clusters of elements that are necessary for any given mode and the number and complexity of these elements increase as you move from traditional face-to-face education, to paper-based distance education and on to the newly emerging forms of online or Web-based education.

A successful learning experience in any one of these modes will depend on the alignment of the elements that make up that mode of delivery. A typical dictionary definition of alignment talks about 'placing in line', 'bringing into line', or 'arranging groups or forces in relation to one another'. Burdett (1994) has pointed out that such simple definitions fail to capture what he terms the 'magic' of alignment, that is, the outcome in terms of performance that is achieved when all sections of an organization, people and resources, are aligned to achieve an agreed goal. Without proper alignment, resources can be wasted, energy dissipated and the overall outcome can fall well below what was expected by all stakeholders.

The human resource development and leadership literature has for many years recognized alignment as a key aspect of strategic change (Cobb, Samuels and Sexton, 1998). It has also recognized that different elements of alignment reside at different levels in the organizational hierarchy. Furthermore, the level of alignment of the elements determines the extent to which strategy, structure and culture creates an environment that facilitates the achievement of organizational goals (Semler, 1997).

The notion of alignment poses some interesting questions for the stakeholders in online programme development. How can this understanding of the importance of alignment be applied to the delivery of education programmes, particularly those being developed for online delivery and learner-managed learning? Can a model be developed that sets out the relationships between key stakeholders over a range of issues? Such a model would need to reflect hierarchical as well as lateral alignment.

In the university setting three major stakeholders in developing an online programme can be defined: learners, lecturers and the administrators. Each needs to understand and relate to the needs of the other two stakeholders on a range of issues if appropriate learning programs are to be delivered. As an example of a hierarchical issue consider the role of a mission statement – that is, the description of the highest goals of the organization and the underlying reason that unites the stakeholder groups. If delivering quality online learning is to become a new component of the mission statement then each stakeholder group must align its expectations and actions with this new dimension if it is to be successfully integrated into the existing mission statement.

Let us now consider some scenarios for other issues. What about the level of financial resources needed to develop and deliver new online programmes? Do senior administrators appreciate the financial costs involved? Are they prepared to allocate the necessary financial resources to allow for development in a set time frame and at the level of quality implied in the mission statement?

What about issues involving lecturers and students? Take, for example, the existing equipment and software skill level of learners or potential learners. If these are not correctly known or anticipated by lecturers, then the online materials developed will either be too simplistic or, more likely, be too sophisticated thereby causing basic access problems as well as problems in dealing with materials once accessed.

This preliminary analysis suggests that a model could be built for any organization moving from traditional modes of education to online education and that the model should identify stakeholders, key issues and the level of understanding/skill/resources that are present. If these levels could be mapped onto a series of stakeholder diagrams then areas of poor alignment could be identified. If this were done early in the process then there would be an opportunity to redirect information and resources so as to improve alignment and hence the overall outcome of the project.

Alignment might appear to be a simple concept and the process of achieving appropriate levels of alignment a relatively straightforward task but as yet there is little evidence that the concept or its application are being applied to the process of moving education online.

Conclusion

Our experience of developing online courses is developmental and supports the view that there is still a lot to learn about how to get the best out of an evolving medium. In many respects it will probably always be 'work in progress' given the rapid rate at which technology is progressing. Nonetheless it is interesting to note that the two key issues that affect the development of online learning are the same problems that confront any institutional delivery of education. The first of these is the dominance of teacher-centred approaches that needs to be challenged if the best of what technology offers is to be realized. The second of these is the requirement for the alignment of the needs of all stakeholders in the design and delivery of courses. Progress in both these areas falls short of the potential for learner managed learning that online technology offers. The challenge is to change existing educational paradigms currently used in universities.

References

Burdett, J O (1994) The Magic of Alignment, *Management Decision*, **32** (2), pp 59–63.

Cobb, J C, Samuels, C J and Sexton, M W (1998) Alignment and strategic change: a challenge for marketing and human resources, *Leadership and Organisational Development Journal*, **19** (1), pp 32–43.

Fisher, K, Phelps, R and Ellis, A (2000) Group Processes Online: Teaching collaboration through collaborative processes, unpublished paper, Southern Cross University.

Foley, G and Schuck, S (1998) Web-based conferencing: pedagogical asset or constraint?, *Australian Journal of Educational Technology*, **14** (2), pp 122–40.

Hase, S and Kenyon, C (2000) From andragogy to heutagogy, unpublished paper, Southern Cross University.

Hase, S, Cairns, C and Malloch, M (1998) *Capable Organisations: Implications for vocational education and training*, NCVER, Adelaide.

Knowles, M (1970) *The Modern Practice of Adult Education: Andragogy versus pedagogy*, Associated Press, New York.

McLoughlin, C and Oliver, R (1995) Who is in control? Defining interactive learning environments, *ASCILITE '95-Learning with Technology*, pp 395–403.

Palloff, R and Pratt, K (1999) *Building Learning Communities in Cyberspace: Effective strategies for the online classroom*, Jossey-Bass, San Francisco.

Rowntree, D (1974) *Teaching through Self Instruction*, Kogan Page, London.

Semler, S W (1997) *Human Resources Development Quarterly*, **8** (1), pp 23–40.

Stephenson, J and Weil, S (1992) *Quality in Learning: A capability approach in higher education*, Kogan Page, London.

Part 2

Researchers

The two items in Part 2 present reviews of current research on online learning. Despite the high level of investment in new online learning programmes by corporations as well as educational institutions, there is surprisingly little systematic research into its overall effectiveness as a learning medium. There are, however, many small-scale evaluations or case studies of individual initiatives from which lessons can be learnt. Coomey and Stephenson concentrate on what is being learnt from specific case studies, whereas Jackson and Anagnostopoulou focus on learning support environments in the context of constructivist approaches to teaching and learning. Both discuss the pedagogical issues arising from the research, and both confirm the view expressed in Part 1 that existing pedagogical approaches are, in the main, likely to transfer to the new medium. Coomey and Stephenson present a useful paradigm grid to help users and designers match their online learning with lessons from research reports from similar paradigms. They also claim to see evidence of a migration from didactic to positivist approaches stimulated by the medium itself.

4

Online learning: it is all about dialogue, involvement, support and control – according to the research

Marion Coomey* and John Stephenson**
*Ryerson Polytechnic University, Canada and **Middlesex University, UK

Editor's introduction

What does the research tell us about what works well in online learning? Coomey and Stephenson reviewed current research to find out. Designers of online learning, the review reveals, should pay considerable attention to learner control, dialogue, learner support and opportunities for direct learner involvement. There are wide variations, however, in the 'flavour' of these common themes according to the overall purpose of the learning activity, from instructional mode at one extreme to open-ended exploratory mode at the other. The chapter explores the implications of these different modes for the design, structure and management of online learning and proposes a framework to help practitioners locate their own practice and construct appropriate programmes and systems based on lessons from the review.

About this report

Web-based online learning is too recent a medium to have been the subject of a systematic and comprehensive research programme to test its overall educational effectiveness. However, there is a growing number of small-scale research reports, case studies and reviews of practice. This chapter is based on a systematic review of such reports. The authors were seeking advice on good practice and any indication of new approaches to teaching and learning being engendered by online learning. One hundred research reports and journal articles were included in the review. Most were published in the period 1998–2000. The articles were equally distributed across three types: overviews of current practice and research, conceptual propositions and individual research reports. The overviews and conceptual pieces were themselves based on other research reports, thereby extending the total experience available.

Though extensive, the scope of this review is inevitably limited. Many interesting developments are too recent to appear in research reports. Pre-1998 items describe practice before the full potential of Web-based learning began to be exploited, and innovative practice within the business world is not normally shared via research reports. Samples often contained less than 15 learners and the quality of programmes is unknown. In many cases there is little information on learner and teacher familiarity with the medium. A number of cases involved computer and multimedia students with a predisposition to using the medium effectively. Nevertheless, the evidence within the 100 items is rich and varied, and sufficient to give an indication of what might be happening more generally.

Many of the detailed accounts focused on *benefits* for learners, such as increased understanding, closer engagement with content, learner motivation, collaboration, skills development, increased learning and greater efficiency, and *detriments* such as technical problems, learner motivation, isolation, learner readiness and contact with teacher. In our analyses we concentrated on lessons learnt and recommendations based on experience, which in turn we coded as advice on the design and structure of software, content, activities, process management and the organization of online learning.

Review of outcomes: four common features

Within the limitations outlined above, four major features of online learning were widely identified as essential to good practice. These features were: dialogue, involvement, support, control (DISC). Most 'lessons learnt' focused on the importance of *structuring* the learning activity and *designing* the materials in order to promote dialogue, secure active involvement of the learner, provide personal or other support and feedback and enable the learner to exercise the degree of control expected. A very brief selection of comments on each is presented below.

Dialogue

Dialogue appears in many forms in online courses: e-mail, bulletin boards, 'real-time' chat, asynchronous chat, group discussion and debate. The literature supports the idea that, for any type of dialogue to be successful, its use must be carefully structured into the course. Instructors and course designers, for instance, cannot assume that learners will be able to jump into group discussions, argue in online debates, or answer questions posed online, just because they are told to participate (Bonk, Angeli and Hara, 1998; Funaro, 1999; Mason, 1998). Gregor and Cuskelly (1994) suggest that if interaction between students is not structured into the course, they will not volunteer to do it.

Beaudin (1999) and Bonk (1999) present frameworks for dialogue in which a responsive moderator with a list of clearly defined questions guides the dialogue and keeps the chat on topic. Doherty (1998) and others talk about asynchronous dialogue as an opportunity for active participation and for in-depth reflection and thoughtful responses.

Involvement

Involvement includes responses in structured tasks, active engagement with material, student collaborations, student direction, flow and motivation. Dee-Lucas (1999) finds that students who use systems with more clearly defined hypertext, with more choices and more defined and refined searches find solutions to tasks faster. Chan and Repman (1999) describe a state of total absorption by the student in online learning activities as 'flow'. Flow, they say, is associated with challenge, clear feedback, learner control and concentration. The need for structuring learner involvement into the system is illustrated by Wilson and Whitelock (1998) who note that the majority of students did not collaborate online with other students or become involved in extra work that was available to them because they said it was too time consuming.

Support

The need for support is the most frequently mentioned feature of online learning. Support includes periodic face-to-face contact, online tutorial supervision, peer support, advice from experts, feedback on performance, support services and software tools. Typical evidence is presented by Alexander (1999), Ewing (1999), Funaro (1999), Mason (1998), Oliver (1995), Thompson and McGrath (1999) and Warren and Rada (1998).

In almost all cases students say that effective procedures for instructor/tutor/peer feedback are the most important features of a successful online course. Students used to more traditionally delivered courses seem to expect more traditional feedback and are frustrated if they do not receive the level of attention they expect. For tutor support to be effective, Lewis and Vizcarro (1998) argue that the structure should make the role of tutor 'clear and distinct'. In distance learning and graduate programmes about multimedia, online students seem more prepared to receive non-traditional support. When the course structure allows students to develop strong working groups, they then perceive the course to be 'congenial' and see themselves as a community (Rimmershaw, 1999).

Control

Control, in this context, refers to the extent to which learners have control of key learning activities and the extent to which the learner is encouraged to exercise that control. Control can cover responses to exercises, pace and timing, choice of content, management of learning activities, learning goals and outcomes, overall direction and assessment of performance. Oliver (1998) cautions against giving control to those with little prior experience without carefully structuring the experience. Oliver reports that: 'There are many students who feel that they learn by being taught and when this aspect is removed from an instructional setting and the onus placed on the student there may be some who will not appreciate the different teaching style despite its more effective learning potential'. McConnell (1995) finds that Masters students in an online learning course repeatedly noted that they have limited control over the time expended on the course. As one student puts it, 'It's just sort of eaten into my whole life'.

Variations upon the messages

The DISC themes (dialogue, involvement, support and control) occur across the board. They feature in reports of cases covering a wide range of student types (part time and full time, school children, undergraduates and graduates) and subject matter (basic skills, education, psychology, sociology, mathematics, the sciences, multimedia, computer science). They feature in both campus-based and distance cases. However, a closer examination of the evidence indicates variations in the flavour of the DISC features according to whether the intended learning is teacher controlled or learner led, or whether the learning activity is tightly specified or open-ended.

For example, there is a considerable difference between dialogue in which every element of the participation was designed by the instructor (Advaryu *et al*, 1999) and a Masters course (McConnell, 1995) in which students choose what to work on and then engage in ongoing asynchronous chat during which they can 'reshape conversations based on their ongoing understandings and reflections.' The former is highly teacher controlled and the latter is learner led.

Similarly, with involvement, support and control, there are pronounced differences in the literature in courses where the instructor shapes the participation versus the learner directing the participation. Alexander (1999) describes involvement in a course in which students are directed to respond to two particular focus statements on their own and then in groups. In contrast, students on a human movement course (Spratt and Smithers, 1999) must become involved in their own time, searching the Web for fitness tests, taking those tests and posting the results to a database.

Support is also offered in vastly different ways online. Warren and Rada (1998) describe highly structured support in a course where the instructor made specific e-mail comments each week about how students should cover content. McConnell (1995) presents an example of learner led support in a programme where students read each others' work and provide peer feedback.

Teacher-led control is noted in a class where students were guided through a highly structured interface to reach a collaborative solution (Baker and Lund, 1997) whereas Dee-Lucas (1999) talks about students who are given an unstructured interface allowing for individual control in navigation.

The paradigm grid for online learning

The variations in the locus of control and task specification illustrated above, and their general occurrence across most of the examples in the study, suggest that much of current experience of online learning falls within four paradigms:

- teacher-controlled, specified learning activities;
- teacher-controlled, open-ended or strategic learning;
- learner-managed specified learning activities;
- learner-managed, open-ended or strategic learning.

These four paradigms can be illustrated as a grid, as shown in Figure 4.1.

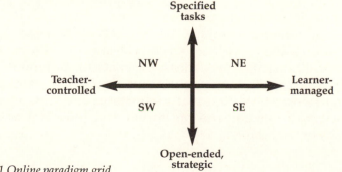

Figure 4.1 Online paradigm grid

Characteristics of the four paradigms

The four paradigms were checked against the data within the 100 reports and were found to accommodate most of the examples cited. Each of the DISC features had different characteristics in each of the paradigms, with implications for the structuring and design of good practice. These DISC features are described below. For ease of reference, each paradigm is described according to its compass bearing – NW, NE, SW and SE.

The north-west quadrant (teacher determined, task specific)

In this sector, the teacher tightly specifies the activities and outcomes, including deadlines, timings, exchanges and online content (often text based), leaving the learner with little scope for initiative, except in carefully controlled situations.

Characteristics of the north-west quadrant include:

- *Dialogue.* Teacher defines/controls online dialogue and interaction. Student responds to teacher's questions and mini tasks. Dialogue with peers is specified as part of task. The focus of dialogue is usually task-oriented problem solving.
- *Involvement.* Little or no scope for learner to influence content. Activity is strictly defined and related to a pre-set task The site is structured to lead the learner directly to specific information. Students can access information from a Web site before, during or after lectures.
- *Support.* Assumed to come only from the teacher via e-mail, phone calls or face-to-face meetings that are scheduled. The main feedback comes from the instructor.
- *Control.* Learner control is confined to responses to tasks. There is some control over sequencing, and level of engagement. The teacher controls the reading materials, the content to be learnt and deadlines.
- *Teacher role.* Instructor.

The north-west sector embraces what Mason (1998) describes as 'content with support' and Paolucci and Jones (1998) as being 'instructor led'. Dee-Lucas (1999) describes situations with 'learning goals that depend in part on accurate recall of the text'. In analysing the content of online courses, Bonk, Cummings and Jacobs (1999) find that the majority are 'little more than photocopied syllabi. In effect, instructors are employing the Web to support traditional classroom structures'.

Advice for the north-west quadrant

- Provide easy access to technical support. This lesson is common to all sectors (Alexander, 1999; Bonk and Cummings, 1998).
- Structured hypertext that clearly directs students to desired goals results in more efficient use of time and clearer interpretation of task (Dee-Lucas, 1999).
- Refer to online discussions during 'real' class time (Funaro, 1999).
- Make online participation a requirement. Create reasons to participate (Funaro, 1999).

The north-east quadrant (learner determined, task specific)

In this sector, the learning tasks and perhaps also the learning goals are specified *but* learners have control of how they work towards and achieve the set goals and the tasks. A typical example from the north-east sector would be a course that included case studies provided by the teacher with considerable learner discretion on how to engage with them. Schlais, Davis and Thomson (1999) describe a business course in which the text is online and there is a set path of instruction but the students also become involved in creating a simulated business in which they must create a product and sell it for profit. That interaction is structured but involves a lot of freedom. There are several examples in the literature of case studies in which students work within an otherwise traditional, lecture-based class, on group projects that require the learners to collaborate to find task solutions (Bonk, Angeli and Hara, 1998; Gregor and Cuskelly, 1994).

Characteristics of the north-east quadrant include:

- *Dialogue.* The teacher sets out the general responsibilities and procedures, but not participation, content or use. Scope is confined to the task, but the systems and protocols support student-managed dialogue with other students, peers and experts.
- *Involvement.* Task-focused self-managed groups. Groups can be self-selected and/or self-moderated. The learner is able to relate or adapt tasks to his or her own circumstances and aspirations.
- *Support.* The tutor provides advice on the nature of the task, learning goals and so forth. Support is mainly by e-mail contact, or tutor-moderated discussion groups. Students provide feedback to members of their own groups and others.
- *Control.* Conduct of tasks is up to the learner. Emphasis is on navigable links to a wide variety of sources. There is use of resources outside the

programme and wide discretion over activities, content and learning outcomes.

- *Teacher role.* Coach.

Design features in this sector include flexible time scales, use of case studies, opportunity for learner to set outcomes and goals, multi-level open linkages and the availability of agents or tools for self-managed learning. Paolucci and Jones (1998) describe this sector as one where the 'instructor has control over content and learning activities and indirect control over technology and student has control of content through hypermedia'.

Wegner, Holloway and Garton (1999) say that 'students not used to this method of inquiry evidently experienced some discomfort making the transition from teacher centered to learner centered learning'.

Advice for the north-east quadrant

- Keep groups small (Alexander, 1999).
- Assign students roles and make those roles clear and explicit (Barros *et al*, 1998).
- Groups with appointed leaders tend to solve tasks more effectively (Oliver and Omari, in press).
- Provide training in how to use social behaviours online (Hackman and Walker, 1995; Marjanovic, 1999). (This lesson also applies to the SW and SE sectors.)
- Develop strategies that enhance two-way interaction (Bonk, Angeli and Hara, 1998).
- Make it a requirement that students respond to others' contributions (Gregor and Cuskelly, 1994).
- Motivation increases when students realize that their work will be displayed (Bonk and Dennen, 1999).
- Course structure allows students to always know what they are doing and what needs to be done next (Sumner and Taylor, 1998).

The south-west quadrant (teacher-determined open-ended strategic learning activities)

In this sector, the programme or teacher sets the overall direction, generalized outcomes, purpose, field, scope or level, and the learner is able to explore, access and use any specific material relevant to that direction *or* the instructor begins the course with teacher-determined and task-defined activities as in the north-west sector but after the 'set' learning is completed the students continue to explore the subject area in an unstructured way. The learner-managed element of the north-east sector is structured and controlled by the teacher with freedom for the learner to explore.

In one example of an elective course in a Masters in Education programme (Alexander 1999), students follow up a week of intensive class sessions with asynchronous debate from their homes. Ogborn (1998) describes a system called 'world maker' in which students create ecological models using real objects and the goal is pure discovery. The students find out through their own trial and error what works in the environments they create and what does not, within a more traditional, teacher-supported classroom.

Characteristics of the south-west quadrant include:

- *Dialogue*. A combination of dialogue styles found in the north-west quadrant during the instructor-led segment of the course and in the south-east quadrant during the learner-managed segment of the course. It could be managed by the teacher and is focused on the overall direction and purpose of the study. It involves use of asynchronous dialogue but with instructor setting out roles for students, making students participate as leaders or respondents in discussions or asking students to categorize their responses.

- *Involvement*. It could start out as solo activity with the student learning rules/concepts/theories from online texts and possibly traditional lectures. Text may be online but there are also locations for students to write and place their 'discoveries' (links, data and content). Once students have mastered 'the basics', they create something new of their own. Group activity is mainly confined to the course group.

- *Support*. Tutor support could be online or occasionally face to face. There is a range of support: traditional feedback in the first phase of the course (north-west quadrant)/instructor acting as facilitator, offering suggestions but not answers during the 'discovery' phase of the course (south-east quadrant).

- *Control*. The learner has control of specific learning goals within the generalized goals. Learners manage their own unstructured discovery activities within given parameters. They are free to set their own personal goals within the generalized activity.

- *Teacher role*. Guide.

Mason (1998) calls this sector 'wrap-around', with the teacher's emphasis on providing supportive navigational material such as study guides, wrapped around existing texts and resources with the students interacting through e-mails and postings. Paolucci and Jones (1998) describe the instructor as mediator in this sector. He says the instructor and learner are a dyad with the instructor having indirect control over learning activities and both having control over technology and content. And there are difficulties if learners are more used to, and expect, the level of direction they enjoyed in more familiar north-west quadrant situations. Lewis and Vizcarro (1998), for instance, note that a conflict for teachers lies in the 'desire on the one hand to force students to be autonomous in their actions whilst on the other hand providing adequate guidance'.

Advice for the south-west quadrant

- Structure the learning environment to promote co-operation within groups (Ewing, 1999).
- Provide examples and instruction of ways to work online in groups (model ways to have a lively dialogue) (Funaro, 1999).
- Creation of labels to allow students to structure dialogue (Sloffer *et al*, 1999).
- Keep dialogue on topic through carefully designed questions, guidelines for learners, and online summaries (Beaudin, 1999).
- Categorize messages, summarize threads of discussion (Advaryu *et al*, 1999).
- Provide steps in the problem-solving process (Oliver and Omari, in press).

The south-east quadrant (learner-managed, open-ended activities)

In this sector the learner is in control of the overall direction of the learning, including learning outcomes and longer terms goals. Personal goals ('reasons for being there') are as important as specific learning outcomes. There may still be a finishing time in most cases but finding your way to the end point involves a lot of learner freedom of choice.

In Mason's examination of online course models (1998) she discussed the Open University's Masters in Open and Distance Education programme. Students integrate comments from discussion conferences into assignments and then 'reflect on what they have learnt from the various elements of the course, including discussion, reading and joint work'.

Characteristics of the south-west quadrant are:

- *Dialogue*. Self or collaboratively (peer-group) directed. There is wide discretion over choice of discussion groups, from peers to 'public' specialist interest groups. Asynchronous dialogue with other specialists. External sources of specialist assistance.

- *Involvement.* Total involvement in the learning activity. The student could be working alone or in a team. Learners relate the learning to their own personal, vocational and academic needs.
- *Support.* Contacts with supervisor initiated and monitored by the learner, facilitated by the system. The teacher is in the background, offering advice on procedures and resources. Feedback is sought from a variety of sources and experts. The structure and design of the online learning facilities provide a framework of support within which the learner has considerable discretion.
- *Control.* The learner determines the goals and outcomes and monitors progress.
- *Teacher role.* Facilitator.

Mason (1998) calls this situation 'integrated' with an emphasis on 'collaborative activities, learning resources and joint assignments... the heart of the course is online discussion and processing information and carrying out tasks'. Paolucci and Jones (1998) talks about the 'technology as tutor' with the learner exercising control 'through use of the system'. Bonk, Angeli and Hara (1998) found that by structuring electronic learning activities, 'students will have more time to reflect on course content and to make in-depth cognitive and social contributions that would be nearly impossible in a traditional classroom'.

Sloffer *et al* (1999) say that the key component to learner centred environments *is* inquiry: 'a questioning that derives from puzzlement, a difference between what the individual expected and what he or she observed'.

Advice for the south-east quadrant

- The role of the tutor, and the amount and level of tutor participation, should be clearly defined (Lewis and Vizcarro, 1998).
- Embed prompts and other ways for students to interact with the content in order to make the thinking process clear (Henderson *et al*, 1998).
- Provide synchronous events (along with asynchronous events) to maintain student enthusiasm and a 'real time' sense of participation (Mason, 1998).
- Develop criteria for students to assess each others' work (McConnell, 1995).
- Remember that 'free for all' open discussions do not usually work (Mason, 1998).
- Provide guidelines and carefully designed questions (Beaudin, 1999).
- Create a structure to make teams collaborate (solve problems through a

voting system; write collaborative assignments by dividing tasks into sections) (Marjanovic, 1999).

- Beware that learners could become so involved in browsing that they might not be thinking about the learning related to specific subject matter (Ewing *et al*, 1999).

Implications of the study

Horses for courses

This review of current experience of online learning and the paradigm grid should be of assistance to anyone seeking to take account of case study reports when structuring and designing online programmes. Both authors of this report have heard colleagues referring to 'what does and does not work according to research' without reference to the paradigm of the case on which the research is based. The grid could be a useful means of helping researchers to communicate their findings for the benefit of developments elsewhere. The observation, for instance, that online materials and user activities must be tightly structured, clearly signposted and closely supervised will be helpful only if the readers of the case study are seeking to develop an online north-west experience for their own learners. If the readers want to develop a programme for south-east learners, then such advice would lead to disappointment for the teacher and frustration for the learners. Similarly, if a teacher follows the advice from case studies within the south-east sector when building a programme for north-west learners, student confusion and disorientation will certainly follow. Therefore, the grid and the DISC elements within each sector of the grid can help instructors and designers create online courses that relate directly to their students' learning needs and their own content requirements.

Transition strategies

The study also points to the importance of designers of materials referring to the normal paradigm experienced and expected by students when designing online programmes. Students used to clear instructions and narrowly defined tasks, for instance, will need considerable help with online learning in any sector other than the north west. Any teacher seeking to exploit the full freedom of the Web, for instance, should first identify the learner's normal learning paradigm. If, as is likely, any of the learners are steeped in north-west culture, the teacher or designer will have to pay particular attention to managing the shift to, say, the south-east quadrant. This will require the provision of carefully signposted and well-structured means of securing the transition to new patterns of dialogue, interaction, support and control.

Migration to learner-managed learning

The range of teaching and learning paradigms described in this study is comparable to that found in non ICT-based learning contexts. It reinforces the argument of others in this book (for example, Alexander and Boud) that teachers using online learning merely re-create their normal pedagogical stance. The north-west sector is comparable to traditional didactic teaching, instruction or formal training, whilst the SE sector equates with the open-ended learner-managed mode that is increasingly appearing in higher education, the workplace and continuing professional development programmes. New technology, it might appear, is replicating existing approaches to teaching and learning by other means.

However, it would be misleading to conclude from this evidence that educationally nothing is changing. The paradigms may be the same but the technology of online learning appears to facilitate a migration from traditional didactic modes to more learner-managed learning modes if teachers and designers wish to take such a journey. By focusing attention on dialogue, involvement, support and control, online learning addresses features that facilitate such migration (Stephenson and Yorke, 1998). Intelligent or intuitive 'agents' or software tools that anticipate needs, provide ease of access to relevant information at the right time, acknowledge personal learning styles, facilitate self-management of progress and forward planning, will make it easier for the teacher to assume a less directive role (Aroyo and Kommers, 1999). The most significant feature of online Web-based learning for those seeking to promote more learner autonomy is its capacity to take learners beyond the provision of their teachers and to engage with a greater variety of materials, learners, experts, support tools and fields. As Bonk (1999) observed, Web-based learning:

> offers a chance for students to enter into dialogues about authentic problems, collaborate with peers, negotiate meaning, become apprenticed into their field of study, enter a community of experts and peers and generally be assisted in the learning process.

Universities in the UK, Europe, North America and Australasia are developing online versions of their existing programmes. Increasingly, these initiatives will move from HTML texts of lecture notes towards a fuller exploitation of online learning tools, agents and protocols. By focusing attention on dialogue, involvement, support and control, and through learner-focused agents and procedures, online learning may be the means by which managing one's own learning becomes a common feature of all undergraduate experience. As Doherty (1998) has observed:

Adaptive transformative pedagogy may be the greatest challenge and the true future of higher education and the learner will be at the core. The student will be paramount in mediating his or her own learning. Learner control will emerge as the dominant characteristic of 'every time, every place for everybody' learning.

References

Advaryu, S, Tzy-Peng, K and O'Grady, G K (1999) *Online Role-Play: Facilitating an online asynchronous environment,* Conference paper, Fifth International Conference on Technology Supported Learning, Online EDUCA, Berlin.

Alexander, S (1999) Selection dissemination and evaluation of the TopClass WWW-based Course Support Tool, *International Journal of Educational Communication,* **5** (4), p 283.

Aroyo, L and Kommers, P (1999) Intelligent agents for educational computer-aided systems, *Journal of Interactive Learning Research,* **10**, (3/4), pp 235–43.

Baker, M and Lund, K (1997) Promoting reflective interactions in a CSCL environment, *Journal of Computer Assisted Learning,* **13**, pp 175–93.

Barros, B, Rodriguez, M and Verdejo, F (1998) Towards a model of collaborative support for distance learners to perform joint tasks, in *The Virtual Campus: Trends for higher education and training,* eds F Verdejo and G Davies, Chapman & Hall, New York.

Beaudin, B (1999) Keeping online asynchronous discussions on topic, *Journal of Asynchronous Learning Networks,* **3** (2), http://www.aln.org/alnweb/journal/jaln-vol3issue2.htm

Bonk, C J (1999) Breakout from learner issues, *International Journal of Educational Telecommunication,* **5** (4), pp 387–410.

Bonk, C, Cummings, J and Jacobs, R (1999) *Twenty First Century Syllabi: Dynamic tools for promoting interactivity,* unpublished manuscript, Center for Research on Learning and Technology Report, Indiana University, Bloomington.

Bonk, C J and Dennen, V P (1999) Teaching on the Web: With a little help from my pedagogical friends, *Journal of Computing in Higher Education,* **11** (1), pp 3–28.

Bonk, C J, Angeli, C and Hara, N (1998) *Content Analysis of Online Discussion in an Applied Educational Psychology Course,* unpublished manuscript, Center for Research on Learning and Technology Report, Indiana University at Bloomington.

Bonk, C J and Cummings, J A (1998) A dozen recommendations for placing students at the center of Web-based learning, *Educational Media International,* **35** (2), pp 82–89.

Chan, T and Repman, J (1999) Flow in Web based activity: an exploratory research project, *International Journal of Educational Telecommunications,* **5** (4), p 225.

Dee-Lucas, D (1999) Hypertext segmentation and goal compatibility: effects on study strategies and learning, *Journal of Educational Media and Hypermedia,* **8** (3), pp 279–314.

Doherty, P (1998) Learner control in asynchronous learning environments, *ALN Magazine,* **2** (2), http://www.aln.org/alnweb/magazine/alnpaga.htm

Ewing, J M, Dowling, J D and Coutts, N (1999) Learning using the World Wide Web: a collaborative learning event, *Journal of Educational Multimedia and Hypermedia*, **8** (1), pp 3–22

Ewing, J M (1999) *Enhancement of student learning online and offline,* http://www.norcol.ac.uk/departments/educas/JimEwing/webversion/studentlearning/htm

Funaro, G M (1999) Pedagogical roles and implementation guidelines for online communication tools, *ALN Magazine*, **3** (2).

Gregor, S D and Cuskelly, E F (1994) Computer mediated communication in distance education, *Journal of Computer Assisted Learning*, **10**, pp 168–81.

Hackman, M and Walker, K (1995) Perceptions of proximate and distant learners enrolled in university level communication courses: a significant non-significant finding, *International Journal of Educational Telecommunications*, **1** (1), pp 43–51.

Henderson, L, Putt, I, Ainge, D and Combes, G (1998) Comparison of students' thinking processes when studying with WWW, IMM and text based materials, in *The Virtual Campus: Trends for higher education and training,* eds F Verdejo and G Davies, Chapman & Hall, New York.

Lewis, R and Vizcarro, C (1998) Collaboration between universities and enterprises in the Knowledge Age, in *The Virtual Campus: Trends for higher education and training,* eds F Verdejo and G Davies, Chapman & Hall, New York.

Marjanovic, O (1999) Learning and teaching in a synchronous collaborative environment, *Journal of Computer Assisted Learning*, **15**, pp 129–38.

Mason, R (1998) Models of online courses, *ALN Magazine,* 2 (2), http://www.aln.org/alnweb/magazine/alnpaga.htm
http://www.aln.org/alnweb/magazine/alnpaga.htm

McConnell, D (1995) *Learning in Groups: Some experiences of online work,* Springer-Verlag, Berlin.

Ogborn, J (1998) Cognitive Development and Qualitative Modelling, *Journal of Computer Assisted Learning*, **14**, pp 292–307.

Oliver, R and Omari, A (in press) Exploring student responses to collaborating and learning in a Web-based environment, *Journal of Computer Assisted Learning.*

Oliver, R, Omari, A and Herrington, H (1998) Exploring student interaction in collaborative World Wide Web computer-based learning environments, *Journal of Educational Multimedia and Hypermedia*, **7** (2/3), p 263.

Oliver, R (1998) Training teachers for distance education programs using authentic and meaningful contexts, *International Journal of Educational Telecommunications*, **4** (2/3), p 147.

Oliver, R (1995) Measuring users' performance with interactive information systems, *Journal of Computer Assisted Learning*, **12** (3), pp 89–102.

Paolucci, R (1999) The effects of cognitive style and knowledge structure on performance using a hypermedia learning system, *Journal of Educational Multimedia and Hypermedia*, **7** (2/3), pp 123–51.

Paolucci, R and Jones, T H (1998) A research framework for investigating the effectiveness of technology on educational outcomes, http://www.sapioinstutite.org

Rimmershaw, R (1999) Using conferencing to support a culture of collaborative study, *Journal of Computer Assisted Learning*, **5** (3), pp 189–200.

Schlais, D, Davis, R and Thomson, K (1999) *Linking Good Neighbors and Faraway Friends into a Shared Student Centered Learning Environment*, European Association of International Education (EAIE), Fifty-third Annual Conference, Maastricht.

Sloffer S, Duber, B and Duffy, T M (1999) *Using Asynchronous Conferencing to Prompt Critical Thinking: Two implementations in higher education*, unpublished manuscript, Center for Research on Learning and Technology Report, Indiana University, Bloomington.

Spratt, C and Smithers, M (1999) *The Nature of Interactions in an Online Learning Environment*, Conference Paper, Fifth International Conference on Technology Supported Learning, Online EDUCA, Berlin.

Stephenson, J and Yorke, M (eds) (1998) *Capability in Higher Education*, Kogan Page, London.

Sumner, T and Taylor, J (1998) Media Integration through meta-learning environments, in *The Knowledge Web: Learning and collaboration on the Net*, eds M Eisenstadt and T Vincent, Kogan Page, London.

Thompson, M and McGrath, J W (1999) Using ALNs to support a complete educational experience, *Journal of Asynchronous Learning Networks*, **3** (2), http://www.aln.org/alnweb/journal/jaln-vol3issue2.htm

Warren, K J and Rada, R (1998) Sustaining computer-mediated communication in university courses, *Journal of Computer Assisted Learning*, **14**, pp 71–80

Wegner, S B, Holloway, K C and Garton, E M (1999) The effects of Internet based instruction on student learning, *Journal of Asynchronous Learning Networks*, **3** (2), http://www.aln.org/alnweb/journal/jaln-vol3issue2.htm

Wilson, T and Whitelock, D (1998) Monitoring the online behaviour of distance learning students, *Journal of Computer Assisted Learning*, **14**, pp 91–99.

For a full set of items reviewed, please contact: Marion Coomey, mcoomey@acs.ryerson.ca

5

Making the right connections: improving quality in online learning

Barry Jackson and Kyriaki Anagnostopoulou
Middlesex University, UK

Editor's introduction

Jackson and Anagnostopoulou have recently undertaken a review of current research with a view to selecting a virtual learning environment for Middlesex University. The research included extensive consultation of external sources of evaluative information and a pilot implementation. The evidence of this study suggests that pedagogical practice and, more importantly, pedagogical conceptions are not necessarily changed by the use of online approaches. It is the teacher's pedagogical conception and not the technology that appears to be the principal variable affecting the nature and quality of teaching. The authors argue that the development of online pedagogy will be best supported by development of conceptions of learning, in teachers and students, which support deep approaches to learning rather than promoting particular pedagogical practices.

Without appropriate pedagogy, use of high capacity communication services cannot provide significant improvements in learning outcomes. In general it is the pedagogy that provides for learning, not the technology or the software alone.

(Carr, 1999)

Introduction

This chapter is written in the context of rapid changes in higher education, many of which are international in scope. The broad features of these changes will be recognizable to anyone working in higher education across the globe: the pressing need to provide a greater proportion of young people with higher education in order to build social and economic development; the promotion of lifelong learning, including retraining and updating for all, as a feature of future economic prosperity; the growing globalization of commerce and of knowledge itself; and the need to address all these issues with greater cost efficiency. Discussion of these issues is accompanied by the expectation that ICT is at the same time both a potential solution and part of the problem. We see an exponential increase in the takeup of ICT, and particularly online technologies, harnessed to solving the problems that higher education and training seek to address.

We will argue that both the main barriers and the main pathways to improving the quality of student learning online lie not with the use of particular technologies but with the pedagogical assumptions and conceptions underlying their use. In this regard the technology itself is transparent: the principles likely to provide good learning experiences are much the same in the real classroom as in the virtual campus. The route to improved learning online is therefore the same route that leads to improved learning by any means – a focus on the particular situated experience of particular learners in specific learning situations, informed by research.

During the evaluation work we have been conducting this year we have encountered scant recognition of the situated nature of learning, nor of its complexity. Much of the literature on online learning has no real grounding in theories of learning. Where reference is made to theories of learning this is often done in a superficial way. There is little evidence of familiarity with the research literature on learning, which makes it clear that the single most important factor shaping learning outcomes is the way in which students approach a learning task, and that the approach is conditioned by a complex of factors that are largely context specific. What this research tells us is that what works here may not work there, that all the conditions in a learning situation need to be understood and aligned if learning is to be effective.

This means that many of the assumptions underlying the development of online pedagogy are up for question.

Pedagogy and technology – three examples

Most of the necessary functions of a learning situation can be implemented by a number of means – it is possible to have one-to-one discussions through e-mail, telephone or video-conferencing, for example. Conversely, different technologies may be more or less well suited to different tasks. However, it is misleading to assume that the use of a particular technology (say online learning) necessarily and of itself brings about improved learning. There are many practitioners for whom using online technology does not stimulate any reframing of their conception of learning and teaching, with damaging consequences for their students.

We wish to illustrate here, through three examples, the complexity of pedagogical practice in relation to the use of online approaches. Our examples are intended to throw light on the difficulties presented by the assumption that online learning *per se* has particular pedagogical character-istics.

Example 1 – Extended Learning Environment Network (ELEN) project

The Extended Learning Environment Network (ELEN) project is a project that aims to disseminate into mainstream courses, across eight higher education institutions in the United Kingdom, the use of a Web-accessed learner management system complete with related materials to support learning of generic key skills and specialized subject knowledge. The project aims to offer online support to groups of campus-based students that could benefit from a communication and courseware delivery system.

Evaluation of the ELEN experience is at an early stage, and data on student approaches and levels of learning outcomes are not yet available. However, the data that are available support an interpretation that the pedagogical conceptions held by teachers have a distinctive effect on the nature of the student learning experience, regardless of the technology used.

Primary findings have indicated a spectrum of student experiences of using learning technology during the project, ranging from indifferent to extremely positive. The experiences of two contrasting but representative students will be used to illustrate this.

Student A found the ELEN experience useful and contributed importantly to his learning. He reported that the generic 'key skills' materials that were on the system were extremely relevant and were easily linked to the subject he was studying. He encountered a few technical problems but the use of communication technology meant he could keep in touch with his tutorial group, even when on placement, and felt well supported by his peers and tutor throughout the module.

Student B, on the other hand, could not see the relevance of the key skills materials to her main area of study. The ELEN component of her module was not compulsory and did not count towards her assessment so she expressed little motivation to engage with the activities on the system. Moreover, there was no reason to use the discussion group facilities available on the system because she could keep in touch with her tutorial group on campus. She found the overall experience interesting but did not see it as providing added value to her learning experience.

Student A and Student B had been allocated to different tutorial groups and therefore their experience of ELEN was orchestrated by different tutors. Focus groups and interviews have concluded that Student A's and Student B's experiences were strongly representative of their respective group's experience (Group A and Group B). Possible variation in Student A's and Student B's personal learning goals, motivation and conceptions of learning might be expected to account for some of the variation in experience but evidence from students across the sample leads us to believe that individual variation is less significant than the variation between Groups A and B.

In order to analyse the findings of the ELEN evaluation and its associated issues, we have found it useful to focus on Robson's (2000) framework for evaluating open learning courses. Robson reminds us that in addition to the concepts held by the individual learners themselves, there are pedagogical concepts inherent in the resources and tools, as well as those held by stakeholders. He further suggests that these implicit concepts or theories may be consistent or conflicting with one another and are capable of influencing the teaching and learning situation, even in a one-to-one teaching situation. These are theories of learning:

- held by the learner;
- held by the educational establishment;
- held by the academics/teachers;
- inherent in the learning materials;
- inherent in the technology.

In the ELEN implementation the theories embedded in three out of the five loci are common across the pilots. Briefly these are:

- *Theories held by the learners.* Within our evaluation the spread of student experiences appears to correlate sufficiently closely to the groups to which students were allocated for us to largely discount individual differences as explanations for the variation in reported experience.
- *Theories held by the educational establishment.* All participants in the study were either employees or students of the same university. The espoused theory of the institution in which the participants worked/studied is therefore common for all – the university is publicly committed to theories associated with the social construction of learning through student-centred activity and increasing autonomy.

- *Theories inherent in the learning materials.* The way in which these materials are written and designed to include information, interactivity, predefined connections by association and feedback reflect the writing model and the learning theory held by the author(s). In the ELEN project all participants made use of the same learning resources in the area of generic key skills.

- *Theories inherent in the technology.* It may be thought that the tools used for a technological intervention are impartial and objective but software design is in fact guided by the educational theories held by its developers. Learning theories embedded in the technology reflect the pedagogical concepts held by the software developers at the time. The 'Virtual Campus' technology provided a single environment for the delivery of materials and student management. Its context, tasks, tools and the interface, which Soloway *et al* (1996) describe as the four components of a learning environment, are rooted in theories of constructivism and socio-culturism with contributions from information-processing psychology.

If we discount individual differences for our two groups of students, the only source of variation in learning theory encountered in the ELEN experience is the variation between conceptions held by the tutors. It is the way in which the technology was orchestrated by tutors with different conceptions that has brought about different learning experiences for students. The way in which the 'Virtual Campus' technology and the key skills materials were introduced, used, embedded and supported by the tutors was central to the students' experience. Each tutorial group participating in the ELEN project had a slightly different experience depending not only on the learning theory held by each tutor but also to what extent it was successfully implemented. Evidence emerging from interviews with sample students and tutors indicates support for the view that the variation in students' experience of learning within the ELEN environment is best explained by the variation in the situated practice of individual tutors and, also, that the variation in tutors' practices can be correlated with conceptions of learning held by the tutors.

Example 2

In this section we describe an example of how variation occurs in the pedagogical use of a single virtual learning environment in ways that do not necessarily accord with the expectations of the literature.

Virtual learning environments (VLEs) have been described as 'learning management software systems that synthesise the functionality of computer-mediated communications software and online methods of delivering course materials' (Britain and Liber, 1999). There are many available VLEs with similar sets of features and a range of capabilities.

Milligan (1999) has attempted to classify VLEs, depending on the tools they have to support various learning situations, into the following range: traditional, extension, learner centred, collaborative and home-made. He also suggests that some systems are better suited than others to particular educational contexts. Table 5.1 illustrates Milligan's categories mapped on to a hierarchical model of online courses developed by Mason (1998). It also lists some representative VLEs for each category.

Table 5.1 Models of online courses

Range (Milligan)	Model of online course (Mason)	Representative products
Traditional	Content + support	WebCT Top Class
Extension	Wrap-around	MERLIN PIONEER
Learner centred	Integrated	Learning landscapes COSE
Collaborative	Integrated	coMentor
Home-made		CVU Nathan Bodington

Our example here focuses on WebCT. This software is identified as typifying a 'content plus support' online course model. At Coventry University WebCT has been implemented university-wide as a standard learning environment and as a minimum, each module is required to match Mason's 'content plus support' model by providing basic module information online. Each module leader is then given the opportunity to increase the content of their sites in ways relevant to their subject if he or she wishes.

Within the same institution it is now possible to encounter a spectrum of learning scenarios online:

- *Content plus support*. Every module site incorporates a module summary, a list of learning outcomes, knowledge base and assessment criteria, and the formative and summative assessments for the module. The above combined with basic teaching resources (such as online teaching notes and PowerPoint slides) are seen by students as a 'safety net' for their work (Chadwick and Bayley, 1999).

- *Wrap-around (for example Module 103LAI: Italy from the Risorgimento to the Second Republic)*. This module involves a combination of theory and discussion, with all participants progressing through set learning resources. All online components of this module are fully integrated into the curriculum and in this case WebCT was used as a reinforcement tool (Orsini-Jones and Davidson, 1999). It not only provides students with the basic information about the module but also incorporates lecture summaries, information about study skills in face-to-face seminars and opportunities for online discussions on seminar topics. Students' reflection on their learning and any unanswered questions were also posted on the system.

- *Integrated (for example, Module 304LAI: Italian Language. Advanced translation skills online)*. In this module students make use of few set resources and instead concentrate on their personal experience in relation to that of their peers. The learning experience is based on considerable communication and collaborative work (Orsini-Jones and Davidson, 1999). WebCT was initially used as a resource area to stimulate debates and offer theoretical support and a bulletin board facility was used to document minutes of face-to-face discussions. Each student group was asked to agree evaluation criteria and standards for their coursework, which were suggested, discussed and documented online. WebCT provided the necessary facilities for students to construct their own resources and share work. The completed coursework was then transferred to WebCT in hypertext format; the students' input dynamically created the course content, which also provided a valuable resource available for use with the next cohort of students. Students were required to reflect upon their completed work and write a group presentation after receiving feedback from their peers about their contributions. The persistence of all module material and recorded interactions on the Web encourages peer observation and comparative evaluation of students' personal performance against that of their peers.

Example 3

Our third example is a report of a teacher reflecting on his practice in introducing Web technology into his courses (Knox, 1997). It illustrates a teacher who finds appropriate online pedagogy through experiment, reflection and redesign. His courses are successful but do not always conform to the advice that the literature on online learning offers. Things don't always go right, but the teacher has a means of knowing that, and is able to respond: 'We floundered badly. About three weeks into the course, I knew it wasn't working and thanks to private messages from a few of the students, I knew why'.

Knox describes at least two features of his apparently successful courses that seem to run counter to the theory-derived advice on online learning. The basis of his course is his lectures, written out as Web pages. The Web pages are linear and have very few external hyperlinks. Knox recognizes that this is sufficiently contrary to assumed good practice to warrant some explanation. The Web lectures, initially chosen for convenience and familiarity, have worked as a format for his particular students. He takes pains to present each lecture as a series of short pages, breaking between pages with a caesura, a dramatic moment, which propels the reader forward to the next page. His explanation for removing hyperlinks is best expressed in his own words:

> The student comes to the web site with roughly the same expectations she/he brings to a textbook. She expects to be able to understand quickly what the work is about, to be able to move through it readily, to have an idea of the boundaries of the work, and to be informed by the content. A site that is filled with hyperlinks violates almost all these expectations. *While in theory we are offering the student the opportunity to explore, in practice the site consists of an unknown number of reading assignments.*
>
> (Knox, 1997)

In Knox's report we see that effective online teaching occurs when the teacher is able to align the technology to a deep and continuously tested understanding of the actual students' experiences, in context.

Discussion of the examples

The three examples above illustrate some interrelated features and generate several implications:

- that the students' experience of, and the value they place on, an online learning experience is determined largely by the way in which the learning technology is presented, or 'orchestrated' by the teacher, and that in turn is determined by the conception of learning and teaching that he or she holds, rather than any implicit features of the technology;
- that a particular online technology can be orchestrated in a number of ways, some of which provide a richer learning experience than others; whether the richness is exploited is largely dependent on the approach taken by the teacher, which of course is determined by the conceptions that he or she holds;
- that the technology should be able and flexible enough to afford the application of several, possibly conflicting, learning theories or else its uptake, use and success in aiding the process of putting them into practice will be limited;

- that the potential for rich learning experiences online is mostly exploited by teachers whose conceptions of learning and teaching predispose them to consider deeply and continuously the needs of the learners in any situation, regardless of technology;
- that those teachers have not arrived at their conceptions of learning as a result of using online learning – the conceptions pre-exist. The same is true of teachers whose conception of learning is narrow and didactic or is formula-driven. Online learning does not, by itself, change teachers' conceptions of learning;
- that advice and guidance available from the literature is often misguided, because it is ill-informed about the nature of learning.

How is good pedagogical practice to be derived for online learning?

There is a vast and growing body of information and advice now available, both in print and online. However, it offers little clear advice. As Bonk and Cunningham (1998) state: 'The lack of pedagogical guidance about integrating tools for collaboration and communication into one's classroom or training session leaves educators across educational settings with mounting dilemmas and confusion'. Recent reviews of this large volume of literature have concluded that it contains little useful research on the effectiveness of online learning, and that where research does exist it is generally of questionable quality (Phipps and Merisotis, 1999).

One of the features of the literature on online pedagogy is that, where pedagogical improvement on existing practice is claimed, the evidence base for the measurement of improvement is questionable. It is notable that independent measures of student learning, such as those associated with the Structure of the Observed Learning Outcome or SOLO taxonomy (Biggs and Collis, 1982; Biggs, 1996, 1999; Dahlgren, 1984), are rarely to be found in evaluations of effectiveness of online pedagogy. An additional difficulty here is that most reports on the effectiveness of online learning evaluate online learning in comparison with 'traditional' pedagogical practice. This is problematic because there is considerable evidence that current 'traditional' practice does not sufficiently achieve the outcomes that it sets out to achieve (see, for example, Dahlgren, 1984; Chapter 3 of Ramsden, 1992).

Where effectiveness is demonstrated, it can often be attributed to a pedagogical improvement rather than to the use of the technology itself. For many authors, however, it appears difficult to divorce pedagogical improvement from the application of technology. This may in part be explained by the fact that much of the literature has its origins in computing research rather than in educational development or learning research. As a consequence many authors have limited knowledge of what research tells us about learning. Where authors have little understanding of how pedagogical change can bring about improvements in learning, regardless of technology, it is easy for them to mis-ascribe the role of the technology itself.

Improvements in learning through online approaches, when observed, are generally the product of reflective teachers who have conceptions that encourage them to develop effective teaching interventions regardless of technology rather than features of the particular online pedagogy such as discussion groups or interactive exercises or hyperlinked resources. Conversely, arguments claiming that pedagogical improvements inherently follow from the use of online technologies are dangerously misleading.

Phipps and Merisotis draw a similar conclusion from their study:

> ... although the ostensible purpose of much of the research is to ascertain how technology affects student learning and student satisfaction, many of the results seem to indicate that technology is not nearly as important as other factors, such as learning tasks, learner characteristics, student moti-vation, and the instructor. The irony is that the bulk of the research on tech-nology ends up addressing an activity that is fundamental to the academy, namely pedagogy – the art of teaching.

(Phipps and Merisotis, 1999)

Conclusion – routes to pedagogical improvement

If the key to the development of effective online pedagogy is the devel-opment of effective pedagogical practice itself, then we can discern some possible routes for improving quality. This chapter is not the place for an extended review of what we know about student learning, but it is appro-priate to make some reference to the literature on learning. This makes it clear that the single most important factor influencing learning outcomes is the approach that the student takes. Students may take a deep or a surface approach to a learning task, and their approach will be determined by a number of factors in the learning situation. These have been comprehen-sively discussed by Prosser and Trigwell (1999).

The research tells us that, in each learning situation and task, attention must be paid to understanding and aligning the various components of the situation if effective learning is to result. This cannot be arrived at by formula: a recurrent finding is that we can never assume that the impact of an intervention on student learning is what we expect it to be. However, we can assume that there are some very simple principles which, if applied, will encourage a deep approach, and that there are some factors that need to be reduced if a surface approach is to be avoided. Examples of these principles can be found in Gibbs (1992) and Biggs (1999).

A similar set of principles has been derived independently in America and is very widely used in higher education institutions (Chickering and Gamson, 1987). An updated version that includes consideration of online learning technology has been written (Chickering and Ehrmann, 1997).

The route to ensuring quality of online pedagogy may therefore be best pursued by ensuring that designers and, more importantly, implementers of online learning, are familiar with the research on learning, understand its implications, and take care to apply the principles that are derived from it.

References

Biggs, J and Collis, K F (1982) *Evaluating the Quality of Learning: The SOLO taxonomy*, Academic Press, New York.

Biggs, J (1996) Enhancing teaching through constructive alignment, *Higher Education*, **32**, pp 347–64.

Biggs, J (1999) *Teaching for Quality Learning at University*, SRHE and Open University Press, Buckingham.

Bonk, C J and Cunningham, D J (1998) Searching for learner-centered, constructivist, and sociocultural components of collaborative educational learning tools, in *Electronic Collaborators: Learner-centered technologies for literacy, apprenticeship and discourse*, eds C J Bonk and K S King, Lawrence Erlbaum Associates, Mahwah NJ (quoted in *Teaching at an Internet Distance, The Pedagogy of Online Teaching and Learning*, URL: http://www.vpaa.uillinois.edu/tid/report/tid_report.html).

Boud, D (ed) (1981) *Developing Student Autonomy in Learning*, Kogan Page, London.

Britain, S and Liber, O (1999) *A Framework for Pedagogical Evaluation of Virtual Learning Environments*, URL: http://www.jtap.ac.uk/reports/htm/jtap-041.html

Carr, J (1999) *The Future is Already Here. A National Strategy for Australian Education and Training to Maximise Opportunities Offered by High Capacity Communication Services*, URL: http://www.educationau.edu.au/archives/Broadbnd/Report.htm

Chadwick, S and Bayley, V (1999) *Teaching and Learning in a New Environment: Using WebCT in the design and delivery of a business enterprise degree programme*, presented at Enable99 Conference: Enabling Network Based Learning, URL: http://www.enable.evitech.fi/enable99/papers/chadwick/chadwick.html

Chickering, A W and Gamson, Z F (1987) *Seven Principles of Good Practice in Undergraduate Education: Faculty inventory*, URL: http://cougarnet.byu.edu/tmcbucs/fc/fulltxt/7pr_int.htm

Chickering, A W and Ehrmann, S C (1997) *Implementing the Seven Principles: Technology as lever*, American Association for Higher Education, URL: http://www.aahe.org/technology/ehrmann.htm

Dahlgren, L O (1984) Outcomes of learning, in *The Experience of Learning*, eds F Marton, D Hounsell and N Entwhistle, Scottish Academic Press, Edinburgh.

Gibbs, G (1992) *Improving the Quality of Student Learning*, Technical and Educational Services, Bristol.

Knox, E L S (1997) The pedagogy of Web site design, *ALN Magazine*, **1** (2), URL: http://www.aln.org/alnweb/magazine/issue2/knox.htm

Mason, R (1998) Models of online courses, *ALN Magazine*, **2** (2), URL: http://www.aln.org/alnweb/magazine/vol2/issue2/Masonfinal.htm

Milligan, C (1999) *Delivering Staff and Professional Development Using Virtual Learning Environments*, JTAP Online, URL: http://www.jtap.ac.uk/reports/htm/jtap-044.html

Orsini-Jones, M and Davidson, A (1999) From reflective learners to reflective lecturers via WebCT, *Active Learning*, **10**, July, pp 32–38.

Phipps, R and Merisotis J (1999) *What's the Difference? A review of contemporary research on the effectiveness of distance learning in higher education*, The Institute for Higher Education Policy, Washington DC, URL: http://www.ihep.com/PUB.htm#diff

Prosser, M and Trigwell, K (1999) *Understanding Learning and Teaching: The experience in higher education*, SRHE and Open University Press, Buckingham.

Ramsden, P (1992) *Learning to Teach in Higher Education*, Routledge, London.

Robson, J (2000) Evaluating online teaching, Open Learning, **15** (2), pp 151–72.

Ryan, S, Scott, B, Freeman, H and Patel, D (2000) *The Virtual University*, Kogan Page, London.

Soloway, E *et al* (1996) *Learning Theory in Practice: Case studies of learner-centered design*, ACM CHI '96, Human Factors in Computer Systems, Proceedings, Vancouver, BC, URL: http://www.acm.org/sigchi/chi96/proceedings/papers/Soloway/es_txt.htm

Part 3

Practitioners

The items in Part 3 have been contributed by some of the most experienced practitioners in the field of online teaching and learning. They are drawn from the United States, Australia, Belgium and the United Kingdom. Each presents at least one example, which is described in some detail. Ron Oliver of Edith Cowan University, Perth, Australia (Chapter 8) and Dennis Schlais and Richard Davis of California State University, United States (Chapter 9) describe attempts to extend online learning to develop high level 'soft skills' such as critical thinking, collaborative skills and group-based problem solving. Schlais and Davis also describe an exciting initiative in international collaboration. Curtis Bonk and his colleagues at Indiana University, in the United States (Chapter 7) take a systematic look at four contrasting examples of online learning and present a view of the emerging roles of teachers in this medium. Robin Mason of the Open University, one of the world's leading institutions in distance learning, reports on two programmes attempting to develop conferencing skills entirely online (Chapter 6). Jef van den Branden, of EuroPACE, Leuven University, Belgium (Chapter 10) looks at attempts to use online learning to build a cross-European network to support research students. Within these five chapters, readers will find a multitude of pointers for use in their own practice as well as insights into some of the pedagogical underpinnings of online learning.

6

Effective facilitation of online learning: the Open University experience

Robin Mason
Open University, UK

Editor's introduction

In this chapter, Mason draws on the Open University's extensive experience of tutoring online in a review of conferencing networks in two contrasting higher education courses, one at entry level, the other at post-graduate level. Unusually for the Open University, the two programmes are delivered without any face-to-face contact. Mason concludes with some lessons on how best to facilitate online learning, including tutor roles, course design and extended resources.

Background

The UK Open University (OU) began using computer conferencing in 1988 and now has nearly 100,000 students online, either studying courses that require networking or accessing a range of administrative, social and additional course resources. This represents a large volume of activity by a large number of students, but it is important to note that it is still less than half the OU's total student body that is involved in any form of online learning.

The approach to educational technologies that the OU has always taken is to monitor its students and potential students regularly and extensively to determine ownership of or access to media that could be used in teaching and to evaluate the effectiveness of its initial uses of new media. As student willingness to purchase various technologies increases and, more significantly, as students indicate an interest and openness to learn through new media, so we increase our use of specific technologies.

This approach was very evident with the advent of video recorders in the 1970s and 1980s, where we were able to exploit the stop/start and replay advantages of videos over broadcasts when the home ownership of video recorders reached 90 per cent.

The same approach applies to the use of computer networking. At first those courses that could make a strong case for requiring students to use a networked computer were the early pioneers. With the encouragement of our student association, the data from our student surveys, and the evaluations of existing courses, we are making increasing use of online tutoring and course and administrative resources on the Web.

We have ambitious plans to put 'tasters' of courses on the Web so that prospective students can more accurately choose the courses that fit their needs. We also have a range of pre-course materials on the Web – how to study, how to write essays, various mathematics and IT background materials. Students can view their records, request information and advice, book summer school places and a host of other administrative functions.

Open University courses use networking to different degrees. At the simplest level, some courses, especially in curriculum areas where student access to IT is not high, offer optional online tutoring or e-mail contact with a tutor. Where access is high, tutoring is offered online, and face-to-face tutorials are much reduced. Students may be required to work collaboratively in small groups and to submit joint assignments. In addition, extra course resources are provided on a course Web site, although the majority of the course is still delivered through purpose-written printed material sent to the students through the post. Finally, on a few courses, both the content and the tutoring are delivered online. We do not intend, for the immediate future, to 'put all our courses online'. We produce very high quality printed course materials and it would be a poor use of networking technology – in our view – to put large amounts of text online when students will simply print it out to make their study more flexible.

This paper describes the findings from our past 12 years of online tutoring and then concentrates on the more recent lessons we have learnt from the courses that do use the Web to deliver both content and tutoring.

Early findings

The business of training students (and tutors) how to use a conferencing system was, when we started, a much more involved and protracted undertaking than it is now. While we are still not at the point where we can expect undergraduate students to be experienced online learners before they start a course, we are approaching this on post-graduate courses. Compared to the old command line systems of the 1980s, the Web is almost 'plug and play', although the dedicated team who run the OU helpdesk might disagree!

While the basic mechanisms for getting online have improved, the need for students and tutors to adapt their learning and teaching styles to the online environment is, surprisingly, still a significant hurdle. As we found in our very earliest evaluations (Mason, 1989), some people take to the online environment immediately and find it a remarkably stimulating and liberating medium for learning; others need a lot more training and encouragement as well as time and practice to feel comfortable or even grudgingly positive about using networks for study. Finally, a small minority is very resistant whether for practical or philosophical reasons.

One of the first observations we made was that simply providing an environment in which students and tutors could interact did not guarantee successful engagement. What happened was that the most confident, 'talkative' and computer-literate participants dominated the discussion areas to the exclusion of the more tentative thinkers, those with less easy online access and those who were so busy they could not quickly see where to make their contributions. Some discussions were valuable learning exchanges but they were lost amongst an overload of more ephemeral, social or irrelevant messages. We could see the potential but needed a much more structured approach for facilitating equality of participation.

In common with most other online teachers at institutions elsewhere, we discovered that students and tutors complain about lack of time, too many messages to read and too much demand for interaction. In our case, the nature of the tutoring role, honed over 20 years of print-based supported open learning, no longer fit the demands of the online environment. We needed to help tutors make their online work more effective and less time consuming.

We have experimented with a range of structures, activities and approaches to address these problems over the years, and continue to do so, as the medium itself evolves and social attitudes and experience of the online world mature. The following list gives some examples:

- A wide range of social conferences and interest groups are managed online by our student association.
- Technical support both by telephone and online is provided by a dedicated team of specialists.
- Tutors are advised by the course team which conference(s) they are expected to moderate and all other conferences are optional for them.
- Course teams provide materials for tutors that include example messages they can use, ideas for discussions, dates for specific activities and resources for preparing their inputs.

- Special guest lecturers are used to relieve the burden on tutors and to provide a stimulating learning environment for short, targeted periods.
- Self-help groups are encouraged where students can exchange the kind of study support many distance learners need to maintain motivation.
- Large courses have created a new specialist tutor role to support and coordinate the inputs of tutors in each region.
- An extra, non-tutoring 'host' has sometimes been used to help in the time-consuming first weeks of a course to welcome individual students, sort out initial difficulties and moderate the plenary conferences.
- Tutors are encouraged to set parameters around their online availability, for example, by indicating the likely pattern of their logons.
- The university has devised a code of conduct for online interaction that is well publicized and lays out what is and is not acceptable practice.
- New practices for monitoring the activities of online tutors have been devised so that a minimum standard can be maintained across every course.
- Many structured activities and small group projects have been devised for the online component of courses.

Current developments

There are three areas of development that currently preoccupy OU staff involved in online teaching: collaborative small group activities, real-time events online and innovative online assessment. Two courses in particular have led the way in these developments and both are presented almost entirely online.

T171 'You, your computer and the Net' is an entry-level course about information and communication technology (ICT) that was first offered in 1999 to 850 students and in 2000 attracted an overwhelming 12,500 students. The course is designed for a wide range of students, some of whom may be completely new to computers or to online work and others who may wish to hone existing skills. Course resources include an extensive Web site of course materials and study guidance, links to further reading, a CD ROM containing course software, and two set books together with introductory booklets designed to help students get started. The course aims to enculturate students into ICT (Weller, 2000) and to provide them with the skills to use new technologies as tools. Students are required to study from the custom-written content on the Web and from the set books, but the degree of freedom afforded them increases as the course progresses.

There are four tutor-marked assignments during the course and an end-of-course assessment replacing the conventional exam. Students have to construct their work as HTML documents and submit them electronically.

The other course, H802 'Applications of IT in Open and Distance Education', forms part of the OU's MA in Open and Distance Education. The course offers practical experience in online activities, collaborative work and Internet searching and was presented for the first time in 1998 to 60 postgraduate students worldwide. The course has very few purpose-written materials and has been designed around collaborative small-group work, Web activities and several set books. It uses a Web-based virtual campus, which has three categories of resources within an integrated environment: a conferencing system, an online study guide and a full text webliography of resources, papers and links to online journals. The approach is largely constructivist and collaborative, the emphasis being on online activities and peer learning, rather than on solitary reading of course materials, and students are expected to make use of a range of Web resources.

Collaborative small group activities

Unusually for the OU, both the courses described here have no face-to-face tutorials and most students never meet except online. As the subject matter of both courses concerns the technology itself, the experience of working collaboratively online is part of the course content.

With H802, we developed the concept of an online debate, choosing carefully a polemical statement that contests central course issues, which has good resources available to substantiate both sides of the argument, and which is significant enough to warrant discussion over a three-week period. We assign specific roles to each person in the group (which could be as small as four, or as large as 10), such as moderator of the discussion, proposer of the motion, opposer of the motion, documentalists (who summarize relevant ideas from the set readings), researchers (who go to find relevant papers and resources on the Web), commenters (whose specific task is to discuss ideas put forth by the opposer and proposer), and finally rapporteur (who is responsible for summarizing the discussion at the end of three weeks).

From previous courses, we were well aware that there is a wide range of abilities, interests and time in which people will engage in online activities. This led us to the concept of different options for different types of learners. On H802 we focus student participation in small group conferences, but offer the option of reading and even participating in the discussions of other small groups.

Each subgroup has their own conference thread for discussion of the current activity, and while they can follow the messages of other sub-groups and can even participate in the sub-groups of other tutors, this is optional. From a perusal of the history function within the conference system, which indicates who has read any particular message, it is apparent that over half the students read some messages from other groups, and occasionally a student will comment outside their own group. In some activities the sub-groups will have different topics; in other activities the groups will all be doing the same work. Students can expand the course by following several topics, or where the same topic is discussed by all, they can see the variety of ways in which different people tackle the question. This facility – this depth and breadth as it were – seems to work well as a way of streamlining student participation at the same time as providing opportunity for individual difference.

(Mason, 1999)

On T171, the course conferencing environment consisted of tutor group conferences in which each tutor and the 12–15 students assigned to every tutor were expected to raise course-related issues and problems. In addition there were course-wide subject conferences run by central academic staff to discuss the major topics in each module. Finally, there were technical support conferences on topics such as word processing, networking, and databases. Specialist staff moderated these. Many students did not contribute to these national conferences, but they did read messages, and this can be very beneficial. Some students reported that they felt they had to read all messages in every conference, and consequently spent a lot of time reading irrelevant messages.

Feedback from the evaluation of the pilot presentation (Mason and Weller, 2000) led to revised guidance to students.

Active discussion has long been one of the aspects that is difficult to provide in distance education, with tutorials and summer schools being the usual means of achieving this. In T171, we deliberately wanted to provoke discussion on a range of issues, so 'embedded conferences' were placed within the Web-based course material. Here students were encouraged to go to the conference and discuss issues such as the role of Microsoft in the industry. As well as providing further interest to the material, this helps students test their understanding of concepts through dialogue, which can then be refined iteratively.

However, many OU students choose to study at a distance precisely because they prefer to work alone, so there is an issue as to what degree the course should force people to participate. As OU students are adults, we preferred to give them the opportunity to do as much, or as little, conferencing as they wanted or needed.

Real-time events

The first real-time event run on H802 was a 24-hour text-based chat in which one hour in every six was led by one of the four tutors. In this way, we hoped to cater for global time differences. We did not want the event to turn into a free-for-all greeting session, so we designed a group task – to mark an anonymously submitted assignment on the same topic as their most recently submitted assignment. Students took to this task with alacrity; the marking scheme was used to go through each of the sections, to make comments on the quality of the work and to arrive at an agreed mark by the end of the hour. About half of the students took part in one or other of the four sessions and a number of them reported how useful it was to look at assignments from the tutor's perspective. One of the outcomes of the event was that a real-time chat system was designed and added to the facilities of the course, and it continues to be used by students on occasions for social and semi course-related issues. The big advantage to this kind of real-time event is that it is accessible to everyone with the usual Web browser. It requires relatively little tutor time and, if well conceived, can add an element of course cohesiveness even on a global scale and a modest educational benefit for a minimum cost.

A real-time audio event has the potential to add more course telepresence and more educational benefit although at somewhat more cost. We used software designed in-house by our Knowledge Media Institute, called KMi Stadium, which supported one-way audio from the tutors and a real-time text-based whiteboard for students' comments. In practice it was incredibly interactive: the tutors could only just keep up with commenting about the issues raised by the 15 students who took part. Everyone found it a stimulating experience and the combination of audio and text allowed the maximum participation in the time.

Other OU courses (in the Business School and in modern languages) have begun to use a new real-time software tool, again designed by KMi, called Lyceum. This provides multi-way audio and shared screen using ordinary Internet access. Real-time sessions can be initiated by tutors and eventually by students. Second language practice, role-plays, debates, self-help groups, problem-solving sessions and student presentations are just some of the many possible uses we see for real-time technologies.

Online assessment

Not only has networked technology opened up new possibilities for course assessment but online course designers also need to rethink their assessment strategy to assess the kind of skills developed by learners in online courses:

information handling skills, resource-based learning skills and collaborative and small-group learning skills (Macdonald *et al*, in press). Assessment is used on both T171 and H802 as a way of encouraging students to participate in online collaborative activities, and also to reflect on their experience. For example, the first assignment on T171 requires students to summarize an article and then to share and discuss their summary online. As evidence of participation, they have to include two of the messages they contributed during the online discussion in their assignment. The evaluation of this assignment showed that it had a positive effect on the quality of contribution and acted as a focus for tutorial support, as well as developing online discussion skills. The next assignment builds on these skills by requiring students to work in small groups to develop a Web site with a home page and links to individual Web pages. Marks are not given for the collaborative product but for the students' analysis of the effectiveness of group work.

On H802, the aim of the course designers was to integrate assessment directly into the online activities and into the collaborative discussions.

> Our thinking is that assessment can be used as a way of validating the importance of contributing to discussions and to team activities, and to encourage students to view assessment as a summary of their work rather than an addition to it. We have allotted as much as 30 per cent of the marks for students' use of ideas from conference messages (their own and other students'). Some assignments are a 'write-up' of the collaborative activity they have just carried out; others are an application of the course activities to their own institutional context.

(Mason, 1999)

Both courses have moved away from the traditional three-hour end-of-course examination. H802 requires an extended essay offering students the opportunity to reflect on all aspects of their experience of learning online. T171 has the same approach except that students produce their reflections as a series of Web pages.

Conclusions

Our experience of how best to facilitate online learning can be summarized under the following four categories:

- *Context*. The context within which online learning is offered must be appropriate in the first place. The advantages of the media must be made obvious to both staff and students through exploiting the unique features and minimizing the disadvantages.

- *Course design*. Uses of online technologies need to be well structured to avoid overload and assist navigation through resources. The assessment strategy should be integrated with the course activities and reflect the aims and objectives of the course.
- *Tutor role*. Tutors need to develop their facilitation skills to be successful online. Ways of limiting the demands on their time need to be sought, otherwise 'interaction fatigue' leads to early burn out.
- *Extended resources*. The more extensive the online facilities offered by the institution (for example, library, registration and payment, counselling, course information and so forth), the more effectively we can take advantage of what networking offers learners. While we are not necessarily aiming to provide 'one-stop shopping' online, we must encourage students to regard networked technologies as a useful tool for all aspects of lifelong learning.

References

Macdonald, J, Weller, M, and Mason, R (in press) Meeting the assessment demands of networked courses, *International Journal of Telecommunications*.

Mason, R (1989) An Evaluation of CoSy on an Open University Course, in *Mindweave: Communication, computers and distance education*, eds R Mason and A Kaye, pp 115–45, Pergamon, Oxford.

Mason, R (1999) *IET's Masters in Open and Distance Education: What have we learned?* CITE Report No. 248, The Open University, Milton Keynes and available at http://iet.open.ac.uk/pp/r.d.mason

Mason, R and Weller, M (2000) Factors affecting students' satisfaction on a web course, *Australian Journal of Educational Technology*, **2** (1),
URL: http://cleo.murdoch.edu.au/ajet/ajet16/mason.html

Weller, M (2000) The use of narrative to provide a cohesive structure to a web based course, *Journal of Interactive Media in Education*, July 2000,
URL: http://www.jime.open.ac.uk

7

Finding the instructor in post-secondary online learning: pedagogical, social, managerial and technological locations

Curtis J Bonk, Jamie Kirkley*, Noriko Hara** and
Vanessa Paz Dennen****
**Indiana University, **University of North Carolina and
***San Diego State University, USA*

Editor's introduction

The authors of this chapter have extensive experience of using online learning in a university context. They identify four key action areas to which the online instructor should pay particular attention: pedagogy, social interaction, management and technology. These four action areas are explored in courses that range from online support for face-to-face tuition to working in fully integrated learning environments. Readers seeking to introduce online learning into their mainstream campus programmes will find this chapter full of helpful practical advice.

Where is the online instructor?

Instructors need a voice in the online learning debate. They need to help institutions decide the level of Web integration in particular courses. They need to take a lead role in various program and policy deliberations. They certainly need to help point out where the Web can prove interesting and powerful as a teaching and learning resource as well as provide sound critique of where there are known and potential limitations. In effect, they need to be vocal about how to use the Web as a pedagogical device and make student learning more relevant, exciting, and powerful (Bonk, Hara, Dennen, Malikowski and Supplee, 2000; Koschmann, 1996). But where are university instructors and corporate trainers in all the critical online decisions and deliberations?

Within the vast expenditure of energy across university and corporate settings attempting to sort out policies, agreements, and new technology tools, we need to first consider the faculty or instructors who will be teaching those courses as well as the students who will be taking them. Without such efforts, we lose quality instructors and many opportunities for true innovation in the adult learning environments. Many college instructors and corporate trainers simply need more information about the ranges of Web uses in their instruction. They need to:

- see examples of how to use the Web to bring in online guests;
- hold chapter discussions from a distance;
- have students reflect on field experiences online with peers throughout the world;
- attend virtual conferences or fieldtrips;
- share materials online with other faculties;
- prepare exams and assessments;
- explore online media resources (Bonk, 1998; Bonk and King, 1998; Bonk and Sugar, 1998; Riel, 1993).

As is clear, activities such as online peer mentoring programs (Bonk, Malikowski, Angeli and East, 1998), debates and role-play require significant planning and task structuring. Unfortunately, most online learning courseware and systems lack such tools and activities. Even after these ideas are grasped and useful tools are created, institutions need to support the innovative faculty members and trainers in using these tools and sharing their experiences (for example, for course-sharing opportunities see the World Lecture Hall at http://wnt.cc.utexas.edu/ccdv543/wlh/index1.html, Merlot.org, and CourseShare.com).

In addition to the above issues, college instructors and corporate trainers need useful frameworks for utilizing the Web in instruction (Bonk and Dennen, 1999). Bonk and Cummings recently described three important Web-based instruction frameworks. First, they linked a dozen guidelines for using the Web as an instructional tool to the 14 learner-centred psychological principles from the American Psychological Association (Bonk and Cummings, 1998). These principles included giving students choice, taking on the role of facilitator, providing prompt feedback, creating recursive tasks that build on each other, using writing and reflection and fostering interactivity and engagement. Secondly, they provided a means to think about the types of interaction structures that the Web affords (Cummings, Bonk and Jacobs, 2000). Interactions among three key online learning participants – instructors, students and practitioners – should be investigated and made more explicit. Just how does one's syllabus indicate the possible types of inter-actions between these three types of participants? Their third framework high-lights 10 distinctive levels of Web integration commonly used (Bonk, Cummings, Hara, Fischler and Lee, 2000). Such levels range from syllabus sharing to including materials from a course on the Web, to having online discussions, to placing an entire course on the Web, to coordinating an entire program on the Web. While the four courses discussed in this chapter primarily address the higher levels of Web integration, there are many smaller-scale and simpler applications of the Web in higher education instruction.

Table 7.1 Summary of the pedagogical, social, managerial and technological roles of the online instructor

	General components and questions (Ashton *et al*, 1999; Mason, 1991)	Ideas from situations 1–4
1. Pedagogical role	**Components:** Assume role of facilitator or moderator (for example, ask questions, probe responses, encourage student knowledge building and linking, summarize or weave discussion, help identify unifying themes, and support and direct interactive discussion, design a variety of educational experiences, provide feedback, offer constructive criticism and rationale, provide explanations and elaborations, utilize direct instructions when appropriate, elicit comments and reflection, referring to outside resources and experts in the field). **Questions:** Who is responsible for different learning activities? Is there much debating and reflection? What activities might foster greater interaction?	**Ideas:** Create problem or project based learning environments, foster peer interaction and feedback, encourage perspective taking and online peer feedback, try innovative techniques (starter-wrapper, debates, online field reflection, electronic cases, structured controversy, team activities), post favourite Web links, monitor and encourage activities with rich peer interaction and feedback and ask many probing questions.
2. Social role	**Components:** Create a friendly and nurturing environment or community feel, exhibit a generally positive tone, foster some humour, display instructor empathy and interpersonal outreach (eg include welcoming statements, invitations, and apologies), and personalize with discussion of one's own online experiences. **Questions:** What is the general tone of the course? Is there a human side to this course? Is joking allowed?	**Ideas:** Employ online cafés as well as student profiles pages, digitize class picture, support casual conversation (eg, discuss survival tactics, online concerns, instructor anecdotes, etc), embed jokes and puns when appropriate in responses, and try to create an online community (eg, share personal stories, invite visitors and foreign guests).
3. Managerial role	**Components:** Coordinate assignments (eg explain assignments, set plans for receipt of assignments, assign partners and groups, set due dates and extensions for assignments), manage online discussion forums (eg set pace, focus, agenda), and handle overall course structuring (eg organize meeting times and places, set office hours, clarify grade distributions, explain the relevance of the course, correct course materials and discuss potential course revisions). **Questions:** Do students understand the assignments? Do they understand the course structure? Are they lost or confused anywhere?	**Ideas:** Consider initial live meetings or online chats, provide detailed syllabus and clear expectations, post online calendar of events or assignments page, provide online gradebook, FAQs, and summary of administrative matters, monitor ongoing discussions and interrupt when off track, assign e-mailpals or constructive friends, provide weekly e-mail feedback, use electronic portfolios to provide overview of how well students are doing and track user logins.
4. Technological role	**Components:** Assist with user technology and system issues, diagnose and clarify problems encountered, notify when a server is down, explain system limitations. **Questions:** Do students have the basic skills? Does their equipment work? Do necessary passwords work?	**Ideas:** Find existing courseware systems or create custom tools, train early, have orientation task and early assignments to test system, explain any custom or unusual tools, have students vote on preferred technologies, be flexible when problems are encountered.

In addition to these frameworks, a fourth scheme (see Table 7.1), first proposed by Mason (1991) and then expanded upon by Ashton, Roberts, and Teles (1999), indicates that it is vital to understand the multiple roles of the instructor in online learning, including the administrative, pedagogical, social and technological roles. Therefore, in this chapter, we document distinct course situations from four different instructors teaching online college courses. We each provide a short vignette based on our online teaching experiences and then explain how we coordinate assignments, discussion, interaction and technologies.

Situation 1: teaching on the Smartweb

Pedagogical actions

The first author has been teaching undergraduate educational psychology on the Web for the past four years. His course, titled 'the Smartweb', is intended for pre-service teachers. Porting this course over to the Web was not particularly easy due to the content-heavy nature of the course and the fact that it simultaneously included both field and laboratory experiences. However, he was fortuitous to write a paper on instructional strategies for the Web (see Bonk and Reynolds, 1997) prior to teaching the course because it helped with course planning as well as the selection of many rich pedagogical activities (Bonk, 1998).

The Smartweb contains tools for Web link suggestions, student profiles, chapter activities, commenting on peer work, accumulating student work in an electronic portfolio, commenting on and rating peer Web link suggestions and profiles (see Figure 7.1). Because of the range of activities and tools, it is important to establish clarity in the expected tasks. As a result of this need, there is a detailed online syllabus as well as two initial meetings to train students in the tools and provide an explanation of the rationale of the course. The pedagogical considerations in the Smartweb are immense. First of all, a deliberate decision was made to provide extensive student feedback. For instance, at the beginning of the semester each student is matched up with an e-mail pal according to his or her confidence in the course. Those who feel highly confident are matched with those who are not. This Web site does not contain password protection, so students provide feedback to each other using avatar names. The e-mail pal provides weekly feedback on one's weekly chapter work that appears in students' online portfolios. In addition, one's e-mail pal is available for advice and can provide reminders on upcoming tasks and due dates. In effect, e-mail pals provide a second level of task structuring or online support.

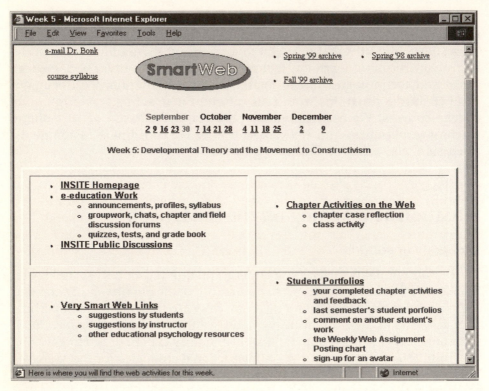

Figure 7.1 The Smartweb interface (situation 1)

The utilization of peers in online instruction is also one way to reduce the heavy workload on the instructor or trainer, thereby enabling him or her to focus attention on key individuals in need of help. Here, the instructor provides feedback on student chapter work, weekly discussions, field reflections and case scenarios. He also strategically provides substantive chapter feedback near the beginning of the semester in order to determine if any students are encountering difficulty with the technology or the course material. In addition, throughout the semester, he also posts weekly weaving comments in the online discussion with specific references to individual student posts.

Social actions

Like the pedagogical role, the social side of the Smartweb is an important indicator of the online course's success or failure. Social actions might include instructor empathy, interpersonal outreach (for example, welcoming statements, invitations and apologies), discussion of one's own online experiences and humour. There are many examples of social activity in the Smartweb. In fact, the Smartweb instructor always opens the virtual café with a greeting.

Smartweb students are then asked to post a self-introduction in response to the opening greeting. During the initial live meeting, students are also asked to complete the information in the student profile section (for example, name, hobbies, strengths and weaknesses, major, hometown, computer experience and so forth). Near the end of this session, a digital picture is taken and later loaded to the Web site with first name and initial of last name indicators. Such tools are meant to provide some shared history and semblance of a learning community.

There is also a heavy focus on student responsiveness and interactive commenting in the Smartweb. For example, students are encouraged to rate peer Web links and evaluate peer discussion or reflection comments. Their Web link ratings appear next to the link suggestion. Students are also encouraged to comment on each other's profiles with a three level rating system (three stars indicating lots in common; two stars indicating at least one thing in common; one star indicating that one simply wanted to comment). In addition to interactive commenting, humour is pervasive on the Smartweb. In fact, a student once suggested that 'a sense of humour' be listed as a prerequisite for the course. The instructor attempts to insert extensive humour not only in his weekly discussion comments and weaving statements but also in any e-mail messages to students. In addition to humour, social acknowledgements are highly prevalent in the Smartweb (for example, 'I agree with everything said so far' or 'Glad you could join us'). Many students begin messages with a social acknowledgement of someone's idea or point of view and then they take the discussion in a new direction (see Bonk, Daytner, Daytner, Dennen and Malikowski, in press).

Certainly, the social climate is central to student online learning. Instructor empathy or concern for student work helps foster a student-centred climate. From this perspective, the instructor must be flexible in pressing situations and give some choice regarding assignments. Of course, the management style, to which we now turn, is also important.

Managerial actions

While the pedagogical role primarily relates to direct instructor involvement in class activities and the social role concerns or class climate or tone, online managerial actions involve overseeing task and course structuring. Managerial actions include coordinating assignments (explaining assignments, coordinating receipt of assignments, assigning partners and groups, setting due dates and extensions for assignments). In the Smartweb, there are many ways for students to find out about the assignment structure and associated due dates.

An initial class meeting or two with students helps spell out the requirements and expectations. Student e-mail pals also provide some assistance on when assignments are due. And, as indicated earlier, they also submit weekly feedback on each other's work. Posting prior student work to the Web serves to model general task expectations and standards, while lowering student anxiety. Furthermore, this archiving of student work or classroom legacy instils pride in students whose work is posted.

In addition to peer mentoring and record archiving, the Smartweb system helps coordinate student weekly activity. For instance, on the Smartweb homepage (see http://www.indiana.edu/smartweb), there is a calendar-like interface. This calendar serves as a reminder that student work needs to be posted each week. Once students post their work, it is stored in their own electronic portfolio under an avatar name. They select their avatar from the 42 names to maintain some anonymity because, as indicated, the Smartweb, for the most part, does not use password protection. A blue dot at the top of their portfolio under a particular week indicates that they were successful in posting. Indicators of peer feedback are provided on the left-hand column of each student portfolio. Both types of indicators are hyper-linked to the respective posting.

A 'Web Assignments Posting Chart' indicates who has successfully posted his or her work as well as whether there is any peer feedback. Once again, there are dots to indicate postings are complete. This serves several purposes. First of all, it provides an overview for the instructor as well as students and guests regarding students who have completed their weekly postings and also received peer feedback. Consequently, instructors can readily determine who needs additional prompting and scaffolding in the course. Along these same lines, students can determine how well they are progressing from a task completion basis in comparison to their peers.

Another means of task coordination is to post important assignment information in the 'administrivia' discussion within the computer conferencing discussion. Here the instructor posts lists of e-mail pals, weekly discussion starters and wrappers, and a listing of team members for any small group work. This area is useful if students forget their role or assignment for a week or the e-mail addresses of their partners. In addition to the administrivia topic, managerial actions are even more vital in weekly online chapter discussions. For example, an instructor might point students to other messages, comment about posting length or format, define the audience, note on- and off-task participation, and direct students to different topics and folders for posting. He typically posts near the end of a weekly posting cycle in order to allow students some responsibility for teaching and learning.

At a general level, managerial actions involve coordinating the course (for example, organizing meeting times and places, office hours, defining grade distributions, explaining the relevance of the course, correcting course materials and discussing potential course revisions). Electronic mail is the tool of choice here. E-mail can inform students of interesting activity in the

Smartweb, detail student grade distributions on an exam, remind students of upcoming events and reflect on overall progress to date. It is also used to coordinate live group meetings and luncheon discussions. E-mail might also be used to announce technology problems that students are currently encountering and times in which the system may be functional again (for example, when a server suddenly goes down or is under scheduled maintenance). The use of e-mail by the instructor is a common event, perhaps occurring three or four times per week on a whole-group basis and 15 to 25 times per week in reply to specific individuals or inquiries. The group e-mails are usually quite long and numbered by key points in order to assist in student comprehension.

Technological actions

The technology required to participate in the Smartweb is fairly basic – a computer with a modem and an Internet connection and appropriate browser. However, because the Smartweb was built using specialized tools, it is vital to train students on how to use key features. Training takes place the first two Saturdays of the semester in three-hour blocks in order to lower student anxiety about the course as well as their computer skills. During the first week, students learn about the course requirements and explore aspects of the Smartweb system including posting a self-introduction in the café as well as in the student profile area. In the ensuing week, students complete their chapter work and field reflections and are asked to report technological problems that they encountered at the start of the second training session.

Some students fail to complete their work in a timely fashion, so completion of the first three weeks of Smartweb work is worth 30 points. Assigning some point value early in the semester is a way to force most students to test out the technology that they have available at home and in school. Of course, technology problems can be encountered when browsers and other tools are upgraded. During the first year or two of Smartweb activity, student posts would take between 15 minutes and an hour to appear in student portfolios. As a result, some students would get nervous that their work did not post and would submit it a second or third time, thereby causing their personal portfolios to bulge and requiring someone to manually delete the extra posts.

Technology issues are diverse. One student in the Smartweb lost two hours of work on a quiz because he was working in the education library late at night and it closed before he completed it. Another student had his apartment burgled during spring break, including his computer. More typical is the student whose computer simply dies or catches a virus during a key moment in the semester. Such technology issues are never totally resolved, so instructors and students need extra patience and flexibility.

Smartweb summary

Given the complexity of the Smartweb, the instructor is vital to any success and certainly cannot hide. The instructor must decide on when and where students will complete their work, interact with peers, link to outside resources and extend the course in new directions. Just what degree of student choice and responsibility for his or her learning will be allowed? What forms of instruction will the instructor rely upon? What hats will he or she wear each day or in any particular interaction? These are just some of the critical issues that need to be addressed as more teaching and learning takes place online. A continual discussion of these issues is provided in the next three course experiences.

Situation 2: online problem-based learning – scaffolding the ill-structured problem-solving experience

Introduction

For the past four years, the second author has taught an online graduate class entitled 'F500: Teaching with the Internet Across the Curriculum' (see http://www.indiana.edu/ f500). The majority of students in this class are teachers and technology coordinators working full-time and taking courses part-time, so it is critical that the course address real-world problems as part of the learning process. As a result, this instructor has used a problem-based learning (PBL) approach (Barrows, 1985; Finkle and Torp, 1995) to design and teach the course. Using problem-based learning in an online environment presents some unique challenges (Kirkley, in preparation).

The goal of the course is for students to experience two weeks 'in the life of a school district superintendent dealing with issues related to Internet rights and responsibilities'. Some examples are students accessing the *Anarchist's Cookbook*, letters from parents who are upset about their child's name being published on the Internet, an unflattering newspaper article about a school principal and computer log files of students in a biology class who are surfing heavy metal band sites. Each piece of information provides part of the issue or problem in which the superintendent, Mr Smith, needs assistance in order to implement a district-wide Internet policy.

Pedagogical structuring

The technological tools available to support problem-based learning currently are quite limited. While there are many asynchronous conferencing tools available, few have features that efficiently support the PBL process for brainstorming, problem investigation, idea analysis and convergence, debating, collaborative writing and team production.

For this course, the instructor uses two tools that explicitly address the PBL process: 1) the Web; and 2) an asynchronous conferencing tool called ACT (Duffy, Dueber and Hawley, 1998). The Web is used to set up the problem or case study that details a school district dealing with a myriad of issues related to adopting the use of the Internet in schools. (See Figure 7.2.) The learning goal for the students is to gain a better understanding of these issues and write a report to the superintendent, advising him on how to deal with various issues such as acceptable use policies, teacher professional development, and student rights and responsibilities.

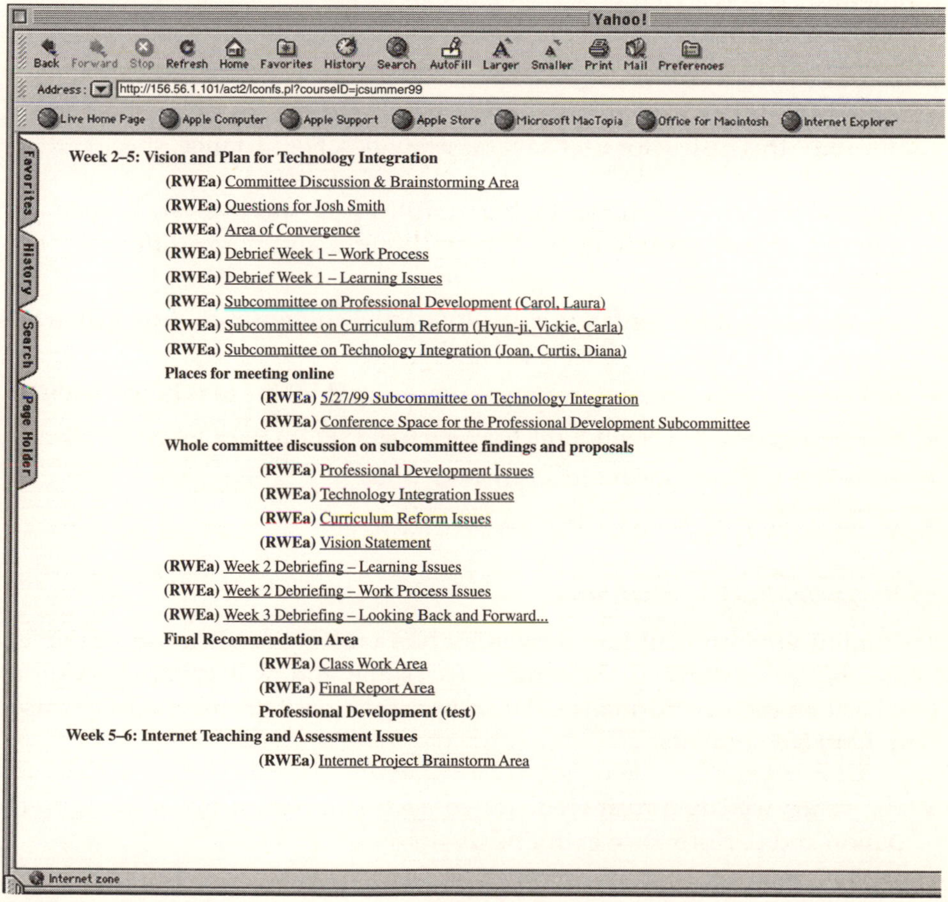

Figure 7.2 The structure of the asynchronous conferencing system (situation 2)

To make the PBL process more concrete, the instructor establishes conferences that visually match the PBL learning process. For example, the first conference is set up so students can brainstorm and define the problem. Fortunately, the branching structure of asynchronous conferencing supports student brainstorming. That is a definite strength, but it is often difficult for students to reach convergence or vote on issues. Therefore, the instructor often creates a separate conference called 'convergence' intended to help students come to an agreed process. Work conferences were also set up for each small group to use for researching the problem. A group work area and final report conference complete the set up.

Students indicate that they like the authentic nature of the problem as well as the visual layout. Of course, it is important to conceptualize the screen display so that the learner is not overwhelmed in a limited spatial environment such as the Web.

Social issues: creating community

Much of the focus here is on community building. To create a sense of community, this instructor uses several strategies. For instance, she:

- creates an open environment where multiple perspectives are valued (for example, she asks students what they thought and poses different viewpoints);
- creates a computer conference just for casual conversation (the instructor also posts there);
- provides a supportive environment where student input is highly valued;
- makes suggestions for students to work together on various projects;
- makes sure missed ideas are addressed; and
- invites visitors to join discussions.

Managerial issues: feedback

The online environment can be one that has a feeling of uneasiness at times. Students need extensive reassurance (personal and as a group) as well as feedback on their performance. Below are strategies that the instructor uses with her F500 students:

- she sends weekly e-mail feedback to each student on his or her participation and performance in online discussions;
- she posts weekly messages with feedback for the class as a whole;
- she asks for weekly feedback from students on instructor performance;
- she asks for feedback on the design of class assignments.

One of the most important management tactics is the creation of clear rubrics and evaluation instruments posted to the class Web site during the first week of class. A second and related managerial aspect of the course is making sure that all course expectations and goals are clear. This instructor has found that the more she teaches this class, the more she records information about her teaching style, student expectations and theoretical commitments. Third, she has found weekly e-mails to be a powerful form of feedback because students respond quickly to them.

Given these tips and caveats, someone might ask, 'Where is the instructor in an online PBL environment?' As with face-to-face PBL, the instructor in an online PBL environment acts as both a tutor and coach. Of course, the instructor has to be careful not to dominate the conversation and learn how to balance coaching, guidance, and fading into the background when appropriate. To provide motivation, this particular instructor posts messages weekly to reassure and encourage students that they are on track (if they are). She also assures them that the issue they are addressing is important to many others. Another motivational role of the instructor is to find another class or practising K-12 teachers actually dealing with similar problems. In fact, outside experts sometimes join in the online conversations and serve as consultants to her students.

While managing the class was not particularly easy the first time, after teaching the PBL unit online several times it has naturally become easier. Some techniques used to ease the burden are standardizing e-mails, creating a FAQ page of her expectations and typical student questions, and improving the design of the assignment and supporting materials.

Technological issues

A major issue faced by students in this class when using a conferencing tool is the delayed aspect of asynchronous communication. When groups have to make decisions, it often takes three to four days before an agreement is reached. That is a huge amount of time in a project that lasts only two weeks. Given the frustrations that such delays can cause, it is not surprising that some of them recommend the addition of a chat tool here to make the work process flow more smoothly.

Conclusions

In conclusion, PBL can be employed successfully online. Students are willing to collaborate and work together regardless of distance, and the instructor's role remains one of facilitator and coach. The role of the instructor is to set up the problem, coach and facilitate, motivate and reassure, and support student reflection and problem solving. However, online problem-based learning can sometimes be frustrating for students who wish to have more structure, especially in the online environment where there is a lack of face-to-face contact. Consequently, we need not only to design new courses and tools and continue sharing our pedagogical ideas and decisions but also to begin to research the impact of various approaches and strategies in the online learning environment.

Situation 3: face-to-face computer information systems courses with online support

The third author has been teaching technology-related courses in the computer information systems programme (CIS). These courses are not online courses but incorporate Web-based technology to facilitate learning. In this section, two specific courses will be described: one is an introductory level course called 'Introduction to Microcomputers'; the other is a more advanced course called 'Create an Internet/World Wide Web Site'. The former course used a commercial Web-based courseware, e-education from JonesKnowledge.com, and the latter one used a Web site developed by this particular instructor.

Pedagogical actions

The 'Introduction to Microcomputers' course was a required course for all students in the CIS program as well as for any business majors. As a result, the computer literacy level of the students varied. As a means to help structure the course for those with less computer experience, this course used a commercial Web-based courseware, e-education (http://www.e-education.com), to post the syllabus online, provide online tests and to manage the grade-book online (see Figure 7.3). The online tests were convenient for the instructor because the system automatically transferred the students' grades to the online grade-book. However, the students were not favourable to the online tests, partly because most of them were not comfortable with using computers (see the managerial actions section for additional details).

The 'Create an Internet/World Wide Web Site' course was an elective course in the CIS program. Consequently, the students elected to take this course and were, for the most part, motivated to learn the associated content. This course used a Web site developed by the instructor, which contained general information about the course and instructor, syllabus, handouts from the class, detailed assignments descriptions, study resources and student work. It was mainly used as a communication tool between the instructor and the

Figure 7.3 Interface for e-education Web site for CIS252 course (situation 3)

students, which is at Level 4 of the Ten Level Web Integration from Bonk, Cummings *et al* (2000). In particular, the students found it useful to have the weekly handouts available on the Web. Also, the instructor's expectations of the assignments were explicitly communicated via the Web site. Furthermore, posting students' work fostered their pride and motivation and also allowed them to give each other timely and relevant feedback.

Social actions

Since both courses were traditional face-to-face courses that used technologies, a part of the class time (for example, lab time) was used to make students comfortable enough to ask questions of the instructor and each other. As Walther (1996) indicated, it might be possible to reach the same comfort level by face-to-face and computer-mediated communication.

However, face-to-face communication can more quickly foster student social-ization. Thus, a combination of the face-to-face classroom and online envi-ronment was intended to develop strong bonds among the students. Given these more technical types of courses might have fewer transferable compo-nents to the Web, it was necessary for the students to have hands-on practice during class and to allow them to ask questions whenever they encountered problems. In this way, either the instructor or other students could provide immediate help. Based on her prior research (Hara and Kling, 2000), the instructor knew that if either of these courses were provided entirely online, the students would be less likely to obtain immediate solutions and might feel overly frustrated.

Managerial actions

The 'Introduction to Microcomputers' course used course management tools, so it was easy to create an online test by using this courseware. However, some of the students were not very familiar with computers when the instructor used an online test for the first time, so some of them were confused and lost. Thus, it might prove beneficial to have non-graded online tests before the actual tests. One of the main advantages of using the courseware was that it included an online grade-book that allowed the students to view their current scores online.

In contrast to such a pre-structured course, the Web site for the 'Create an Internet/World Wide Web Site' course provided a reference point for the students to manage assignments by themselves. In addition to the course syllabus, there was an assignment page where the students had access to descriptions of each assignment as well as all the relevant due dates. Thus, the students could constantly check the assignment page and the instructor could refer to the page when she explained the assignments.

Technological actions

Comparing the technologies used by these two courses (one used a commercial courseware and the other used a self-developed Web site), both had advantages and disadvantages. Of course, the advantage of using a commercial courseware is that it reduces the development time of a Web site. The tools are ready to use for instructors. This is especially beneficial for those who do not have extensive technical skills or access to technical support. Moreover, if all the instructors in the same department or university used the same courseware, then their students do not have to keep learning new tools. However, the downside of using a commercial courseware is that it may be costly as well as difficult to customize key components or fulfil individual needs. It can also limit instructor and student creativity.

Situation 4: teaching a self-paced instructional media and technology applications course in an interactive manner

Slightly more than a year ago, the fourth author inherited an online course following a fairly traditional correspondence model. The course, which focuses on instructional media applications and is targeted at masters-level students, was originally designed with a course Web site that simply provided assignments and resources for students. Students were required to read the textbook, complete the assignments and submit them to the instructor for feedback via electronic or regular mail. Ideally, students were supposed to finish the course requirements within one semester. The instructor needed to keep close watch over who was falling behind, and conducted a great deal of private communication with individual students regarding their progress. Students did not feel they were part of a group or cohort and thus often fell behind. Attempts to encourage student interaction had been made at using a class listserv or a basic Web-based bulletin board, but these efforts generally fell apart by the third week of the course.

It seemed that while the course was well designed in terms of readings and assignments, it did not have much value added from being on the Web. A student could print out all of the Web pages on the first day of class and never use the Internet again. Determined to make the Web course a worthwhile experience and to increase course interactivity, the instructor began to make some changes to the course. Today it remains a self-paced course and the course Web site still provides assignment information, but it also makes significant use of a Web-based conferencing tool and requires both student discussion and peer feedback activities.

Pedagogical actions

In terms of pedagogy, three major changes occurred in the course related to:

- orientation time;
- bi-weekly discussions;
- student portfolios and peer feedback.

As indicated below, these changes increased the interactivity of the course and created an online community of learners.

Orientation time

Time is now allowed at the beginning of the course for students to get used to the discussion tool and meet each other. Upon entering the course, students find an introductory discussion topic that encourages them to share a little about themselves and reply to another student. By using this task, students get to know each other and they learn how to send a message and a reply. Other orienting tasks in the discussion forum include sharing a favourite Web link and a discussion about online course concerns and survival tactics. By providing these orientation activities during the first week of the course, all students can participate and begin developing relationships and a shared history, regardless of whether they have already acquired the textbook.

Bi-weekly discussion

Every other week a new discussion is started in the online forum. Each time, students have two different discussion topics to choose from and are encouraged to participate in both. The discussion topics are tied to general themes covered in the course but do not require reading any particular part of the book. Most topics ask students to draw upon their own experiences and interests in their response. This flexibility makes it possible for all students to contribute to the discussion regardless of their background or what assignment they are working on at the time.

Not only are discussion questions carefully crafted to allow each student to share a unique response, but they are also designed with directions for responding to classmates. Early experimentation in the discussion area showed that many students were often at a loss for what to say to their classmates; they tended to simply respond to the instructor. In response, students now receive recommendations for how to interact in a particular discussion such as finding and sharing Web resources, playing devil's advocate, providing alternative solutions to a problem, linking concepts between different peer responses and asking probing questions.

Student portfolios and peer feedback

Although students may be working on different projects at different times, there is still value to seeing each other's work and receiving feedback from someone other than the instructor. Originally, students submitted course work directly and privately to the instructor; now students post their assignments to a public portfolio area on the course discussion forum. Students are encouraged to review portfolios other than their own and provide peer feedback. Instructor feedback is e-mailed privately to students.

Having public portfolios has increased the quality of student work and has contributed to a sense of a learning community in the class. Students view the assignments as a way to share ideas with the class as well as a form of assessment. They have been encouraged to try new things by seeing what others have done. For example, a Fall 1999 student who was rather timid with computers taught herself how to use Hyperstudio. Upon posting her assignment, she attributed her new confidence and skills to the motivation she had received and examples she had seen from classmates.

Social actions

This course has a social element that runs throughout the semester and is encouraged highly and modelled by the instructor. The orientation activities set the tone for socialization, which is deemed an important part of building an online community. At the same time, students are encouraged to fill out their user profile, a pre-formatted Web page that allows uploaded photos, links to Web sites and space for other pertinent information. Throughout the semester the instructor and students share what is going on in their lives, often as an aside to discussions, because it helps add a more human element to the electronic medium.

This course does not have a specific area such as a coffeehouse for online socialization. This decision was based on the instructor's belief and prior experience that students who engage in significant social behaviour tend not to visit areas of the course explicitly established for online socialization. Nevertheless, allowing socialization is important to these online students, who do not have break times during which they can chat and who do not run into each other on campus. One student even sent a private message to the instructor at the end of the course thanking her for allowing students to 'talk' freely in the conference; she had been taking another online course in which social discussion of any nature was deemed 'off-topic' and highly discouraged.

Managerial actions

The structural changes in the course have also assisted class management. The student portfolios prevent the instructor from getting an overloaded e-mail inbox and from accidentally deleting or losing student assignments. The electronic portfolios also make it easy to see at a glance how the students are doing. The development of an online learning community with rich discussion has lessened the amount of private e-mail between students and the instructor, because some students will often answer each other's questions.

The Web-conferencing tool used by this course, SiteScape Forum (SSF) (see Figure 7.4) is not a course-management tool and thus does not offer support for tests or a grade-book. However, it does have a few built-in features that

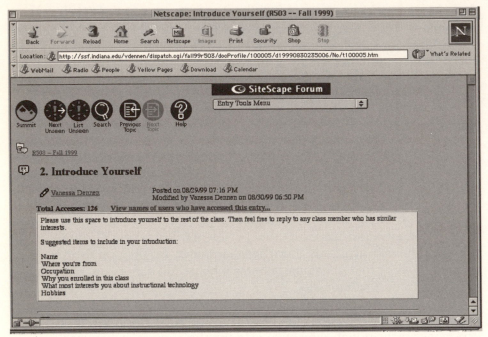

Figure 7.4   SiteScape discussion forum interface and example of introduction directions (situation 4)

are useful to instructors and students alike. The 'list unseen' and 'e-mail notification' features of SSF, for instance, make it easy for both the instructor and students to track new course activity. Everyone can receive e-mail updates about new postings to the forum on a regular schedule – once per day was the schedule used for this course – thereby providing a regular reminder to check in and participate. Upon logging in, there is a 'list unseen' button that, when clicked, will provide a listing of all unread messages. Additionally, the instructor can modify, move, or delete any messages as needed, and also track recent user logins.

Technological actions

In terms of technology, all that is required is a computer with an Internet connection, Web browser and e-mail account. The SSF software is accessed via the World Wide Web and no extra plug-ins are required. However, some students come to the course without a great deal of computer experience. The orientation activities give students a chance to become familiar with the technology and the basic skills needed in the course, such as sending messages, replies, links and files. Early in the semester, the class group decides on a preferred format for sharing documents and develops guidelines and instructions for the less technologically experienced students to follow. Many students find that their technology confidence builds throughout the course; they often try new computer-based tools for their course assignments, particularly as the end of the semester nears.

Self-paced course conclusions

Self-paced, Web-based courses need not be isolating experiences. As seen in this case, online interaction between students in a self-paced course can have many benefits, including but not limited to:

- improved quality of student work;
- improved course completion rate;
- the development of a community of learners.

As indicated, however, students will need adequate time to learn the technology. Successful online interaction also requires careful development of discussion questions as well as opportunities and guidelines for sharing assignments.

Final comments across the four online situations

The courses reviewed here are attempts to explicate the role of the instructor in online environments. Have we found the instructor? With proper structuring of online events and activities, it is extremely hard for either the instructor or the students to hide in the online class. Have we provided the means to identify and clarify what an instructor might decide to do to be successful in such venues? We certainly hope that this chapter will help others locate the critical roles of the instructor in online learning. Have we seen any interesting themes or trends? As pointed out in Table 7.1, there are certainly key issues that we all face such as when to intervene, how much structure to provide in online assignments, and how much responsibility students might enjoy when teaching online. What is clear is that the framework from Ashton *et al* (1999) provides a useful look at the structure and functioning of online learning and the role of the instructor. Ashton *et al* suggest that future research explore the pedagogical, social, managerial and technologies roles of the instructor from the start to end of an online course as well as across instructors, across offerings of the same course and across different courses.

The courses reviewed here are not only intended to 'find the instructor' in online learning but also provide pointers to successful online classroom management and interaction. Given the relative newcomer role of Web-based instruction, it is vital to know the pedagogical, social, managerial and technical hats that online instructors wear. Of course, this is just a small glimpse of the world of online teaching and learning and we are sure that there are many more interesting stories still untold. None the less, we hope that you find our discussions of online instruction across our four settings beneficial to a wide variety of teaching and training settings.

References

Ashton, S, Roberts, T and Teles, L (1999) *Investigation of the Role of the Instructor in Collaborative Online Environments*, poster session presented at the CSCL '99 Conference, Stanford University, http://www.sfu.ca/cde/Teles/tele/handout.htm

Barrows, H (1985) *How to Design a Problem Based Learning Curriculum for the Preclinical Years*, Springer, New York.

Bonk, C J (1998) *Pedagogical Activities on the 'Smartweb': Electronically mentoring undergraduate educational psychology students*, paper presented at the American Educational Research Association Annual convention, San Diego CA.

Bonk, C J and Cummings, J A (1998) A dozen recommendations for placing the student at the centre of Web-based learning, *Educational Media International*, **35** (2), pp 82–89.

Bonk, C J, Cummings, J A, Hara, N, Fischler, R and Lee, S M (2000) A ten level Web integration continuum for higher education, in *Instructional and Cognitive Impacts of Web-based education*, ed B Abbey, pp 56–77, Idea Group Publishing, Hershey, PA.

Bonk, C J, Daytner, K, Daytner, G, Dennen, V and Malikowski, S (in press) Using Web-based cases to enhance, extend, and transform preservice teacher training: two years in review, submitted to: *Computers in the Schools (Special Issue: The World Wide Web in Higher Education Instruction)*.

Bonk, C J and Dennen, V (1999) Teaching on the Web: with a little help from my pedagogical friends, *Journal of Computing in Higher Education*, **11** (1), pp 3–28.

Bonk, C J, Hara, H, Dennen, V, Malikowski, S and Supplee, L (2000) We're in TITLE to dream: envisioning a community of practice, The Intraplanetary Teacher Learning Exchange, *CyberPsychology and Behavior*, **3** (1), pp 25–39.

Bonk, C J and King, K S (ed) (1998) *Electronic Collaborators: Learner-centered technologies for literacy, apprenticeship, and discourse*, Erlbaum, Mahwah, NJ.

Bonk, C J, Malikowski, S, Angeli, C and East, J (1998) Case-based conferencing for preservice teacher education: electronic discourse from the field, *Journal of Educational Computing Research*, **19** (3), pp 269–306.

Bonk, C J and Reynolds, T H (1997) Learner-centered web instruction for higher-order thinking, teamwork, and apprenticeship, in *Web-based Instruction*, ed B H Khan, pp 167–78, Educational Technology Publications, Englewood Cliffs, NJ.

Bonk, C J and Sugar, W A (1998) Student role play in the World Forum: analyses of an Arctic learning apprenticeship, *Interactive Learning Environments*, **6** (1–2), pp 1–29.

Cummings, J A, Bonk, C J and Jacobs, F R (2000) *Twenty-first Century Syllabi: Dynamic tools for promoting interactivity*, Indiana University, Bloomington, IN.

Duffy, T M, Dueber, W and Hawley, C (1998) Critical thinking in a distributed environment: a pedagogical base for the design of conferencing systems, in *Electronic Collaborators: Learner-centered technologies for literacy, apprenticeship, and discourse*, eds C J Bonk and K S King, pp 51–78, Erlbaum, Mahwah, NJ.

Finkle, S and Torp, L (1995) *Introductory Documents*, available from the Center for Problem-Based Learning, Illinois Math and Science Academy, 1500 West Sullivan Road, Aurora, IL 60506–1000, USA.

Hara, N and Kling, R (2000) Students' distress with a Web-based distance education course, *Information, Communication and Society*, **3** (4).

Kirkley, J (in preparation) *Guidelines for Problem Based Learning in a Distance Education*, Indiana University, Bloomington, IN.

Koschmann, T (ed) (1996) *CSCL: Theory and practice of an emerging paradigm*, Lawrence Erlbaum Associates, Mahwah, NJ.

Mason, R (1991) Moderating educational computer conferencing, *DEOSNEWS*, **1** (19), pp 1–11.

Riel, M (1993) Global education through learning circles, in *Global Networks*, ed L Harasim, pp 221–36, MIT Press, Cambridge, MA.

Walther, J (1996) Computer-mediated communication: impersonal, interpersonal, and hyper-personal interaction, *Communication Research*, **23** (1), pp 3–43.

8

Exploring the development of critical thinking skills through a Web-supported problem-based learning environment

Ron Oliver
Edith Cowan University, Australia

Editor's introduction

Oliver describes his experience of using Web-based 'settings' to develop critical thinking and problem-solving skills as part of a campus-based programme at Perth, Western Australia. The aim was to determine the extent to which immersion in such a course, which involved a high degree of practice of tasks associated with critical thinking and information management, contributed to the development of such skills, and to identify factors that could be seen to promote their development. The results showed that the development of these generic skills was not a necessary outcome of the course and that some deliberate interventions may be necessary to ensure these learning outcomes are achieved in such learning environments.

Introduction

A recent area for our research at Edith Cowan University has been to explore the capability of learning settings to support the development of generic skills. The feedback to date has confirmed many of our expectations that particular forms of Web-based learning settings hold particular promise for the development of generic skills as complementary outcomes of tertiary level courses. In our most recent studies, we explored students' practice and development of generic skills with a Web-enabled problem-based learning setting (Oliver, Herrington and McLoughlin, 2000). The results, based on students' self-reporting of their learning behaviour and activities, suggested that many opportunities were provided for the development of a broad range of skills. What we were not able to show in these studies was evidence for the development of particular generic skills or for the influence of particular learning strategies on their attainment. The current research project was planned to explore the ways in which a problem-based learning setting might influence the development of students' critical thinking skills.

Critical thinking skills

A number of papers and reports at the government level have attempted to define the range of generic and transferable skills that are desirable outcomes of higher education (for example, Mayer, 1992; Dearing, 1997). Typically the set includes communication skills, number skills, team skills, learning skills and skills in the use and application of information and communication technologies (ICT). A number of writers have attempted to conceptualize the skills into more focused and discipline-oriented forms. Clanchy and Ballard (1995) proposed that generic skills comprise three main forms, thinking skills, research skills and communication skills. Bennett, Dunne and Carre (1999) offer a four-component model to conceptualize key skills in the higher education sector with a framework comprising broad managerial skills. They argue that the important key skills are fundamentally those associated with being able to manage oneself, others, information and tasks and they contend that the bulk of all generic skills can be embraced within the four categories of this framework.

Critical thinking skills are a component of this larger set of generic skills, which have in recent years gained prominence in discussions of graduate attributes and important outcomes of education. Critical thinking describes the process of identifying issues and assumptions in an argument, recognizing important relationships and drawing conclusions based on the available information and data (for example, Kaasboll, 1998). The need for critical thinking skills as an outcome of formal education has emerged as an important issue for universities and institutes of higher education on feedback and advice from employers (for example, Guthrie, 1994) and from considerations of the needs of the lifelong learner (for example, Candy, Crebert and O'Leary, 1994). More recently, the growing use of technology for information storage has renewed interest in this notion and has expanded the set of skills in ways that reflect the importance of accessing and using electronic information (for example Bruce, 1998). Critical thinking skills are inherent in the ability to make meaningful use of electronic information.

Developing critical thinking skills

There are a number of opinions on appropriate ways to develop students' generic skills. Once the need for a particular skill has been identified, one strategy is to provide purposeful instruction to support its development (for example, Greenan, Humphreys and McIlveen, 1997). Many writers argue that this is not the best option. Candy *et al* (1994), for example, reason that generic skills should be at the heart of all university teaching and that their development should be sought through integrated teaching approaches. In such settings the skills development is through learning activities and strategies related to the subject domain, an approach often claimed to promote the development of transferable skills (for example, Bennett *et al*, 1999).

Research suggests that the more effective settings for developing transferable generic skills are those that promote more than the surface learning that purposeful instruction tends to achieve (for example, Biggs, 1999). Deep learning is more often achieved by learning strategies that create cognitive engagement and higher order thinking than others that support more passive forms of learning activity. Other writers argue that more autonomous learning settings promote the forms of learning process conducive to the practice and development of generic skills (for example Boud, 1988; Gibbs *et al*, 1994). Contemporary thinking posits that university learning can be significantly strengthened through workplace-based *practica* and applications (for example, Seagraves, Kemp and Osborne, 1996). A number of writers also argue the place of experiential and authentic learning as strategies that facilitate learning and transfer (for example, Brown, Collins and Duguid, 1989).

Problem-based learning (PBL) is among the more common forms of learning strategy that are frequently used to create forms of experiential and authentic learning. This learning strategy is frequently used as an approach supporting the necessary learning conditions for generic skills development. It is a strategy that we have explored in the past as a vehicle for generic skills development and that shows considerable promise and prospect (for example, Oliver, Herrington and McLoughlin, 2000).

The Web-based PBL learning setting

The Web-based system that we have developed to support our PBL learning settings is comprised of several dynamic bulletin boards and management routines. The system provides support for the following problem-solving process:

- a number of problems are provided for students to solve throughout the course;
- each week a problem is solved by groups of students who communicate among themselves to develop a solution that is posted to the Web when completed;
- the groups can view each other's solutions and provide some peer assessment through a simple voting scheme;
- tutors mark the solutions and students can view their grades, which form a cumulative total across all problems.

There is only minimal teacher support and scaffolding provided within the system and students are expected to use their own initiatives, skills and resources in the solution of the problems. It was our intention in this study to explore ways in which our PBL environment encouraged the practice of critical thinking and supported students' practice of tasks associated with developing information skills through the collaborative problem-solving activities.

Methodology

The study was undertaken with a group of 75 students studying in the third year of their university undergraduate multimedia degree course. The unit aimed to develop students' skills and understanding in the use of contemporary ICT for open and distance learning. It involved both practical and theoretical components. The theoretical component of the course was delivered in a flexible mode to both on- and off-campus learners and involved a number of teaching and learning elements that each week comprised a lecture and seminar session of one hour's duration for the 13 weeks of the course where the weekly topics were introduced and discussed, and a weekly and Web-enabled collaborative problem-solving activity.

The weekly seminars were used to introduce the students to the general topic of the weekly problem and to provide some background and motivation for the learners. Each of the problems was constructed as an open-ended task, which attempted to convey some form of authentic application of the material and information. Students were given some preliminary information sources with which to commence their inquiry but were expected and encouraged to supplement these with resources obtained through their own inquiry and exploration. Each problem was solved by a group of three to four students across a week with the solution being posted to the public bulletin board.

The students were formed into groups with a maximum size of four within their classes and they stayed in these groups throughout the semester. Students were required to work collaboratively to solve the problems and were free to choose the various roles that each might play. Students received feedback on their solutions in several ways. On completion of their problem solution each week they were required to read the solutions of other groups in their class and to choose which groups they felt provided the best solutions. Students were able to view the outcomes of this voting system. The tutors marked each solution and gave a mark based on three criteria: how well the problem was contextualized and decomposed in order to frame a solution; the quality of the solution suggested; and the quality of the arguments and supporting information provided. Again these marks were shown on the bulletin board. As the problems progressed, students were able to see how their group was faring against others in their class and amongst the whole cohort.

Students were given some instruction and guidance in the problem-solving process as part of the lecture in the first few weeks of the course and after the first two problems had been completed. After this time, they were left to their own devices and a number of data-gathering processes employed to monitor their behaviours in the learning settings. In the first six weeks, students received only marks as a measure of their problem-solving success and in the final four weeks they were given marks plus brief written feedback on their solutions. Questionnaires were given to all students at the end of the course to collect data that described the problem-solving strategies that their groups employed. Several willing students completed reflective journals that provided data on their impressions of the learning settings and their learning processes.

Results

The study used a number of data sources to gather information about the ways in which the students used the learning environment, their levels of practice of tasks associated with the development of critical thinking and their success in the problem-solving tasks that provided evidence of their critical thinking.

Problem-solving strategies

Feedback from the students confirmed previous studies (for example, Oliver, Omari and Stoney, 1999) that students using this problem-based approach tended to use consistent methods from week to week and that among the various groups, several distinct forms of problem-solving activity were popular. The majority of the students favoured an approach where, each week, different students from within the group took responsibility for different roles. Table 8.1 shows the group results and indicates the form of approach used by that group.

Table 8.1 Group scores (out of 15) for the weekly problems

Problem	1	2	3	4	5	6	7	8	9	10	Average
Group 1(S)	9	6	9	8	9	10	10	8	12	6	8.70
Group 2(S)	7	12	10	8	9	9	10	11	9	8	9.30
Group 3(S)	9	9	12	8	10	9	9	11	11	10	9.80
Group 4(S)	11	13	10	10	9	9	7	12	8	8	9.70
Group 5(T)	12	11	12	11	9	11	12	9	8	10	10.50
Group 6(I)	9	5	7	7	9	9	11	9	7	5	7.80
Group 7(T)	10	9	11	11	10	10	11	11	8	9	10.00
Group 8(S)	9	9	10	10	10	13	10	11	11	11	10.40
Group 9(T)	12	13	12	10	11	11	13	13	10	10	11.50
Group 10(I)	8	9	9	–	7	9	12	–	–	–	9.00
Group 11(S)	10	12	11	11	11	11	11	13	13	13	11.60
Group 12(S)	9	11	11	9	9	–	–	12	10	12	10.37
Group 13(T)	8	11	10	12	10	10	13	11	13	13	11.10
Group 14(S)	12	8	8	–	8	8	5	9	9	8	8.33
Group 15(S)	10	8	9	10	11	9	10	9	11	8	9.50
Group 16(I)	9	7	8	9	–	7	10	8	8	–	8.50
Group 17(I)	9	7	8	–	8	–	7	–	7	8	7.85
Group 18(S)	10	8	8	8	9	8	8	10	8	7	8.40
Group 19(S)	10	9	9	9	10	9	11	9	8	9	9.30
Group 20(S)	9	9	8	–	8	7	8	8	7	–	8.00
Average	9.65	9.4	9.75	9.44	9.32	9.39	9.89	10.2	9.37	9.12	9.55

Shared tasks (S)

Most teams established a weekly leader whose role it was to coordinate the research of the other members and to develop the solution based on feedback from team members. Students who used this approach tended to assume the leadership role up to three times in the semester and in most instances were the principal developers of three solutions. Among groups who used this method, most learners indicated that they contributed on a weekly basis to the data-gathering process and recognized that this involved them in searching the Web for relevant resources, reading and sifting information from the given resources and providing summary data to their team leader for the week. In most instances, the materials were passed between the members and their leader through e-mail. The majority of students using this approach indicated positive responses towards its impact on their learning and their level of satisfaction of the learning achieved.

Team roles (T)

In four of the 20 groups, students assumed the role of team leader for all projects and coordinated the research and problem-solving activities accordingly. The team leaders helped to refine the problem and directed their members to research particular areas and to supply information in particular forms. The groups that used this process tended to be those where the members were relatively well known to each other ahead of this class and who had some experience working collaboratively previously. There was general comfort among the students in these groups with the activities and a majority of students indicated that they enjoyed the problem-solving process and learnt much from it.

Individual efforts (I)

Four groups indicated that they commenced the semester with the intention of sharing tasks but, for practical reasons, found themselves taking substantial responsibility for individual problems with which they received little help from their colleagues. These groups established a system of one person doing the bulk of the work for one problem and then expecting another in the group to do likewise for the next problem. This process was not successful for many of the students and was often the result of participation in a group where collaboration was not totally achieved and many learners expressed dissatisfaction with the learning activity because of problems with group members. In several instances group members failed to post the solutions and also failed to assess the solutions of other groups.

Level of participation

Table 8.1 shows some interesting results. In the first instance, the table shows that a majority of the groups completed all the given problems and only three groups completed less than 80 per cent of the problems that were set. This was an important factor to explore because in student-centred settings, students' motivations to complete required tasks can wax and wane due to the levels of autonomy accorded them. In group work where students need to rely on each other, there is an even greater likelihood of tasks not being completed caused by dysfunctional teams. There was no particular coercion applied to students to complete the problems apart from including the problem-solving activities as a component of the assessment for the course. Even with this incentive, a number of the groups failed at times to submit their solutions to several problems.

The groups that failed to submit results were primarily those where collaboration was weak and where students assumed individual rather than collaborative roles in the problem-solving process (Groups 10, 16 and 17). Interviews revealed that failure to submit was frequently a matter of disorganization and poor communication caused by a lack of collaboration. It appeared that we need some strategy in this process to encourage and support teams whose members have difficulties collaborating because the lack of collaboration appeared to impinge on their level of problem-solving activity and their levels of success in such endeavours.

Problem solutions

The weekly problems were assessed by the tutors according to three main criteria: problem decomposition; the solution proposed; and the arguments supporting the proposal. Students were coached in appropriate ways to present their solutions in ways that clearly identified these aspects in their responses. The use of a template of this form encouraged the students to tackle the problems in a consistent fashion and in the interviews the students indicated that the use of the approach helped them to focus on the problem and to determine possible solutions.

The feedback from the students suggested that they found the strategies that were suggested very useful in the problem-solving process and their responses indicated a strong perception that their practice using this heuristic had helped to develop their skills in the problem-solving process. Observation of the problem solutions tended to support such perceptions. The bulk of the problem solutions were well presented and demonstrated that they were based on the use of a sound method that focused on decomposition of the problem, through an inquiry process to a determination of appropriate solutions and supporting arguments.

There were, however, a number of solutions presented each week that suggested that the students, while using this method, were not engaging deeply with the inquiry and problem-solving process. In such instances, solutions were often suggested but the supporting arguments and reasons given were not substantial and not well informed by the available evidence. In terms of grades achieved, a score of nine or more typically indicated a satisfactory and well-argued solution, whereas scores of less than nine had problems in one of more of the identified criteria.

Student achievement

The average scores for each of the groups are shown across the bottom of Table 8.1 and there is no discernible pattern in the scores. The expected increase associated with skills development through practice is not evident.

The average score for all the 10 problems was 9.55 and there was no particular variation from one problem to the next. It is difficult to determine a pattern in the results that could sustain the argument that these results were indicative of a trend towards general improvement across the course. The weekly averages show a remarkably consistent pattern and there is no pattern to suggest that the scores had changed in any consistent way. It appeared that some groups scored consistently higher scores than others throughout the course and between the first and last weeks, overall results were quite consistent.

Possible explanations might have been linked to the level of difficulty of the problems but examination did not sustain this concern. There appeared to be a general fall in levels of interest as the course progressed, tied perhaps to the novelty of the setting wearing thin. Or the possibility existed that the setting did not in fact lead to a development of critical thinking skills but simply served to reinforce those that existed at the start. Feedback from the interviews and questionnaires seemed often to support this assertion. The course gave students every opportunity to practise problem-solving and critical thinking but there were no explicit measures in the process that necessarily led students to improve their performances or their skills in critical thinking.

Responses to written feedback

Student responses to questions and discussions throughout the early stages of the course suggested that students were not really gaining much feedback from the marks that the tutors were giving. In fact, a large number of the students indicated that they commenced subsequent problems before they had checked to see their results from the previous week. The electronic submission system meant that the solutions could be assessed and marks allocated without students actually seeing them. A number of students indicated that the marks did not really provide them with much feedback and that they didn't really pay much attention to the mark for reasons other than checking that they were achieving a passing grade. As a means to provide more feedback and as an attempt to provide some support for assisting students to improve their solutions, the Web-based system was altered to enable the tutors to provide some feedback that could indicate to the students where they had fallen down or perhaps where improvements could be made to their weekly solutions.

At the end of the course students were interviewed to assess the ways in which the feedback had been useful to their problem-solving and critical thinking processes. Their responses indicated that many still made very little use of the feedback, just as previously it was identified that many had paid little attention to the marks received. The reasons appeared many and varied.

For example, in instances where the students exchanged roles, the new leaders didn't really see the advice for the previous problem as particularly relevant to them. The students for whom the advice would have been useful assumed minor roles in the next problem-solving processes and the advice often went unheeded. The students in the groups which had established permanent group leaders, Groups 5, 7, 9 and 13, indicated that they generally did heed the advice and attempted to use the information to improve their subsequent solutions but these tended to be the groups that offered the best solutions anyway and any improvements to their scores were not discernible in the small number of cases present in the study.

Student motivation

The problem-based activity had several forms of motivation built-in. The most important of these were the results forming a component of the unit assessment. Thirty per cent of the marks for the unit were based on the results from this activity with all students in the group receiving the same mark, and non-performers receiving proportionally less in relation to their lack of participation. A second motivating force was the capacity of the system to show students the achievements of their group in relation to all others in the class and in the cohort. Students could view their cumulative totals against others and it was expected that this could encourage those groups whose performances were less than that of others.

Feedback from the students revealed that both these factors tended to have less motivating influence than was intended and expected. For many students, the totals and marks enabled them to ensure that they maintained a passing grade and in fact in some cases provided a disincentive to try harder because all they were keen to achieve was a passing score. They indicated that the assessment component encouraged them to attempt the problems but didn't really motivate them to achieve high scores. Few students indicated that comparisons with other groups had any impact on their levels of performance. Most commented that they were interested in the comparisons but felt that, as they were working in groups, it was difficult for them individually to hold much sway in the score achieved by the group. This was seen as one negative aspect of group work and a factor that probably needed to be addressed if the full potential of the environment was to be realized.

The students who expressed the highest levels of motivation to succeed in the course were all those who were intrinsically motivated and many of these students indicated that the marks component and scores influenced them little. They used the scores to monitor their progress and to check the quality of their responses but claimed in the main to be influenced in their efforts to achieve by their personal standards and interest in learning rather than any other extrinsic factor built into the system.

The impact of the online setting

There have been many instances in the past where teachers have sought to develop students' critical thinking skills in conventional and formal educational settings. The use of the online setting in this study provided many new opportunities through the communication, information access and interactive functions that were supported.

Information

The Web provided the students with a vast source of information for the inquiry tasks that they were undertaking. The scope and extent of the available information provided the learners with numerous opportunities for their own inquiry and research. Whereas conventional settings tend to be limited in the amounts of information and resources provided for learners in this setting there was no limit and this provided strong support for the inquiry tasks that were created to support the critical thinking activities.

Communication

The use of e-mail and bulletin boards in this setting was a very important component of the critical-thinking process. These technologies gave purpose and context to the tasks being undertaken by the learners and provided the means for students to carry out many of the learning activities. Whereas in conventional settings students tend to have limited opportunities for communicating and collaborating, the online setting greatly extends their opportunities and the forms of communication that can be undertaken.

Interactive functions

Yet another powerful function of the online setting and one that provided great support for the critical thinking tasks was the interactivity supported by the Web. In this setting the Web provided the means to support many of the novel elements designed to create critical thinking opportunities for the learners. These included the online assessment procedures, the peer-assessment supports, the display of 'best' solutions, the cumulative assessments and displays, the comparative grading displays and the teacher feedback system. All these functions added varying forms of supports for learners engaged in the critical thinking processes, particularly in support of reflection and interpretation as learning activities.

Summary and conclusions

Generally speaking, the outcomes from this study suggest that although the problem-based learning setting provided many opportunities for the advancement of students' critical thinking skills, for many of the students these outcomes did not eventuate. A number of factors emerged from the study as influences that limited this setting from achieving the anticipated development of critical skills. These included:

- The nature of the learner-managed learning environment limiting the influence of the teacher to be able to motivate, monitor and manage the students' learning processes. The environment appeared to provide many opportunities for the development of critical thinking skills but many students failed to use the opportunities to effect these learning outcomes. In particular many students failed to use the feedback provided to assist their learning.
- The different tasks and roles undertaken by the students within their teams for each problem limited the actual extent of the critical thinking which each student was required to do throughout the course. There were 10 problems; few students actually completed the full problem solving for each, relying on their colleagues on a weekly basis for help and assistance.
- The implicit nature of the critical thinking saw many students under-valuing the problem-solving process and placing more emphasis on immersing themselves in the topic under inquiry and exploring the information and content of which it was composed.
- The tasks included a number of reflective components but these tended to be avoided by the students resulting in little reflection being undertaken on the processes involved, the solutions developed and strategies for improvement.

At the same time the study demonstrated the potential of online settings as a means to support critical thinking processes. In particular the study demonstrated particular advantages being derived from such online affordances as information access, communications support and the various forms of interactivity supported by Web settings. Each of these elements provided particular opportunities for learning and each played a role for all learners. There are many other ways in which these Web functions might be applied in learning settings and future research will probably reveal further opportunities as the technology continues to develop.

There are many writers who argue that critical thinking is a process that can be taught by direct instruction (for example, Greenan, Humphreys and McIlveen, 1997). They posit that there are a number of procedures and steps in the process that can be identified and developed through practice and feedback. In this study we explored the notion that another way to develop these skills might be to practise tasks that involved critical thinking and, through appropriate feedback and reflection, to lead students forward with these skills. The study did not appear to provide adequate opportunities for the practice, the feedback nor the reflection. It is still possible that our contentions were accurate but the system appears to need to be changed before they can be fully tested again.

The findings from the study have not dampened our enthusiasm for the problem-based learning setting because it has shown itself in the past to provide many opportunities for this course as an effective learning strategy and a flexible delivery medium. The setting provides a number of distinct advantages over conventional forms of teaching in terms of creating student-centred settings that make use of the many learning opportunities afforded by the Web and for providing engaging and dynamic learning settings supporting transferable learning. But as a means for developing critical thinking skills, in its current form, it has not been found to be as successful as we had hoped.

The results suggest that it is not so much the learning setting that may have been the problem but more the way in which it was implemented. It is still likely that the same setting implemented under different conditions could return the required results. It would appear that, in order to create opportunities to develop these skills, the setting needs to provide more scaffolds for the development of these skills, for example, more meaningful feedback, more reflection on the part of the learners and more engagement for all students in the process of articulating and developing the problem solutions. This research has identified weaknesses within the current way in which the setting is implemented and it is our intention to develop strategies and supports for the environment that can overcome these. We anticipate in subsequent uses of this learning strategy to effect these changes and to re-explore the setting to determine if we can discover evidence that the setting can in fact be used to develop critical thinking skills.

References

Bennett, N, Dunne, E and Carre, C (1999) Patterns of core and generic skill provision in higher education, *Higher Education*, **37** (1), pp 71–93.

Biggs, J (1999) *Teaching for Quality Learning at University*, Open University Press, Buckingham.

Boud, D (ed) (1988) *Developing Student Autonomy in Learning*, 2nd edn, Kogan Page, London.

Boud, D and Feletti, G (1991) *The Challenge of Problem-Based Learning*, Kogan Page, London.

Brown, J, Collins, A and Duguid, P (1989) Situated cognition and the culture of learning, *Educational Researcher*, **18** (1), pp 32–42.

Bruce, C (1998) The phenomenon of information literacy, *Higher Education Research and Development*, **17** (1), pp 25–43.

Candy, P, Crebert, G and O'Leary, J (1994) *Developing Lifelong Learning through Undergraduate Education*, Australian Government Publishing Service, Canberra.

Clanchy, J and Ballard, B (1995) Generic skills in the context of higher education, *Higher Education Research and Development*, **14** (2), pp 123–36.

Dearing Report (1997) *Higher Education in the Learning Society*, HMSO, London.

Gibbs, G, Rust, C, Jenkins, A and Jaques, D (1994) *Developing Students' Transferable Skills*, The Oxford Centre for Staff Development, Oxford.

Greenan, K, Humphreys, P and McIlveen, H (1997) Developing work-based transferable skills for mature students, *Journal of Further and Higher Education*, **21** (2), pp 193–204.

Guthrie, B (1994) *The Higher Education Experience Survey: An examination of the higher education experiences of 1982, 1987, and 1992 graduates*, Australian Government Printing Service, Canberra.

Herrington, J and Oliver, R (1997) Multimedia, magic and the way students respond to a situated learning environment, *Australian Journal of Educational Technology*, **13** (2), 127–43.

Kaasboll, J (1998) Teaching critical thinking and problem defining skills, *Education and Information Technologies*, **3**, pp 101–17.

Mayer, E (1992) *Key Competencies. Report of the Committee to Advise the ACE and MOVET on Employment Related Key Competencies for Post Compulsory Education and Training*, Australian Government Publishing Service, Canberra.

Oliver, R, Omari, A and Stoney, S (1999) Collaborative learning on the World Wide Web using a problem-based learning approach, in *Selected Papers from the Tenth International Conference on College Teaching and Learning*, ed J Chambers, FCCJ, Jacksonville.

Oliver, R, Herrington, J and McLoughlin, C (2000) Exploring the development of students' generic skills development in higher education using a Web-based learning environment, in *Proceedings of ED-MEDIA 2000. World Conference on Educational Multimedia, Hypermedia and Telecommunications*, eds S Heller and J Bordeaux, AACE, Virginia.

Seagraves, L, Kemp, I and Osborne, M (1996) Are academic outcomes of higher education provision relevant to and deliverable in the workplace setting?, *Higher Education*, **32** (2), pp 157–76.

9

Distance learning through educational networks: the global view experience

Dennis Schlais and Richard Davis
California State University, USA

Editor's introduction

In this chapter, Schlais and Davis argue that education networks create new learning opportunities that require a new supporting pedagogy. They show how an imaginative use of the Web for distance learning can support effective collaborative learning, develop critical thinking skills, expand access to learning resources on a global scale, push academic tutors to rethink their role and challenge the notion of a university. The authors argue that external trends and the distinctive features of online Web-based learning are combining to promote a switch to more learner-managed learning. The authors cite the experience of the Association Global View, an international network supporting online learning in business and management.

New technology and distance education

Among educators, 'distance education' typically means providing educational services only to learners who are not physically at the institution's site. Delivery is often via the Web or some combination of Web/e-mail/taped video/text/or compact disc. This view of distance education limits the potential that can be derived from education technologies. Educators are often constrained in their perspective of distance education as a learning process flowing only outward from the university to the learner. Educational resources follow institutional vision and mission statements, directing faculty and technology resources to flow only in an outward direction to distribute knowledge to their target markets.

In today's technology-rich educational environment learning might take place not only at the institution via distance education programmes but also through the learner's own Web resources. The Web's learning environment creates a learners' market. In addition to their own university, alternative learning resources are becoming more available and more competitive. The same course might be offered online from several vendors (universities). In cases where learning and not degrees have the higher priority, learners can gain knowledge without going through the educational intermediary. Experts, mentors and peers found on the Web provide information, which directly empowers the learner. Students might have just as good a quality learning experience studying investments through CNN Financial News online plus other sites than from taking a formal university investments course. Learners also have an option of finding other learners with similar interests, resulting in cooperative and collaborative learning opportunities that might not be gained in the classroom. This type of situation raises many issues, such as whether the student should be learning how to invest on an 'as needed' basis or whether it is necessary to have the entire course in order to understand its parts as an integrated whole.

Information, knowledge and their delivery are becoming decentralized and, in some cases, fragmented. Educational institutions may see the delivery of information and knowledge from multiple sources, which are delivered in a highly efficient manner, as a threat. But such distribution of knowledge is also an opportunity. Opportunities are numerous for institutions that reinvent themselves and emerge as coordinators and facilitators of the distribution of information and knowledge. This change requires acceptance that the institution and its members do not have exclusive or monopoly control on information, or control of the process in which information is transformed into knowledge beneficial to the individual learners.

When institutions are reinvented, leaders of educational institutions can harness technology to seize opportunities that allow learners to seek knowledge outside of the institutional setting. Networks are bridges that provide learners with access to worldwide information sources. Many textbooks today provide Web links to supplement their content. In comparison to texts and Web links, a network builds bridges that allow for two-way traffic. The seeker of knowledge becomes the provider of knowledge. Professors and students in similar classes worldwide are connected in a network, not only to the same information but also to each other, enabling collaborative learning. In such networked environments, institutions expand educational experiences and opportunities for learning even as they forfeit control.

A global network addresses many needs. Literature in education documents the value of collaborative and active learning. The network is a tool that encourages active and collaborative learning both inside and outside of the classroom environment. Active learning processes for a single student, a team or an entire class can be efficiently coordinated in a network. Simultaneously, the network has the power to leverage scarce educational resources by making the student an educational partner and supplier of knowledge. Knowledge needs to be integrated to enable the critical thought process, something that educational institutions recognize as valuable but elusive. With a network, education leaders might encourage integrative curriculum design within a discipline or across disciplines. A network, by its international design, provides a global perspective much needed by students and their professors to help build a tolerance between people of diverse cultures and value systems. A networked multi-nation educational system facilitated by instructors, coordinated by network administrators and guided by participating institutions will create new and powerful learning opportunities.

New technology and the notion of a university

To begin a review of the Association Global View network the authors explore the question 'what is a university?' The question is asked with no intention of answering, but with the hope of adding a new perspective. A university is a collection of intellectuals in search of reason and truth, intent on passing the acquired knowledge and wisdom gained on to the next generation. A university is a major driver in creating a higher standard of living for the people in the society. Historically, a university has been a very stable, cautious, risk-adverse institution managed by administrators whose task it is to guide a very cautious, narrowly defined, risk-adverse, group of intellectuals who must teach the content of disciplines to numbers of students. Given diverse and challenging demands it is fortunate that universities function as well as they do. University leaders and faculties have been reluctant to change this model. Each university, as a business, has created a differentiated advantage, found target markets and built a brand image, some more successfully than others.

Technology made available in this decade has challenged the university's stable operating environment. In business, the same technology has radically altered entire industries within a few years (such as stock brokerage, communications and broadcasting). The new educational technologies have created new universities that are challenging the brick-and-mortar institutions, relying instead on computers and communication technologies. A university's territory and its markets, formerly secure, are vulnerable.

Resource needs have increased sharply as high-cost technology is added to the brick-and-mortar campuses. Students are becoming more critical and discriminating about the educational value of some information. They openly question the importance and relevance of course content and have become critics on pedagogy and delivery style. What constitutes a modern quality education from a student's perspective is becoming important in influencing pedagogy and the vision of the university.

Active team and collaborative learning – online?

Part of the university's vision is to provide students with a quality education. Historically, students for the most part were less critical than are students of today. They were more passive and learnt what was professed. The pedagogy of today must address complex student needs. It is clear from the literature that active, team and collaborative learning pedagogy can add value to the educational experience.

In the traditional educational setting, the teacher is the source of knowledge and authority. The basic framework for collaborative learning is student involvement in the learning process. The structure of the learning environment allows some of the teacher's authority from the traditional classroom setting to be transferred to the collaborative learning group. Students assume some responsibility for defining the learning task and the methods of search for knowledge. McLellan (1998: 44) states, 'it is valuable to have students take ownership of the class by helping to determine certain things, such as discussion topics, helping classmates determine how to solve technical problems, ideas for carrying out assignments'.

Not all student group work is collaborative. Simply forming a group and asking it to perform a task does not mean that collaborative learning takes place. This group may work cooperatively, but not collaboratively. Collaborative learning is different from cooperative learning. In cooperative learning, student-learning groups operate within a framework that maintains traditional lines of classroom knowledge and authority. In collaborative learning, some aspects of classroom knowledge and authority can be shared by both students and teachers (Flannery, 1994). The main principle underlying collaborative learning is that students are more motivated to learn if they have an active part in the learning process. People are more prone to learn if they have an active role in framing the learning situation (Freire, 1974).

Collaborative learning is a natural process of social interaction and communication (Flannery, 1994; Gerlach, 1994). This type of social interaction, learning and decision making is expected in the workplace of today.

Most occupations require collaborative relationships to achieve organization goals. While most education takes place in a traditionally structured setting of task assignment and a focus on teacher authority, people are expected to act collaboratively in the workplace. As firms become more global, collaboration will become more important. 'To function effectively, companies must develop skills in communicating and collaborating across distances, many times without face-to-face interaction' (Rockett *et al*, 1998: 174). Expanding globalization and new job demands are causing business schools to look at pedagogical assumptions, curriculum and learning processes (Alavi and Wheeler, 1995). A number of studies have examined the relationship between collaborative groups and learning. The motivational aspects of collaboration on learning have been discussed in the literature (Dobos, 1996; Johnson and Johnson, 1985; Johnson and Johnson, 1989; Sharan and Shaulov, 1990; Slavin, 1987). Critical thinking ability can be developed through appropriately structured collaborative learning environments (Adams and Hamm, 1990).

Collaboration and critical thinking

One of the central objectives of higher education is critical thinking. With emphasis in colleges and universities on lifelong learning and learning to learn, collaborative learning can provide the framework for students to develop the ability to think beyond memorizing material. Memorized material might be information but, perhaps, not knowledge. Interpreting information is an important step in transforming information into knowledge (Sharan and Sharan, 1992). Management education, for the most part, is aimed at building knowledge and skills. What is lacking in the education of our future business leaders is the critical thinking ability needed to operate effectively in an individual-empowering information environment. Critical thought refers to an individual's ability to analyse ongoing social arrangements to determine if and how those arrangements enhance human life; to recognize that any one or any set of arrangements is a complex and interrelated part of society which has a history and is evolving over time; and to appreciate that reality is perceived and shaped by powerful forces in society such as the media, work organizations and educational institutions (Prasad and Cavanaugh, 1997).

> Why are critical thinking skills so hard for students to acquire?… Why is it so hard to help students learn anything but facts and ideas that they can treat as facts and ideas?… That is, although they learn to solve the problems, they do not understand the fundamental concepts of the

course... A coupling of collaborative learning with critical thinking can transform education much more effectively than the pursuit of either alone.

(Nelson, 1994: 45)

Web-learning and education networks

The introduction of networks in education offers the opportunity for new kinds of collaborative learning (Kitchen and McDougall, 1998–99; Negroponte, 1995). Computers and related technology – the Internet and World Wide Web – have enabled new kinds of collaborative learning formats. As with collaborative learning in general, in computer collaborative learning work is better done under the control of the learners than under the control of the teacher (Tomlinson and Henderson, 1995).

Internet technology gives instructors the ability to offer students a more complete range of learning methodologies. In addressing Web-based instruction, Duchastel (1996–97) provides 'A Web-based model for university instruction' (Table 9.1). Duchastel advocates the steps shown in the 'Function' column of his model as presented in the table.

Table 9.1 Web-based university instruction model

Function	Contrast with typical approach
1 Specify goals to pursue	Specify content to learn
2 Accept diversity of outcomes	Demand common learning results
3 Request production of knowledge	Request communication technology
4 Evaluate at the task level	Evaluate at the knowledge level
5 Build learning teams	Work individually and in groups
6 Encourae global communities	Work locally

Source: Duchastel (1996–97)

This model recognizes that Web technology enables students to explore for knowledge and to be active participants in producing knowledge, rather than just regurgitating facts. It also recognizes that by using different knowledge sources and cognitive skills, teams may produce different answers or outcomes. Noting the difference between content-driven courses and Web-based courses, he states that 'In an information-rich environment, in contrast [to traditional education], it is more appropriate to guide the students toward expected end-results and let them organize their learning on their own' (p 224).

Gasen and Preece (1995) (Table 9.2) address a range of issues dealing with collaborative learning including group dynamics, pedagogy and administrative issues. The key issues are pertinent to Duchastel's Web-based model when Web-based collaboration is considered.

Table 9.2 Themes and key issues in collaborative team projects

Theme	Key issues
Group dynamics	Who will be in the groups?
	What skills are needed?
	How will group dynamics be supported and developed?
	What technologies can support group processes?
	How does distance collaboration affect group dynamics?
Pedagogical issues	What types of learning activities are needed?
	What will be the scope and focus of the project?
	How will the project be integrated within the course?
	What is the faculty member's role in supporting the learning process?
	What technologies can support collaborative team learning?
Administrative issues	How do faculty and teams keep collaborative projects on schedule?
	How should team projects be evaluated?
	How do technology and distance issues affect the administration of team projects?

Source: Gasen and Preece (1995)

Duchastel's model, Gasen and Preece's themes and key issues in collaborative learning, and the general discussion from this section on collaborative learning should be considered in terms of our leading question, 'What is a University?' Is the technology revolution providing a springboard for radical changes in education and in the institutional structure of education? What type of educational support system would deliver a two-way or a hundred-way collaborative learning environment? What would be the role of the instructor, the student and the institution involved?

The authors do not have answers to the questions but we can offer some insight into the development, operation and administration of an international educational network that is attempting to address those issues, Association Global View.

Association Global View (AGV)

AGV's startup

Association Global View was created in 1991 from the initial desire of two professors located in different countries, United States and France, to provide meaningful global perspectives to their students.

Simulation pedagogy and the transfer of the data between institutions was an immense problem a decade ago. The Web as we know it today did not exist. E-mail was not capable of sending sizeable text or binary files. A development team created communication software to support multi-sited simulations. The software resided at both sites with large blocks of data transferred between the sites using file transfer protocol (FTP).

During the development stage of the simulation, the professors and university administrators recognized that the creation of a collaborative interactive programme between two sites would be difficult. Nevertheless, the administration from both universities endorsed the attempted linkage, although no resources were provided. Both universities shied away from funding commitments, neither being willing to take the financial risk. Each university was concerned that it might expend resources to 'help and aid' another institution that was quite capable of paying its own way.

The programme worked. The students were highly motivated by the use of current technology, by active learning in the simulation, by team learning and by being part of the 'global business community'. Everything they perceived a course should be was met in this experimental, cross-cultural, collaborative learning venture. Institutional concerns about budgets, sharing of risks, copyright and student fees dogged the early development, despite a successful prototype. The development team therefore decided to create a non-university non-profit organization. Association Global View (AGV) was chartered in France with funds donated by members of the development team. Donated funds were supplemented at a later date with student subscription fees to continue operations.

Association Global View staff took over administrative functions of the joint program and AGV satisfactorily addressed many of the concerns about Web-based courses and the administration of collaborative learning cited above in Duchastel's model and Gasen and Preece's themes and key issues in collaborative learning. The role of AGV was one of establishing compatible schedules and common course content between instructors at the two universities to facilitate collaborative cross-cultural learning experiences. A global communication system was created forming a common Web-based message and chat centre. A student and/or university user fee system was created to fund AGV's operational costs. Universities continued to voice support and offered financial support in the form of loans. Association Global View operations were moved to the California site where most of the development was taking place. A new AGV was chartered as a non-profit organization in California.

AGV's technology changes the pedagogy to learner control

Association Global View communications, simulation programmes and administrative functions improved each year with occasional setbacks. Major concerns were consistently expressed by the instructors and AGV staff about the pedagogy. No major adaptations had been made to the business simulation pedagogy to provide for a more pleasing, more effective and more efficient Web-based learning process. In the first few years of operation, professors involved in the programme assumed that if the pedagogy worked on-site in one classroom, it would work in a multi-sited electronic classroom. Over time, some control of content, material and discussion began to shift from instructor to the students.

Collaborative learning through Web teams allowed the learners to influence what they learnt, how they learnt and with whom they learnt. This shift in control or power over learning evolved as the technical aspects of the program evolved. New pedagogy started to emerge that allowed students in the same class worldwide to have a common core of content and experiences. This universal pedagogy allowed students to identify, explore and share related content either by professorial design, student intent or by accident.

Two examples of student-initiated content provide insight into the power of a network, collaborative learning and the freedom of the learner to set one's own learning agenda as expressed above in Duchastel's model, and Gasen and Preece's themes and key issues in collaborative learning.

Example 1

A student team running a simulated business firm in Northern California developed a long-term strategy of funding and building (or acquiring) large-scale virtual manufacturing plants. The strategy was to make it big or lose it all. To lower the risk, the US team developed alliances with French, Dutch and Chinese teams who became loyal buyers of their products. Each foreign partner was requested by the US team to collaborate regarding strategy in order to make the alliance both functional and profitable for all teams. Alliance members held discussions regarding performance measures set by their different professors (across cultures and nations) to determine how best to earn alliance members the highest grades.

Example 2

A simulated manufacturer and distributor from Texas made several errors and found itself facing bankruptcy. The firm located a French firm through worldwide postings, chats and e-mails. The French firm was willing to purchase the Texas manufacturing facilities and in turn supply the Texas firm with the product. The Texas firm immediately reversed its near-bankrupt status and both firms, through an intensive collaborative effort, made substantial profits.

What is so unique about the activities of the students in the two examples is that they exceeded any requirement set by any of the professors in the courses and, indeed, any expectation that such intense collaborative partnering would ever take place. Perhaps even more importantly, the work of the students ranged outside the expertise of some of the professors instructing the course. The students had on purpose or by accident determined in part what they would learn, when they would learn it and with whom they would collaborate. The students had assumed control of a major part of their learning experience through the global network.

Challenges for tutors

The new pedagogy, where the networked learner was partnered with the instructor in the creation and implementation of the content delivery, generated numerous requests for information from students to AGV staff. The students needed help resolving issues beyond their instructors' knowledge or beyond the instructor's control. For example, in the simulation, international lawsuits are common and are now expected when 500 students engage in active learning by negotiating deals for virtual products around the world. The instructor is generally excited about the student's legal learning experience and often provides advice. The problem is that the instructor often cannot afford the time and perhaps does not have the expertise to contact all parties in the lawsuit and mediate a solution. Protocol would suggest that a professor would not be directly involved in another professor's classroom activities even in a virtual sense.

The consensus of AGV administrators, faculty and students was that AGV needed to expand services to provide resources on an as-needed basis to students when the instructor was not able to do so. Advice on such issues as lawsuits, bankruptcies and additions of new capital through investment bankers is now available through AGV staff or from expert professors who volunteer their time.

The development of Web-based interactive pedagogy continued as students began to take advantage of AGV as a learning resource. There are numerous times in a simulation where knowledge is valuable only if it can be had at a specific moment in time. Student teams negotiating around the world often need advice within hours or minutes. Instructors are often not available at the critical time information is needed. Association Global View staff provides professorial backup and advises students on clerical and standard course content – AGV calls this its 'just-in-time learning resource'. Association Global View created a 24-hour turnaround tutor and mentor support programme to facilitate the 'need to know now'. The mentors are generally advanced students who are paid or volunteer to help students in the simulation. It is not unusual for an expert student tutor from the nation of

Moldova to be advising a student from Texas regarding a contract pending with a team in Vietnam. Association Global View staff members collect frequently-asked questions and host online chats for students worldwide. The instructors are not participants in this part of the learning process and often are not aware to what extent the resources are utilized by their own students. This is not to say that the professors have diverted their attention from teaching. They are perhaps, given student motivation, even more involved than normal in the teaching and discussion of concepts, content and applications in the course.

Implications for fees

To date, AGV has held subscription fees equal to the cost of a new textbook and has funded the extra services by increasing the number of participants. There is, of course, some level of service that cannot be provided without increased fees. The fee structure is important in a discussion of new types of learning and pedagogy that extend outside of the university's specific course description. If the network is to continue to explore development of external Web-based pedagogy it will need to find alternative funding sources, or limit participation to students and universities that can pay full fare. Nations such as China and Vietnam would be underrepresented if all fees were set based on costs in the US and/or Europe. Loss of participants from low-income nations would be a loss to the total value created by a global education network. The issue of equity in setting global user fees has been recognized but not resolved at this point in time.

AGV's network expansion

Within a year of developing the prototype simulation, the network of participating instructors grew to three with the addition of a new development partner, the Hogeschool voor Economicshe Studies (HES) from Amsterdam. Other professors soon added to the network but were less interested in development and more interested in the cross-cultural and international aspect of the simulation. The simulation is currently offered once each semester and services over 1,000 students from five to seven nations.

Web pedagogy must have some size limit – the point where the confusion added negates gains in educational value by adding more students from more nations. The development team does not know what that optimum size limit is. Whatever the optimum, the network has unlimited expansion options by simply replicating another independent collaborative group.

The network is expanding as the Web-based pedagogy is transferred to other courses in business. Association Global View worked with professors to create an 'introduction to business' course, which included normal course content with an online text, a globally interactive simulation and globally interactive case and project assignments. Tests on the 'introduction to business' programme at a university in Texas (LeMaster, Davis and Schlais, 1999) suggest that students could gain the same knowledge as in a standard course in one-third of the time. With the additional time, the instructor could substitute other valuable interactive and collaborative Web-based learning activities that both supported and expanded learning opportunities.

The Web-based pedagogy was next transferred to an international case course. In this programme real firms work with a professor to write an academic case about their firm. The cases are posted to an electronic clearing-house administered by AGV. Business professors create teams in their classes. A team is assigned to a case. The same case will also be assigned to three or four other teams around the world. The teams share, cooperate and collaborate to resolve the firm's case in an international setting. Review of the pedagogy found that the collaborative and interactive learning process was as valuable a learning experience as resolving the case.

Several problems exist in the global case course that seem to exist in all Web-based team pedagogy. In the global case course some students used Web-based pedagogy effectively but other students either could not, or did not want to engage in self-directed learning activities. Instructors and AGV staff are currently attempting to provide a learning structure that will insure some minimum performance standards for all students without providing excessive direction for the more independent students.

A business law course at a Canadian university is innovating an interactive and collaborative pedagogy. Student teams in law will serve as law offices for teams in the simulation around the world. For example, a team from China, having been financially damaged by failure of a Dutch firm to deliver virtual product as contracted, will consult with their 'law office' in Canada. The Dutch firm contacted by the Chinese team's lawyers may or may not seek to retain the services of a legal team. In this situation, Chinese, Dutch and Canadians must all communicate and collaborate to resolve an international dispute. Note that business law is not part of the required course content for most of the teams. Teams not engaged in lawsuits are informed about the events by a weekly newspaper and by their instructor. Students pay close attention to other teams' learning experiences. Some experiences are better learnt by observation than by doing.

There are many cross-discipline learning opportunities within a network. The network can be expanded into non-business disciplines expanding opportunities both within and outside a variety of disciplines. Currently programmes are being designed for a broadcasting course and discussions are under way related to art, literature and political science courses.

Value added by global networks

Business firms have formed affiliations and are using B-to-B sites as they reinvent themselves in this new Web-based era. Leading universities are exploring and testing something similar. The result of the exploration and testing may be an education network. A primary concern is that they will only go halfway – that is, connect internally or to the Internet for one-way distant education to gain efficiencies and new markets. If that is all they do, they will miss the great opportunity to build bridges that globally connect professors and students.

The Networked Future of Education

It would seem from the above discussion that educational networks will, to some degree, shape the future of education. The authors, in this regard, remain cautiously optimistic. Based on AGV's experience, there are sources of support and sources of resistance to global educational networks. Forward-looking education leaders support the AGV network concept. One major reason for the support is that AGV programs immediately internationalize their programs with little if any expense. University leaders see an opportunity to leverage scarce educational resources. Students support the AGV network concept as it hones their computer and Web skills, provides a link to the world and makes the student a partner in their own education.

The major resisting forces are providers of education, mainly faculty and textbook companies. Faculties have expressed grave concerns about their new role in an educational network. The new Web-based globally interactive programmes require the faculty:

- to become computer literate;
- to give up some control (security) to students in the classroom;
- to give up some control to AGV;
- to give up some control to unnamed persons (students and professors from foreign nations);
- to become flexible as classroom activities become more diverse and less planned;
- to be willing to admit lack of expert knowledge beyond a narrow field even in a highly integrated discipline such as business administration;
- to draw from their own expertise as needed rather than rely on a textbook and its supporting materials.

Textbook companies have examined AGV's online course materials, which are basically free or have a minimal transaction cost. Association Global View assigns value to its service and only minor value to its text material. In discussions with a major international publishing firm, their representative indicated that the firm's entire business model would need to change before it could partner with AGV and its business model. Traditionally, faculty and publishing firms are closely partnered and thus they form a serious obstacle to new models of learning.

Faculty members who have switched to the AGV model might be classified as independent or maverick professors who place a very high priority on student learning. All faculty participants to date have donated the software and text materials that power AGV. If this process were to continue, networks would become a major source of inexpensive knowledge gleaned from a worldwide group of educators, most of whom might never be published by standard commercial publishers. In some sense, networks of the future might challenge the established process of the creation and distribution of knowledge through commercial publishers. Instead of five 'introduction to business' texts, there might be 50 available. Instead of one on-site 'introduction to business' class, there might be 36 from eight nations with half of them being globally interactive.

Moving even more bravely into the future, it is possible that students of the future could select their entire degree programme from courses offered by 27 universities located in seven nations. Which university would grant the degree? What, in that future point of time, is a university?

References

Adams, D and Hamm, M (1990) *Cooperative Learning: Critical thinking and collaboration across the curriculum*, Thomas Books, Springfield.

Alavi, M and Wheeler, B C (1995) Using IT to reengineer business education: an exploratory investigation of collaborative tele-learning, *MIS Quarterly*, **19** (3), pp 293–312.

Dobos, J (1996) Collaborative learning: effects of student expectations and communication apprehension on student motivation, *Communication Education*, **45**, pp 118–34.

Duchastel, P (1996–97) A web-based model for university instruction, *Journal of Educational Technology Systems*, **25** (3), pp 221–28.

Flannery, J (1994) Teacher as co-conspirator: knowledge and authority in collaborative learning, *New Directions for Teaching and Learning* **59** (Fall), pp 15–23.

Freire, P (1974) *Pedagogy of the Oppressed*, Seabury Press, New York.

Gasen, J G and Preece, J (1995) Collaborative Team Projects: Key issues for effective learning, *Journal of Educational Systems*, **24** (4), pp 381–94.

Gerlach, J (1994) Is this collaboration?, *New Directions in Teaching and Learning,* **59** (Fall), pp 5–14.

Hamm, M and Adams, D (1992) *The Collaborative Dimensions of Learning,* Ablex Publishing Corporation, Norwood, NJ.

Johnson, D and Johnson, R (1985) Motivational process incooperative, competitive and individualistic learning situations, in *Research on Motivation in Education,* eds C Ames and R Ames, pp 249–86, Academic Press, Orlando, FL.

Johnson, D W and Johnson, R T (1989) *Cooperation and Competition: Theory and research,* Interaction Book Company, Edina, MN.

Kitchen, D and McDougall, D (1998–99) Collaborative learning on the Internet, *Journal of Educational Technology Systems,* **27** (3), pp 245–58.

LeMaster, J, Davis, R and Schlais, D (1999) Early integration of the functional areas of business: using a simulation-based approach to teaching introduction to business, *Proceedings of the American Society of Business and Behavioral Sciences,* **7** (8), pp 74–82.

McLellan, H (1998) The Internet as a virtual learning community, *Journal of Computing in Higher Education,* **9** (2), pp 92–112.

Negroponte, N (1995) *Being Digital,* Alfred A Knopf, New York.

Nelson, C (1994) Critical thinking and collaborative learning, *New Directions for Teaching and Learning,* **59**, pp 45–58.

Prasad, A and Cavanaugh, J (1997) Ideology and demystification: Tom Peters and the managerial (sub-) text – an experiential exploration of critique and empowerment in the management classroom, *Journal of Management Education,* **21** (3), 309–24.

Rockett, L, Valor, J, Miller, P and Naude, P (1998) Technology and virtual teams: using globally distributed groups in MBA learning, *Campus-Wide Information Systems,* **15** (5), pp 174–82.

Sharan, S and Shaulov, A (1990) Cooperative learning, motivation to learn and academic achievement, in *Cooperative Learning: Theory and research,* ed S Sharan, pp 173–202, Praeger, New York.

Sharan, Y and Sharan, S (1992) *Expanding Cooperative Learning Through Group Investigation,* Teachers College Press, New York.

Slavin, R (1987) Developmental and motivational perspectives on cooperative learning: a reconciliation, *Child Development,* **58**, pp 1161–67.

Tomlinson, H and Henderson, H (1995) Computer supported collaborative learning in schools: a distributed approach, *British Journal of Educational Technology,* **26** (2), pp 131–40.

10

Scenarios for PhD courses in a European network environment, as supported by EuroPACE

Jef van den Branden
EuroPACE and Leuven Institute for Innovative Learning, Belgium

Editor's introduction

Online learning is increasingly being used to provide expert and cost-effective support for small groups of dispersed learners. This is as true for PhD students as any other. Van den Branden presents a review of three scenarios in which support for small groups of research students is provided collaboratively by video-conferencing, formal networks and information and communications technology (ICT). The three scenarios are drawn from projects commissioned by the European Union and have the additional challenge of collaboration across cultural and linguistic barriers, something that Web-based online learning initiatives need to address.

Introduction

With today's specialization of science and technology, a model of PhD education that relies only on the research for a doctoral dissertation is becoming outdated and to a certain extent also inefficient. The cost of education to society forces universities to make education as efficient as possible (offering the best output within the shortest possible term). Consequently, courses that support PhD students to become more effective in conducting their research tend to become a necessary formal part of the PhD education. This trend, established earlier in the United States, is increasingly to be found in Europe and governments create incentives for universities to follow this trend. The Flemish government in Belgium, for instance, provides extra funding to the university if students are following courses as a formal part of their PhD education.

In its *Standards for the PhD Degree in the Molecular Bio-sciences*, the Committee on Education of the International Union of Biochemistry and Molecular Biology distinguishes the following roles of formal graduate courses (IUBMB, 2000:17–18):

- Transfer of skills (for example, on scientific writing, presentation of talks, professional ethics, time and project management, and so forth) through short courses and workshops.

- Building confidence and promoting a sense of collegiality through generic or specialized courses, interdepartmental teaching and formal student-run seminars.

- Acquisition of the student's general information base in a field of study through formal courses, aiming at the preparation of the candidate for life-long learning or research activity.

- Increase of the candidate's knowledge base, professional training and support for effective communication, through specialized graduate courses.

The scenarios that are being described in this chapter aim at the second and especially the fourth role of the list. Prior to the description, a rationale for the common base of these scenarios, namely a networked university environment, is given. The three scenarios themselves are then outlined through cases in which they were implemented. A brief discussion of the scenarios and connected issues is then given as introduction to the conclusion.

PhD courses in a networked university environment

A problem that immediately arises when implementing the practice of formal PhD courses is that the level of specialization that is needed may not be available within a given university. Moreover, it will probably never be cost effective to develop such courses in a single university due to the limited number of PhD students constituting the target audience.

One reaction to this problem has been to create ICT (information and communication technologies) solutions that are tailored to the specific needs of (small groups of) doctoral students. Specialist knowledge drawn from leading experts in the field can be brought together and distributed as student support, so that each participating teacher only gets a limited work load in return for a full course that can be offered to their own students. The model is not restricted to the PhD level, but the more advanced the course is, the more benefit this model of collaboration offers. Finding these experts is, of course, more likely in the transnational environment of a (European) network of universities than within the regional collaboration of some institutions. Bundling the efforts in a network also provides the opportunity to find the critical mass of students that is needed to make the development cost effective.

This option fits in the larger approach that EuroPACE, a Trans-European network of traditional universities for ICT supported education, introduced into its model of a virtual class and campus. This model, which can be represented as in Figure 10.1, emphasizes the networking between universities to service their own campus students.

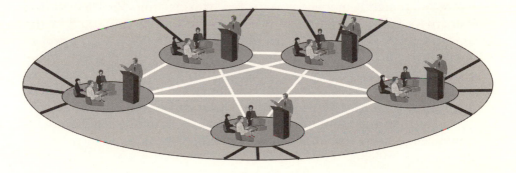

Figure 10.1 Model of virtual class and campus

A number of universities are interconnected by ICT links to support joint activities. Within the network (represented by the larger circle), each university (the smaller circles) is connected to all the others (represented by the white lines). Universities and/or individuals from outside the network can only participate in network activities through connection with a network member university (these potential connections are represented by black lines).

A course can be taught by one teacher for the complete audience of students in the network or by a number of teachers (each teaching their subject topic) residing in different universities. Even team teaching by two or more teachers at the same time is possible. Lectures are either transmitted online (through, for example, video-conferencing) or offered as a Web course. Student support for the whole network can be covered by one university, as a joint activity of staff from various universities, or by local staff for the local students (with backup of experts from other universities of the network).

This model of a virtual class and campus may extend beyond course development and delivery alone. It can include administration and management (technical management, personnel and student administration, financing and accounting, marketing, examination and crediting and so forth), the organization of research (including inter-university research cooperation and communication, contract research and so forth) and service to society at large (knowledge and technology transfer, science communication and so forth). It thus is more comprehensive than its use within PhD courses would suggest. However, it was assumed that this model would prove its usability especially at a (post-)graduate level because the student audiences of this level are mostly small, course subjects highly specialized, and typical subject experts are often not available within each university.

This model, together with the flexible and open learning model and the learning-on-demand model, was tested during the VirtUE (Virtual University for Europe) project that ran from 1996 to 1998 supported by the European Commission's Ten Telecom programme. EuroPACE and its project partners developed some scenarios for the purpose (Van den Branden, 1998). The VirtUE project used three scenarios that were piloted in PhD courses or course modules. All scenarios offered their courses in the transnational environment of a university network. Information and communications technology played an important role for online as well as offline activities, with communication as the crucial element connecting the courses to the research of the doctoral students.

The joint research scenario

The joint research scenario is the most research oriented. It was conceived as an essential part of the doctoral student's research training and is prepared and supported through a distance-learning environment. It may best be described through the case in which this scenario was implemented (Silvana De Rosa, 2000).

The Erasmus-Socrates European Social Representations and Communications (SR&C) PhD Network set up a European PhD programme in the field of SR&C (a leading theory in contemporary social psychology). This programme adopted the European Credit Transfer System (ECTS – http://europa.eu.int/comm/education/socrates/ects.htm) as an instrument to evaluate academic performance in a transparent way. Students are awarded credits for courses and didactic activities involving physical mobility (an international summer school, seminars and advanced courses) and virtual mobility (mainly forum discussions through multi-point video-conferences). Additional credits are given for the quality of their own research programme, conducted at their 'home' university and during compulsory stays at other universities of the network, for which the assessment is jointly made by their 'home' tutors and the co-tutors of the foreign training sites. Finally, credits are also given for bibliographic knowledge.

Distance training has been set up for the doctoral students in the meta-theoretical analysis of the bibliographic corpus on SR&C. The analysis is based on a grid (http://www.europhd.psi.uniroma1.it), is made as a cooperative contribution and should lead to the complete, fully researched bibliography for the domain.

The virtual PhD classes scenario

This scenario offers the virtual campus the equivalent of PhD courses that can be found in many universities today. Two cases from the VirtUE project (Van den Branden *et al*, 1998) are described here, as they are typical of a number of courses and course modules with which we have experimented.

A first case is the computer vision course, designed and developed as a joint initiative of EuroPACE, the European Computer Vision Network and the Catholic University Leuven (KU Leuven). It covered the major applications of computer vision, the rationale for its use, its basic working principles and the current trends in advanced features. The course consisted of six pre-recorded lectures, transmitted through satellite broadcasts of one hour and followed by a live satellite broadcast of a panel discussion between top experts on the topic of the lecture. The audience could ask online questions by phone, fax or e-mail. A Web site was used for information about the course organization, for additional resources, offline communication between participants (including the panellists) and for self-evaluation (quiz).

To offset the large investment (many experts, recording in broadcast quality, satellite transmission), the audience for this course was a mix of graduate students, PhD students and professionals with various backgrounds (engineering, computer sciences, physics and mathematics). This spread in background had a consequence for PhD student participation: although their expressed satisfaction was high, their offline communication remained beneath expectation, in spite of the possibility of having direct access to top experts.

A second example is to be found in the contemporary bio-mechanics course modules. The PhD course comprised four point-to-point video-conferencing seminars between two universities (KU Leuven in Belgium and Eindhoven in the Netherlands), with a mixed audience of seven doctoral students in Leuven and 12 undergraduate students in Eindhoven). Each seminar was composed of a lecture, followed by a discussion on case studies that included relevant reporting of research work by participating PhD students. Each university prepared two seminars.

Despite the mixed audience, students and teachers were satisfied with the content and technical quality of these 'online' seminars, although students (especially the undergraduates) evaluated the video-conference lectures as inferior to lectures in a seminar room or lecturing theatre (less interaction, less vivid presentation). They gave, however, a very positive evaluation for video-conferencing as a tool for the introduction and discussion of the case studies. The video-conference mode enabled participants of both sites to see and become familiar with each other, which served in stimulating later e-mail exchange.

The teaching preparation scenario

Teacher preparation as part of the PhD education is regularly found in US universities (for example http://www.uiowa.edu/~gradcoll/2ndlanguage.html, http://www.edb.utexas.edu/coe/depts/ci/it/Ph.D.html). The last scenario lines up with this practice. Again, the scenario is described through a case.

In the framework of the Joint Call programme, and later the Socrates programme of the European Commission, the Coimbra Group network of European universities developed within its HUMANITIES project a pilot on virtual student mobility in the field of literature (Floor, 1998a). The pilot was later embedded in the VirtUE project and became afterwards an independent Socrates project under the name 'Euroliterature' (http://www.euro-literature.uib.no/index.html). The original four to five universities of the HUMANITIES and VirtUE period were extended to about 20 European universities that were fully or partly involved in its activities.

In each participating university, scattered all over Europe, a course is taught in the conventional way to third- and fourth-year students on subjects that are commonly chosen for the term. A local Web site is set up for local activities (discussion forum, provision of learning resources). The common Euroliterature Web site is the joint communication and information platform. Other joint activities are lectures, given by specialists to all participants through multi-point video-conferences. Intended as a supplementary source of information from outstanding experts, these video-conferences also act as starting points for local and transnational discussion. A final, but most important, part of the activities is the joint paper, which students have to write with peers from other universities in different countries, enabling real experiences of 'cultural diversity'.

PhD students were involved in this project as tutors. They received instructional handbooks and three days' training in the use of educational technology and distance teaching methodologies previous to the start of their activities (HUMANITIES, 1995; Floor, 1998b). Ongoing expert support could be received whenever needed. They were stimulated to introduce their research in their tutoring activities and discuss it with peers and external experts (either teachers from other universities or invited lecturers). This turned out to be beneficial to the PhD students as it provided feedback on their research, raised new relevant research questions for them and gave a good introduction in the professional academic world.

Discussion of the scenarios

As already mentioned, all scenarios are based on transnational networked collaboration, using ICT for development, delivery, support and communication.

The implementation of the 'joint research scenario' in the SR&C Network has a large component of traditional as well as technology based classes and seminars. The basic joint research scenario – the combination of research training through collaborative literature reviews, courses by experts in virtual classes, intensive communication through ICT and the use of ECTS for the establishment of a European PhD – can easily be implemented in PhD education of every subject domain. The scenario was quite successfully accepted within the SR&C Network. The implementation of virtual lectures through multi-point video-conferencing, however, has also encountered resistance. Some universities were reluctant to buy the necessary equipment, with the argument that it was too expensive for the occasional use they expected to make of it. Some lecturers reported being inhibited by the technology while teaching, and others reported that the technology inhibited the establishment of human contacts.

The 'PhD course scenario' enables the construction of a course through complementing inputs of European and even world leading experts on the subject. From a content point of view, such an approach has the potential to create a most attractive and relevant course for PhD students who are working in the field of the course. As these experts are often over-demanded, asking their collaboration for a limited number of lectures and/or forum discussions is more likely to receive a positive response than requesting from them a set of well worked-out course materials. When technology enables them additionally to present their lecture without the need to travel, the advantages of this approach are convincing.

The use of educational technology, however, also has drawbacks. The environment is, certainly, in a transnational context, more costly than conventional teaching on campus (equipment cost, communications cost, necessity of technical staff and so forth). It is true that the multi-medial capacity of Internet technology has promoted this medium as replacement for the formerly used technologies such as satellite, v-sat or video-conferencing, with greater availability of equipment at a better cost–benefit balance. But even then it remains necessary for the universities to make large investments in basic equipment and networks. There are also the limitations in bandwidth of Internet that influence both download times and image quality, one of the major reasons for an organization such as the National Technological University in the United States to maintain satellite broadcasts as a delivery mode for its courses.

To increase this cost–benefit ratio, the target group of PhD students is often extended with undergraduate as well as postgraduate and continuing education students. The last categories offer the additional advantage that direct income is raised through course fees. It should, however, be realized that this practice may limit the usability of the course for PhD students, as non-PhD students have quite different interests in content topics and different motivations (for example, practical versus theoretical) for following the course. The experience of physical distance, inherently connected to distance education, may be reinforced through this introduction of a mental distance between the interests of various categories of course participants.

Information transfer and communication remain essential issues in courses, and consequently language can cause possible communication problems in the translingual context of a transnational dialogue. English may have established itself as the worldwide scientific communication language, but at a more local level, even PhD students often lack sufficient proficiency in English to understand and communicate complex concepts and reasoning. This aspect cannot be neglected in the environment of networked courses. Nevertheless, recommendations are still encountered such as the one reported by the TELESCOPIA project during the Online Educa Conference in Berlin (November 1995), in which it was proposed to impose the use of one common language (English) as the solution to all language problems in open and distance learning (be it connected to better methods for teaching English all over Europe).

Such recommendations ignore the obvious conflict between the 'solution' and the general claims in matters of cultural identity and language, as can be found in reactions of European Union member states, which led in the meantime to the notion of 'Europe of the regions' as complementary to 'Europe of the states'. It should be recognized that imposing a *lingua franca* is an act of power exercise which, just like colonization, imposes standardization unilaterally and consequently raises resistance from the less powerful parties.

In a state-of-the-art overview on language policy versus language management (Jansen and Lambert, 1995), it has been concluded that the naive belief in the existence of perfect communication through the use of a *lingua franca* and the assumption that all partners in international (virtual or distance education) networks have the same goals, expectations and competences must be rejected. In fact, the diversity of goals, expectations and backgrounds is often the very reason why people enjoy studies in a transnational context. The authors therefore suggest replacing language policy with language management. Some guidelines for such language management in virtual instruction networks have been described elsewhere (Van den Branden and Lambert, 1999).

Such language management has been built into two of the described cases: the SR&C and the Euroliterature cases. Both projects are multilingual, with a mix of common language(s) for joint activities, but preparation and follow-up of these activities at the local site (including local Web site activities) in the mother tongue of the students. In the case of Euro-literature, experiments with multilingual video-conferences were conducted. Not only were several languages used for the conferences (eventually with local simultaneous translation) but instruction was also given in insert breaks during video-conferences that enabled participants to have a summarizing interpretation and local discussions in the mother tongue and the preparation of further interactions in the common language.

These scenarios imply training in the use of technology for all the actors. Not only should students, teachers and tutors be trained but so should the often-forgotten categories of technical and administrative staff.

Conclusion

The three scenarios that were implemented proved to have potential for PhD courses of various kinds (joint research courses, virtual classes, teaching training). Their strength relies on the transnational networking, made possible and affordable through well-considered use of ICT. Trans-national networking is attractive, not only while it expands the expertise that is available at the local site, but also while it opens possibilities for communication, feedback and collaboration with remote experts and peers (PhD students) working in the same field of specialization. It may also provide the critical mass that is needed to develop a cost-effective course.

The joint research courses scenario clearly scores the best in terms of response to the needs for education of PhD students. The confrontation of PhD students with undergraduates, (post-)graduates and continuing education students in the same course (the other two scenarios) creates mixed experiences. Where it leads to course contents that are less focused on the interests of PhD students, resulting sometimes in lower responsiveness, it also provides feedback to those that otherwise could be overlooked and thus creates new relevant research questions and even new research lines.

Although well-considered in their conceptual stage, these scenarios were exploratory in nature. Their concepts were mainly based on assumptions and were changed during trials as the result of observation and feedback. The resulting conclusions cannot be anything but tentative. Further and scientifically underpinned investigation is needed to come to valid models. However, first impressions suggest that these networked scenarios are good starting points for complementing the traditional PhD education that is purely based on research work and even for formal PhD courses that are set up by a single university.

References

Azuma, R (2000) *A Graduate School Survival Guide: So long, and thanks for the PhD*, http://www.cs.unc.edu/~azuma/hitch4.html

Floor, P (ed) (1998a) *Beyond HUMANITIES. Long Term Strategy for ODL in University Environments and Virtual Mobility*, Coimbra Group, Brussels, http://www.dipoli.hut.fi/org/humanities/hum3/hum-pub.html

Floor, P (ed) (1998b) *Beyond HUMANITIES. Guidelines for the Implementation of ODL and VIRTUAL MOBILITY Approach in Conventional Universities*, Coimbra Group, Brussels, http://www.dipoli.hut.fi/org/humanities/hum3/hum-pub.html

HUMANITIES (1995) *Tutor Guide*, http://www.dipoli.hut.fi/org/humanities/hum1/humanities/deli/tutguid.html

IUBMB (2000) *Standards for the PhD Degree in the Molecular Bio-sciences*, http://www.iubmb.unibe.ch/Downloads/book.pdf

Jansen, P and Lambert, J (1995) Language as intercultural strategy in open distance learning, in *Handbook of Cultural Factors in use of Technology Learning Environments*, ed J Van den Branden, pp 26–90, EuroPACE 2000, Heverlee.

Silvana de Rosa, A (2000) Distance training of European doctoral students in meta-theoretical analysis of fully researched bibliographic corpus, in *ODL Networking for Quality Learning. Proceedings of the Lisbon 2000 European Conference,* ed A Rocha Trindade, Universidade Aberta, Lisbon (Portugal) 19–21 June 2000.

Van den Branden, J (1998) VirtUE: A Virtual University for Europe, in *Universities in a Digital Era. Transformation, Innovation and Tradition. Roles and Perspectives of Open and Distance Learning. Proceedings of the 1998 EDEN conference*, eds A Szücs and A Wagner, University of Bologna, Bologna, Italy, 24–26 June 1998.

Van den Branden, J et al (1998) *VirtUE. Validation Report of the Pilot Network* , EuroPACE 2000, Haverlee.

Van den Branden, J and Lambert, J (1999) Cultural and linguistic diversity: threat or challenge for virtual instruction, in *Virtual Instruction: Issues and insights from an international perspective*, eds C Feyten *et al*, Libraries Unlimited/Teacher Ideas Press, Tampa.

Part 4

Transition

The items in Part 4 have been grouped together because they describe the challenges that need to be addressed when introducing online teaching and learning into traditional institutions and learning cultures. Sisko Mällinen of Lahti Polytechnic Finland (Chapter 11) sets out her aspirations for new approaches to teaching, focusing on the development of high-level soft skills and the introduction of a more positivist pedagogy with teachers and learners whose traditional practices are hard to change. Her experience will strike a chord with many readers in similar situations. Woodman *et al* (Chapter 12) report on a high-profile innovation in Middlesex University that sought to convert an international programme to online delivery. Despite high investment and proven third party software, traditional practices and attitudes survive. The introduction of new media will not in itself see any significant change in the prevailing pedagogical stance, unless it is accompanied by clear strategies to bring such change about. Both chapters provide advice from which others might learn.

NORTH ARKANSAS COLLEGE LIBRARY
1515 Pioneer Drive
Harrison, AR 72601

11

Teacher effectiveness and online learning

Sisko Mällinen
Lahti Polytechnic, Finland

Editor's introduction

Mällinen reports on teachers at Lahti Polytechnic in Finland moving from traditional delivery methods towards online learning. Not only are many teachers unused to and wary of the technology – they also have to cope with the need to develop students' personal professional skills and accommodate more constructivist approaches against a background of traditional attitudes to teaching and learning. Mällinen argues, with reference to examples, that traditional teachers can begin to make the transition by replicating good classroom practice in their online courses.

New challenges in education

It is difficult to find teachers to design and teach online courses. That was the experience in Lahti Polytechnic when a new online education project started in 1999. The project was partly funded by the European Social Fund, and aimed at staff development of local small and medium size companies via new technologies. Several reasons might have been behind teachers' reluctance to participate in the project, the most obvious being the usual lack of time. Another reason might have been that the Internet was an unknown territory. Teachers did not know how to teach on the Internet.

In fact, the whole concept of teaching is undergoing a change. This is not because of new educational technologies but because society is changing. Students as a consequence need to develop a range of high-level personal skills related to flexibility, critical thinking, communication, self-managed learning and adaptability, along with familiarity with new technology and awareness and appreciation of different cultures (Lasonen and Stenström, 1995; Ruohotie, 1996; Townsend, Clarke and Ainscow, 1999). These skills cannot be taught; they must be learnt. As the labour market becomes less and less predictable – old jobs disappear and new opportunities are created – schools cannot prepare students for specific jobs anymore. What the school can offer is the theoretical basis that enables students to make innovative decisions in new situations. Rote solutions will not work for the new, complex problems. Therefore, education must offer students not just facts and figures but experiences of cause and effect as they process contextual information. To accomplish this teachers will have to learn to work in teams; they will have to be committed to lifelong learning, and they will have to master the new technologies. The old kind of transmission of knowledge does not result in true learning. Now the teacher's role is changing from 'the sage on the stage' to 'a guide on the side'. The teacher becomes the designer and manager of a learning process where students construct their own knowledge networks (Tella, 1997).

From theory to good practice

In addition to these changes in context, new theories of learning are emerging. According to Lehtinen (1997), learning today is:

- constructive;
- cumulative;
- self-directed;
- goal oriented;
- contextual;
- abstract;
- cooperative; and
- different for every student.

Learning is constructing one's knowledge network repeatedly. Students process new information and form new meanings and knowledge structures. Self-directedness implies students taking greater responsibility for their learning. Students take an active role in the learning situation, first finding out what they do not know, then deciding on the best learning strategies and setting their own objectives. To do this students must be aware of their own cognitive processes. Students learn more if they are involved in setting the goals for their learning. Advocates of contextual learning theories argue that new knowledge only makes sense as part of the social and cultural situation. Abstract learning, on the other hand, is understanding new concepts that form the theoretical basis required in making innovative decisions in new situations and solving complex problems. What students learn depends on their prior knowledge, their motivation and interests, and many other things. This cognitive diversity explains how different students seem to be learning different things, although the learning situation is the same. In a way students construct their own learning environments according to their interests and needs (Lehtinen, 1997).

Switching to IT in education

Given the changes in society and new approaches to learning, what can new technology offer the hard-pressed teacher? Information technologies provide new tools for teachers in their everyday work. Computers and information networks are no more than a new kind of chalk and overhead projector. The goals and contents of the course determine the instructional approach. However, in order to make use of the new technologies, teachers have to become conversant with computers and networks. This may be a big step. With all their duties teachers do not seem to find extra time to learn to use new computer programs. Moreover, experience shows that network-based teaching takes up much more time than traditional classroom teaching (Farrington, 1999; Marttunen, 1997).

A good idea is to start small. Teachers can take a look at their courses to see if there is any part that needs adjusting; anything that might benefit from a new approach. What they do not have to do is to produce the whole course in an HTML format following all the principles of the constructive learning theory. Not right away anyway, and not on their own. In the light of what is known about learning and the professional qualifications required in the working life, let us look at some simple ways in which information technologies can help teachers to improve their teaching.

Social interaction skills are increasingly important in a modern world. There is also evidence that learning is improved by interaction with other students. This seems to be one of the most important ways that IT can enhance learning. There are cultural differences, of course, but, for example, for a Finnish student, study- or work-related social interaction does not come easily. Finnish students do not engage in conversations to develop new ideas; they like to listen and contemplate the ideas on their own. They would rather express a well thought-out opinion than discuss half-baked ideas. These observations are based on experiences of cooperative learning projects, not on a scientific study (Lehtinen, 1997). Thus in the case of cooperative learning, for example, there is a lot of chatting going on before the work begins. But after the workload has been somehow divided, each student tends to do his or her share alone. In the end, the different pieces are put together. In the worst cases a couple of students do the work while the others are engaged in unproductive activities.

Using the Internet to connect the students, and providing them with communication tools does not necessarily change the situation for the better unless an extra effort is made to overcome this problem. However, having the tools to express ideas that are difficult to form into words at an early stage, might lower the threshold of communication. Lehtinen (1997) reports on an experiment where students using a computer-aided algebra program (DERIVE) were able to communicate with each other silently by showing their ideas on the screen. This kind of non-verbal communication would be possible with graphic programs as well when working on a design project, for example.

Obviously the goal cannot be to teach silent communication. Activities like the above serve as a first step towards sharing ideas. Another point that Lehtinen is making is the use of communication tools like electronic bulletin boards and chat rooms to encourage students to engage in meaningful discussions about the subject matter. These easily accessed tools make it possible for students to participate in a real-time exchange of ideas in a shared knowledge-building process or, alternatively, read what other students are writing, let it sink in, form their own opinions, and express them when ready. The fact that communication via networks is in a way faceless, and the students can maintain their anonymity to a certain extent, may also make participation easier. E-mail interaction between the student and the teacher can also be more personal and intimate than face-to-face interaction. It can also make it easier for the student to approach the teacher (Farrington, 1999).

Marttunen (1997) gives an example of a simple use of e-mail to develop students' *argumentation skills* and critical thinking. The reason why attention is being paid to argumentation skills specifically is the evidence on Finnish students' poor performance in academic discussions (Laurinen, 1996; Marttunen, 1997; Mauranen, 1993; Steffensen, 1996). Finnish undergraduate students do not often ask questions in class, they do not challenge the lecturer, they are shy to express critical views about the professors' or fellow students' arguments, and, as mentioned before, the simple sharing of ideas in public is not easy for the students. Marttunen (1997) reports of a study made in the University of Jyväskylä. The students used an electronic e-mail environment to discuss the course literature. As all the selected students participated in the e-mail communication, the interaction between the students improved. However, the study also showed that critical argumentation was scarce. Marttunen concludes that Finnish undergraduate students tend to avoid disagreement as it feels impolite. He goes on to suggest that seminar and class discussions could be increased by giving the students an opportunity to comment on the lecture afterwards via electronic communication tools. This way, shy students might also be encouraged to ask questions and offer their often valuable insights and experiences. Again, the desired outcome would be that once the students get used to expressing their ideas, they would feel confident enough to do so in class as well.

The above are examples of using communications networks at a rather low technical level. On the market there is a range of commercial Web-based courseware that makes it possible for the teacher to plan a course where students learn at their own pace, test their learning strategies and develop their independent learning skills. In Lahti Polytechnic a decision was made to use WebCT (developed in the University of British Columbia, Canada), which is basically a program for creating a virtual classroom including communication tools for students and teachers, possibilities for students to present their own material, quiz tools, different tools for teachers for student management and so forth. Apart from educational purposes in the polytechnic, WebCT is also used as a communication tool between the faculty, all other personnel and the students. It can be accessed via the Internet, and thus provides the most up-to-date information about the school activities, cancellations, last-minute changes in the lesson plan and so forth. Students can also contact individual teachers through WebCT. Similarly, teachers can address their messages to specific classes. The WebCT bulletin board is used, among other things, to encourage teacher–teacher interaction and discussion on chosen topics.

In the University of Turku they have developed a Web-based WorkMates program, which offers students and teachers a common forum for presenting their own material and for working together to produce documents. It also has tools for communication and guided information search (Lehtinen, 1997). WorkMates can be accessed anywhere via the Internet provided the computer has a Web-browser. This enables asynchronous working on the same project – working together without being present at the same place at the same time. These programs encourage cooperative learning, following Vygotsky's theory of socially constructed knowledge. The students can comment on and add to each other's documents, and in this way develop their critical thinking skills as well.

With these sophisticated open-learning environments students can be faced with real-life authentic problems as part of their curriculum. The problems can be embedded in the learning process in such a way that working on them gives the students both a contextual experience of solving a complex problem, plus a chance to test the theory and develop their abstract thinking (Lehtinen, 1997).

One example of the use of WebCT in Lahti Polytechnic is the combined marketing and the English language project conducted via the Internet. WebCT was used as a virtual classroom to connect students from two different polytechnics: Lahti Polytechnic and North Karelia Polytechnic. The students were doing a course on marketing with an emphasis on foreign language skills. The two groups of students never met. Two teachers from each polytechnic were involved in the project. It was the students' responsibility to create imaginary companies in teams of three or four students, and to produce the company Web pages with descriptions of their products. The students also introduced themselves with photographs. This was all done in English. All this material was put in the presentation area within WebCT. The students then had to familiarize themselves with all the companies, decide which of them they would like to do business with, and then approach the chosen company/companies with a business letter. The companies had their own e-mail addresses within WebCT. The correspondence led to a business deal with a problem arising at the last minute. The problem was then solved in a video-conference between the companies.

The experiences of the combined marketing and English course were very positive. According to the students the correspondence felt real, and they had to pay extra attention to making themselves understood. This is not always the case when the letter is only written for the teacher to mark. The students were also happy for an opportunity to practise video-conferencing, and the negotiation skills in English. The project would have been even more effective if the other school had not been Finnish too. Even so, the students felt not knowing the other party made the simulation more real than working with one's own classmates.

What can go wrong?

Obviously many things can go wrong, starting with all the problems that the new technology brings. Technical problems aside, there are other pitfalls. Manninen and Pesonen (2000) are concerned about the overemphasis on the constructive theory of learning that almost seems to be equated with network-based learning environments. This could result in too narrow an approach to teaching. The contents and the goals of a particular course often determine the instructional approach. A case in point is the behaviourist concept that immediate feedback gives the best result if the goal is to master a simple procedure or a grammatical structure, for example. There is no reason to abolish lecturing altogether, either. Why should the students not be given a chance to listen to an expert?

The spreading of certain catchwords like cooperative learning and self-directedness can lead to misuse of these concepts. It is possible that teachers who are not familiar with the constructive theory of learning as a whole, misunderstand these words and may, in fact, make their courses worse. Co-operative learning and self-directedness do not mean leaving students alone, giving them group work and more homework, to study independently. In fact, designing and tutoring these learning processes requires more from the teacher than the traditional transmission of knowledge method. For example, a self-directed information search on the net may result in students' impulsive surfing without ever reaching the goal. Students may also end up selecting the resources on the basis of their initial misconceptions of the subject matter. The fractional information on the Internet does not result in understanding if students have no prior knowledge of the subject.

The transmission theory of knowledge is still very much part of the teaching at curriculum and classroom level. Thus the first idea that teachers may have when they start to plan an online course, or part of a course, is how to produce material on the Internet. In other words, how to transmit their knowledge to students via the Internet instead of face to face. As a result, teaching may be reduced to the delivery of materials only.

Another mistake easily made is to tie the teachers' hands – or imagination – to one particular program. If the school has chosen certain courseware, this tends to dominate the planning process, even though it would be perfectly possible to use other programs as well. Accidentally the planning of online learning becomes technologically led. We start asking questions like 'What can I do with this program?' instead of asking 'How can I make the learning process more effective?'

Teacher effectiveness and online learning

'It's the classroom, stupid,' says Reynolds (1999) in one of his articles on school effectiveness. He seems to be right. An electronic learning environment is, after all, a virtual classroom. It is still what the teacher does that matters. So what is it that makes an effective classroom and can it be replicated online?

According to Creemers (1996) the following teacher behaviours contribute to better student outcomes:

- effective class management;
- use of homework;
- high expectations;

- clear goal setting;
- structuring the curriculum content;
- clarity of presentation;
- frequent questioning;
- use of immediate exercise after presentation of new content;
- use of evaluation, feedback and corrective instruction (Creemers, 1996: 52).

Reynolds *et al* (1999) identified five factors that 'travel' across contexts and cultures. These are:

- a controlled environment;
- a strong commitment to academic goals;
- high time on task;
- good teacher–teacher relationships;
- highly interactive classroom teaching in which there is a balance of control–autonomy for pupils.

Effective class management online and *a controlled environment* are as important in a virtual environment as in a real classroom. It means that the teacher does not leave the students to work alone but, instead, actively follows how the students are doing, and steps in if necessary – either to point the students in the right direction, or to give individual tasks, and so forth. The main thing is to know what the students are doing and keep them on task. This kind of class management can be achieved with the help of student tracking functions within the software, or by giving students deadlines, quizzes and so on, to check that they are working on task. Tutoring also includes frequent feedback and evaluation of the work done. In short, the teacher's presence should be strong on an online course. After all, the teacher does not typically give students interesting learning tasks and then walk out of the classroom.

High expectations and *strong commitment to academic goals* refer to the appropriate difficulty level and the contents of the course. There is evidence (Creemers, 1996; Reynolds *et al*, 1999) that a higher goal encourages better achievement. Teachers' high expectations are reflected, not just in the tasks they give to students, but also in the way they communicate with their students. Students do better when they feel that teachers believe that they can be high achievers.

Clear goal setting, structuring the curriculum content, clarity of presentation, frequent questioning, use of immediate exercise after presentation of new content, and use of evaluation, feedback and corrective instruction all apply to any planning of a course content. If there are tasks that require independent work from students, a clear goal becomes even more important. Preferably the goal is set together with the students. Online learning gives students opportunities to choose different learning strategies and perhaps different resources, but the common goal will ensure that learning really takes place.

Making the *structure* of the online course clear is important in two ways. Students need to see how the different tasks promote learning and take them towards the goal. However, they will also have to be able to locate themselves on the Internet so that they do not get lost. Pesonen *et al* (2000) suggest preparing a map of the structure of the course, a map that students can access from all the pages. This map also serves as the table of contents. That is what we usually look at first when we take up a book, too. A presentation of the structure of the course gives students an overview that helps them navigate through the different pages.

Questions, exercises, evaluation and feedback are all forms of *interaction*, either with the material, between students themselves or between students and teachers, ensuring the balance between *control and autonomy for students*. In addition, frequent tasks where students can test their understanding, help keep up their motivation, and provide teachers with diagnostic information on how the students are learning. This *feedback* can then be used to modify the course if necessary. Frequent feedback from the teacher to the students, on the other hand, helps fight against feelings of isolation and reinforces the teacher–student relationship.

What comes to focus in the research within higher education, apart from clarity of presentation, clear goals, feedback, intellectual challenges and high expectations, is the importance of a *good relationship* between the teacher and the students (Ballantyne, Bain and Packer, 1999; Ramsden, 1992; Tang, 1997). Ballantyne, Bain and Packer (1997: 224) go as far as to conclude that 'a good relationship between teacher and learner is crucial for effective learning, at any level of education'. According to Ramsden (1992) the emotional aspect of teacher–student relationship is more important than methods and techniques applied in teaching. A good relationship involves respect for students, stepping down from the stage to help them to learn, and being available for the students even outside of class. Biemans *et al* (1999) conclude that students experience more room to learn when the teacher stimulates them. This is also connected to clarity; the more the teacher stimulates the students, the more he or she is experienced as clear.

The findings of teacher effectiveness research seem to be twofold. On one hand, we learn about effective instructional methods that could be applied to the designing of online courses. On the other hand, the teacher–student relationship is emphasized, especially within higher education. The latter could be related to the actual running of an online course and effective tutoring.

In conclusion

In the discussion about online learning the focus is often on the learning materials or the technology. However, it is equally important to consider the teacher's role as the designer and manager of the new learning environments. Although learning is a student's individual growth process, there is evidence that teachers can make a difference. It is therefore vital for teachers to keep up to date as regards the theories of learning, the goals of education and training and the means of achieving those goals. The challenges for education arise from the changes in the working life and society, and these changes should be reflected in teaching as well. Virtual classrooms, electronic chat rooms and bulletin boards are just sophisticated tools that teachers can use in creating the best possible opportunities for students to learn. What the teacher knows about learning, and the relationship he or she develops with the students, remains just as essential in virtual classrooms as in physical classrooms.

References

Ballantyne, R, Bain, J and Packer, J (1999) Researching university teaching in Australia: themes and issues in academics' reflections, *Studies in Higher Education*, **24** (2), p 237.

Biemans, H, Jongmans, C, de Jong, F and Bergen, T (1999) *The Instructional Behaviour of Teachers in Secondary Vocational Education as Perceived by the Teachers Themselves and by Their Students*, paper presented at the European Conference on Educational Research, Lahti, Finland, 22–25 September.

Creemers, B (1996) The school effectiveness knowledge base, in *Making Good Schools*, eds D Reynolds *et al*, Routledge, London.

Farrington, G (1999) The new technologies and the future of residential undergraduate education, in *Dancing with the Devil: Information technology and the new competition in higher education*, ed R Katz *et al*, Jossey-Bass Publishers, San Francisco.

Lasonen, J and Stenström, M-L (1995) Introduction of educational structure in Finland, in *Contemporary Issues of Occupational Education in Finland*, eds J Lasonen and M-L Stenström, Kopi-Jyvä Oy, Jyväskylä.

Laurinen, L (1996) Pro gradu-tutkielman tekeminen ongelmanratkaisuna – tutkielmaseminaari keskustelu- ja oppimistilanteena, in *Seminaaridiskurssi – diskursseja seminaarista, ed* L Laurinen, M-R Luukkaa and K Sajavaara, Jyväskylän yliopisto, Soveltavan kielentutkimuksen keskus, Jyväskylän yliopistopaino, Jyväskylä.

Lehtinen, E (1997) Tietoyhteiskunnan haasteet ja mahdollisuudet oppimiselle, in *Verkkopedagogiikka*, ed E Lehtinen, Oy Edita Ab, Helsinki.

Manninen, J and Pesonen, S (2000) Aikuisdidaktiset lähestymistavat – verkkopohjaisten oppimisympäristöjen suunnittelun taustaa, in *Aikuiskoulutus Verkossa – Verkkopohjaisten oppimisympäristöjen teoriaa ja käytäntöä*, eds J Matikainen and J Manninen, Tammer-Paino, Tampere.

Marttunen, M (1997) Vuorovaikutus sähköpostiopiskelussa yliopisto-opinnoissa, in *Verkkopedagogiikka*, ed E Lehtinen, Oy Edita Ab, Helsinki.

Mauranen, A (1993) Opiskelijan diskurssimaailmat – vaihto-opiskelijoiden perspektiivi, in *Korkeakouluopetuksen Kriisi*, ed H Jalkanen and L Lestinen, Artikkelikokoelma Jyväskylässä 19. 20.8.1993 järjestetystä korkeakoulutuksen tutkimuksen V symposiumista, Kasvatustieteiden tutkimuslaitos, Jyväskylä.

Pesonen, S, Pilli-Sihvola, M and Tiihonen, J (2000) Verkkokurssin tuotantoprosessi, in *Aikuiskoulutus Verkossa – Verkkopohjaisten oppimisympäristöjen teoriaa ja käytäntöä*, eds J Matikainen and J Manninen, Tammer-Paino, Tampere.

Ramsden, P (1992) *Learning to Teach in Higher Education*, Routledge, London.

Reynolds, D (1999) Platform: it's the classroom, stupid, *The Times Educational Supplement*, 28 May 1999.

Reynolds, D, Teddlie, C and the ISERP Team (1999) *Worldclass School: A preliminary analysis of data from the international school effectiveness research project*, Department of Education, University of Newcastle upon Tyne, unpublished.

Ruohotie, P (1996) *Oppimalla Osaamiseen ja Menestykseen*, Oy Edita Ab, Helsinki.

Steffensen, M (1996) *How Finns and Americans Persuade*, paper presented at the Eleventh World Conference of Applied Linguistics (AILA 96), 4–9 August, Jyväskylä, Finland.

Tang, T (1997) Teaching evaluation at a public institution of higher education: factors related to the overall teaching effectiveness, *Public Personnel Management*, **26** (3) p 379.

Tella, S (1997) Verkostuva viestintä- ja tiedonhallintaympäristö opiskelun tukena, in *Verkkopedagogiikka*, ed E Lehtinen, Oy Edita Ab, Helsinki.

Townsend, T, Clarke, P and Ainscow, M (eds) (1999) *Third Millennium Schools: A world of difference in effectiveness and improvement*, Swets & Zeitlinger BV, The Netherlands.

12

From conventional to distance education: adopting a pedagogy and managing the transformation

Mark Woodman, Maya Milankovic-Atkinson, Chris Sadler, Alan Murphy
Middlesex University, UK

Editor's introduction

Woodman *et al* describe the process by which a university school of computing sciences converted a post-graduate programme into an online format as part of an international collaboration programme called the Global Campus. Institutional constraints, student expectations and traditional attitudes combined to replicate a traditional content-delivery and learner-support model, using third-party software designed around 'steps of instruction' and confining learner control to responding to instruction. Lessons learnt are reported, not least in the context of alternative pedagogical approaches.

Introduction

Our experience of providing online learning materials arises from an international project called Global Campus, which uses mostly Web technologies to offer a distance-learning mode for a masters degree programme, which is also run in the conventional, face-to-face mode. As the originators of educational materials for this programme we are motivated by the advantages brought by the development of flexible learning arrangements for home students as well as the provision of efficiently delivered, high-quality courses to partner institutions abroad. From the outset of the project we have committed to the Web as a technological infrastructure (which is not the same as committing to online use of the Web). We have sustained the essence of distance education: that the lecturer/author does not teach students directly and is not routinely accessible to them. Furthermore, we have consistently committed to an essentially asynchronous model of delivery in which face-to-face tutorials, deadlines for continuous assessment and formal examinations are the only synchronization points. The consequence for students is that they must take more responsibility for their learning than they would have done in the conventional mode. The consequence for the Global Campus team was that we had to devise a pedagogy that was not only useful for Web-based content delivery but would support learners managing their learning.

Fitting into institutional constraints

The degree to which our variation on the distance education theme would require learners to manage their learning, the degree to which learning could be asynchronous, and the degree to which study would be interactively online (rather than simply computer based) depended on factors external to the project. These facets of distance education are compromises due to institutional rules, requirements of the degree programmes, staff resources and expertise, timescales for delivery, and expectations of national academic quality agencies. For example, to satisfy rules and aspirations about quality, the school's academic management determined the frequency, duration and attendance requirement for tutorials, and specified the normal grading ratio between continuous assessment and formal examination. For almost half the modules of the degree programme, students could expect nine hours' Web-based and other study per week, with at most a one-hour weekly tutorial; these figures were doubled for most of the other modules. The pedagogy for the distance-learning mode had to fit this pattern and students were hence constrained in the way they managed their study.

Despite the real constraints described, we aspire to a concept of a programme being defined in terms of its required outcomes and being 'taught' by academics originating or referencing useful resources for students working towards the required outcomes. The advantages of committing to Web-based and eventually to online provision were expected to benefit all stakeholders. Academic management wanted the ability to deliver up-to-date and updateable programmes to overseas students and to reduce the dependence on synchronous teaching at home. Overseas students wanted access to programmes local to them and home students wanted more flexibility and more tangible resources. To achieve these goals, we initially devised a mixed-mode in which Web materials based on CD ROM could be substituted for much online access. This was because we expected students in some target regions to have problems with reliable Internet access and we could not guarantee the performance requirements of a fully online delivery mechanism if and when student numbers would increase. (As soon as is practical, CD ROMs will be phased out.)

Thus, this article is a reflection on how we addressed and continue to address the issues of transforming part of our curriculum to (essentially) online learning; what pedagogy we adopted; how successful our students are when managing their learning and how successful academics are when transforming their courses. The final, concluding section suggests management strategies to support pedagogies and looks ahead to improvements we intend to make.

The Global Campus project

The Global Campus project was established in May 1999 between the School of Computing Science of Middlesex University (MU) in London and the Regional Information Technology and Software Engineering Centre (RITSEC) in Cairo. The Global Campus was originally conceived by RITSEC, who were keen to develop their collaboration with MU further, and a decision was made to launch the popular MSc programme using the distance-learning mode. Middlesex University was to prepare the 'raw' distance learning material and RITSEC would provide technical support by implementing a Web-based learning environment and transferring the MU materials to that environment.

The Global Campus version of the MSc Business Information Technology (BIT) programme was first piloted in Cairo in September 1999, and in February 2000 the programme proper started with additional students in Hong Kong and in London. There is a single MSc BIT programme, so home students have been given the option of studying the distance-learning materials. As a result of MU quality-related requirements, remote students are supported locally by a learning support centre (LSC). Each LSC is formally inspected prior to its involvement in Global Campus so that quality standards are ensured. Learning support centre tutors provide weekly tutorials and assess coursework. End-of-module examinations are assessed by MU. The examinations are held at the same time at all sites and assessments are moderated, discussed and reported at the MU assessment boards.

Currently there are over 80 students active in the distance-learning mode of the programme in Hong Kong and Cairo; there are now 115 in London using the distance-learning material as a resource in a mixed-mode approach. Fifty more overseas students are due to start in September 2000, and negotiations with other potential LSCs are progressing towards a 2001 start date.

The transformation process

Each Global Campus module was divided into learning units, each of which was worth one credit. Hence 10-credit modules were divided into 10 learning units, and so on. This homogeneity was initially thought to be useful because it allowed academics to view units in a way that corresponded to whole or half weeks of conventional teaching. (This strategy proved useful for determining the pacing of some modules, but was inhibiting for others.) Module handbooks for the existing MU MSc BIT syllabus (containing module objectives, lecture notes, tutorial exercises, sample examination papers, coursework, reading lists and so forth) served as a starting point for the authors of the material. Any syllabus revisions that were incorporated during the development of the distance learning materials redefined the syllabus for the programme and hence for home students studying in the conventional mode.

The development of distance learning materials is an iterative, continuous-improvement process. Teams of academics, usually MU lecturers involved in face-to-face teaching of a module, draft learning units as stylized documents. Their structure, styles and additional annotations act as instructions to the RITSEC designers and implementers of the Web materials. Units are repeatedly reviewed, edited and revised prior to and after implementation. Following implementation and testing of online, WebCT versions, CD ROMs are produced as snapshots of sequences of units.

By September 2000 all except the project module of the MSc BIT programme had been deployed in distance learning mode – some 120 learning units. To meet such very tight deadlines, work was shared among academics as authors, reviewers and editors. The authors were both MSc BIT lecturers and others with relevant expertise, either in the subject domain or in distance education. Ideally, the academic responsible for the individual modules in the programme, the module leader, would form and lead a team to produce the Global Campus materials, but this was not always possible and often the Global Campus project staff undertook the team leadership role. To establish a common framework within which this could be achieved authorship packs were designed to aid authors and to achieve a standard pedagogy for the programme. Sample reviews were also designed and distributed. The process improved with experience, particularly after the pilot with the first two modules, when module leaders gave valuable feedback. In response to this, workshops were organized for new authors and modules leaders and more effort has been put into team development.

Pedagogy and adopted materials structure

From the outset the Global Campus team believed that we needed an environment to deliver material as online Web pages. We assumed that in the short term CD ROMs would be used to deliver snapshots of the static material but that the server-based versions would be the master versions. We espoused a constructivist approach to the design of learning materials and wanted the environment to support tools for students to manage their study, and for interacting with each other and with tutors – mostly asynchronously, but with the possibility of synchronous interaction. After a study of available environments we concluded that WebCT (see UC Evaluation of WebCT as an online teaching environment http://www2.canberra.edu.au/cc/flex/webct_report.html) would be satisfactory, although we may have to replace it sooner or later.

Choice of an instructional model

The harder issue to face concerned the core of the pedagogy: how to structure the main body of Web-based materials. The programme is a computing masters programme and so involves lots of practical work. However, it also covers much discursive material, for example on trends and issues of e-commerce. We needed a core pedagogy to address these possibly conflicting requirements. After a non-exhaustive analysis, we concluded that the *I CARE* system pioneered at San Diego State University had what we required. According to its main proponents, Hoffman and Ritchie (1998, 2001): 'I CARE is distilled from basic instructional design practice, adapting various systems or 'steps of instruction' to what seemed to us to be particularly useful components for an online course'.

Very limited learner control

The Global Campus team agreed that *I CARE* would be suitable for our conception of an online course and learner-managed study. *I CARE* had been devised to address the dominance of asynchronous activity in online courses and it explicitly recognized: 'learners' prerogative to organize their course time around work, family and other commitments, while maintaining a modular structure of 'do-able chunks' arranged in a progressive series.

The following extracts (slightly edited to suit our terminology) from Hoffman and Ritchie (1998) summarize how *I CARE* materials are split into sections:

Introduction
The introductory section serves to place the present [unit] in the context of the course as a whole, and enliven learners' prior knowledge with regard to the content that is about to be presented. This section should include clearly stated objectives.

Connect
The connect section is primarily for presenting new information in context. It may consist of online text... Alternatively, it may consist primarily of instructions to read offline text material.

Apply
This is the practice section of the [unit]. It might involve writing a short paper... It could involve a hands-on project.

Reflect
Often the least valued – and frequently one of the most needed – stages in a pedagogically sound lesson is to give students an opportunity to reflect on their newly acquired skills and knowledge. This might take the form of a thoughtful response to a carefully crafted question from the instructor, or a peer exchange about lessons learnt.

Extend
Like the introduction, the extend section has many possible functions. It can provide closure, prompt further exploration and learning, assess students' skills and knowledge.

At some early part of the project, the 'C' meaning became corrupted to 'content'. The change was made for clarity, since 'connect' was thought not to have an obvious meaning for students. In retrospect this was a mistake. First, it did not bring the clarity that was intended. Second, and most importantly, the instruction to students to do something via the verb 'connect' was lost in favour of the noun 'content' that might have condoned the passive role adopted by students (more of this later). For a while, authors also thought that they only had to produce material for that section!

Another departure from the original *I CARE* system was that we allowed a different, less linear flow. All examples of *I CARE* exhibited the following pattern of Web pages: a page of introduction, followed by a single Web page (possibly of considerable length) of 'content'/'connect', which was followed by a page of 'apply', and so on. This might have been satisfactory with packets of study associated with lessons, but not for a week's worth of learner-managed study. Instead, our 'content' section has hyperlinks to computer-based activities in the 'apply' section and to reflective review questions (self-assessment questions) in the 'reflect' section. In addition, we introduced in-line exercises. These involved activities not requiring a computer with the intention either of embedding new knowledge via the activity or of motivating the introduction of new knowledge in what followed. These exercises were breaks in the narrative, *in situ* in 'content', to distinguish them from the more demanding activities in 'apply'. This may have been an unnecessary departure from the original *I CARE* and we are still debating it.

However, that was itself not enough. Embedding the Web pages in an environment resulted in multiple pages, especially for the 'content' sections, each of which may incorporate many diversions. Although students with good hypertext navigational skills are best placed to exploit this structure, we have maintained the possibility of an entirely linear study path.

The *I CARE* model provides consistency and a guaranteed level of quality of Global Campus learning units. Academics were happy to use *I CARE* because it followed the familiar directed transmission model to which their tried and tested assessment methods were added. *I CARE* does not force teachers to exploit educational technology. When our version of *I CARE* material is combined with WebCT for online use, students have available to them well-structured learning resources according to an explicit pedagogy and a set of tools to assist them in managing their learning.

The 'content' section was relatively straightforward to develop, although judging the amount of text needed and the time for exercises and activities remains difficult for most academics. Similarly, pacing and motivating using exercises, asides and the like also need practice. Some activities designed for the 'apply' section did not adequately allow the application of knowledge and development of skills introduced in 'content'; review by colleagues and practice has improved this. The 'reflect' and 'extend' sections were more difficult to design because, in traditional teaching, these would tend to be adjusted spontaneously to student response.

The 'extend' section often involved activities in which students were exhorted to explore related topics on the Web raising the practical problem of ensuring links outside our control remained live. This section has proved difficult to use consistently. It raises a key issue concerning assessment: should students who diligently work only through materials provided for them be rewarded with better grades than those awarded to students who exploited the Web by mastering other relevant material not provided and therefore not assessed by the programme?

WebCT

While WebCT has proved itself to be very satisfactory – we have not yet fully exploited the facilities we required. For most authors, the only work absolutely requiring the online use of WebCT were asynchronous discussions (initiated in the 'reflect' section) and an 'end-of-unit-review' – an automated test that is intended to be a major piece of self-assessment for students and to assist tutors to monitor students (it is not for grading).

The face-to-face tutorials of our version of distance learning are used to help students pace their work, clarify problems, further demonstrate the use of software tools and facilities, explain the tasks for the coursework and discuss the activities and review questions. Some tutorial sessions may address a specific topic or problem and be organized as workshop or seminar. Tutors may briefly introduce the unit topics but are not expected to give formal lectures. They also send weekly reports on the progress, and report any difficulties or problems. The multiple roles of tutors have been hard to get right: they often see themselves as teachers for a module (the distant authors are the teachers) but are more often needed as facilitators (Harisim, 1999) or the orchestrators of some communal learning activities.

Effects of the transformation to a distance-learning pedagogy

We have observed several aspects of the transformation from conventional to learner-managed study, which we either anticipated or subsequently discovered, which, along with the management imperatives we identified, impacted on the pedagogy for online learning. These include:

- *Making content explicit*. Materials previously 'locked up' in the heads of the module leaders have been made explicit for student use (9 MB per module) although they are not always especially clear and there is a maintenance task ahead of us to improve coherence and consistency across authors (and modules).

- *Upkeep*. Motivating and resourcing the upkeep of materials is more difficult than securing their initial generation for a number of reasons:
  - fixing things is always more boring than creating them in the first place;
  - the authors have 'moved on to other things' and are no longer available or interested; the material is 'good enough for the moment' so we can procrastinate;

- from a management perspective it is important to define a clear review cycle, to stick to it, to identify the resources (especially the effort) required and to build all this into people's activity schedules.

- *Review of software.* With hindsight we can see ways in which our original plans and ideas might be modified to improve the learning opportunities for our students. These currently involve some ideas about experimenting with the precise *I CARE* format together with some other ideas that seek to exploit the WebCT environment more effectively. However, with some 120 learning units deployed, a relatively minor general change can become a substantial undertaking.

- *Responsibilities for upkeep.* Work needs to be done on establishing roles and responsibilities that capture the curriculum ownership issues and that substantiate the review imperative.

- *Student engagement.* Student expectations are largely dictated by the requirements that a physically present lecturer may place on their time and effort. Traditionally, a lecturer might expect that it is relatively easy to gain and retain their students' attention, but more challenging to engage their cognitive and critical faculties. Physically removing the lecturer (as the distance learning model presupposes) brings about a situation where traditional attention-getting strategies become irrelevant and the cognitive and critical commitment becomes more immediate and important. Students took their CD ROMs to be hypertext books, not local copies of online materials, and concentrated on simply reading what was on the CD ROMs. Many students wanted printed copies of the material. Another way of saying all this is that distance learners need to assume an active role in the learning process, and they need to learn how to do this more or less straight away, but we academics must help avoid media confusion that we are used to dealing with.

- *Feedback.* The mechanism for direct feedback from students is e-mail. However, it is not realistic to expect a student steeped in passive learning to suspend an activity and launch an e-mail system to compose a written communication in a language that is not their own, to somebody they have never met and whom they are culturally conditioned to regard as an unquestionable authority. We have taken some steps to overcome this problem:

  - we have introduced an induction programme run by MU staff at the beginning of each module – this emphasizes the importance of feedback and encourages students to dispatch an e-mail (there and then);

  - we try to make the e-mail feedback responsive by acknowledging e-mails and following up quickly;

- we are designing coursework and assignments that explicitly involve an online element of computer-supported collaborative working;
- we schedule synchronous 'chat' sessions with the MU lecturer (but the takeup has not been widespread);
- we charge the local LSC tutors with an observational role and encourage them to report back frequently.

Until we resolve this, it will be difficult for us to plan distance learning scenarios that require more student independence than we currently demand. From a management perspective, this issue is one of opening lines of communication and ensuring that they are fully and properly used.

- *Lecture notes are not enough.* The biggest initial transition for the lecturers is the fact that lecture notes, which may have served for several years as admirable support for a spirited series of lectures, must be enhanced by material that can recapture that spirit. In some ways, this is a new mode of expression for lecturers. Specific areas where special attention needs to be given include:
  - the lucid delineation of the learning outcomes of the unit;
  - a more precise (or at least realistic) view of the time and effort requirements of different pieces and types of work;
  - greater clarity about the nature and scope of assessment.

It is interesting to note that these three areas are just those that bear most heavily on the demands made on active learners. Lecturers too need to learn how to promote active learning in their students.

Conclusion and discussion

Our goal was to provide our MSc programme in business information technology in a form suitable for online study. Within a period of 18 months we have achieved that goal, with only a student project module to be completed. The programme has been deployed in Cairo, Hong Kong and London and some 200 students are currently learning to manage their learning with the support of local tutors.

Our initial success and our practice of continuous improvement have been due to three major factors:

- adopting a clear pedagogy for our core Web-based materials;
- committing to a learning environment that supports Web delivery and learner-managed study; and

- managing the transformation to the distance mode by taking an incremental approach that allows academics and students to change their practices gradually.

I CARE has been invaluable. It provided sufficiently clear guidance to authors and a consistent and meaningful structure to students. Its instructional provenance has not, we believe, diminished the prospect we still hold of developing materials to a more constructivist design. Our adaptations of *I CARE* do not appear to be significantly deleterious.

Similarly, WebCT has been an excellent vehicle for delivering what we first needed and for extending and changing the learning environment in response to student feedback and according to our changing judgements. There is a question about the homogeneity of the materials. Undoubtedly, uniformity helped establish our approach and eased the learning curve our authors and implementers had to endure. However, we are aware that opportunities to increase or enliven interactivity may not be being taken.

Crucially, we believe that our approach to managing the production, deployment and operation of our version of learner-managed online learning has properly sought to manage a process of change. Specifically, we began by running a pilot operation. We have not insisted on technologically challenging facilities for learners. We have provided local support for remote students, and we have instigated feedback mechanisms.

In conclusion, we recommend what some might call an *engineering approach* to the development of online learning materials. It is important to commit to a design, the pedagogy, and to a delivery mechanism, the learning environment, so that problems can be identified and resolved or strategies for resolution can be devised. The study that learners undertake is not an experiment for them and so the distance-learning materials should be based on and linked to existing face-to-face teaching. Concomitantly, the management of the process to achieve the desired goals should be sensitive to the process of change (experienced by academics and students) and should incrementally deploy and modify new learning materials and practices.

Acknowledgements

We acknowledge the foresight and guidance of our MU colleagues Norman Revell and Walaa Mohammed Bakry who helped initiate the Global Campus programme with Effat El Shooky in RITSEC. Much of the work reported here, and many of the initial achievements happened because of former team members Kyriaki Anagnostopoulou, Tim Dockerty, Kay Dudman and others.

Many of the recent refinements to Global Campus are due to John Jenkins and Julie Macdonald. Thanks are also due to our many module leaders and unit authors and to RITSEC colleagues, especially Rasha Rostom and Hoda Mansour El Askalany.

References

Britain, S and Liber, O, *A Framework for Pedagogical Evaluation of Virtual Learning Environments*, http://www.jtap.ac.uk/reports/jtap-041.html

Harasim, L (1999) A framework for online learning: the virtual-u, *IEEE Computer*, September.

Hoffman, R and Ritchie, D (1998) Teaching and Learning Online: Tools, Templates, and Training, in *SITE Annual 1998*, CD-ROM edn, Society for Information Technology and Teacher Education, Association for the Advancement of Computing in Education, Charlottesville, VA,
http://www.cssjournal.com/hoffman.html

Hoffman, R and Ritchie, D C (2001) An instructional design-based approach to developing online learning environments, in *Web-Based Training*, ed B Khan, Educational Technology Publications, Englewood Cliffs, NJ.

Part 5

Designers and producers

Part 5 is given over to commercial producers of online materials. Online learning is a highly technical activity and requires specialist skills. Much of the early running has been made by the commercial sector and small-scale multi-media companies have flourished. In the absence of pedagogical advice from those commissioning the products, these small companies exercise their own judgement about what is appropriate. All three authors in Part 5 argue for better understanding between teachers, designers and producers working in teams. Martin Good, chief executive of a successful company producing online learning materials, would like to see designers getting more involved with pedagogical issues (Chapter 13). Keith Shaw, currently advising Ufi Ltd (the UK's University for Industry project) deals with the tension between quality learning systems and value for money (Chapter 14) and Quentin Whitlock (Chapter 15) argues for better training of materials designers. Collectively, the three authors give some useful insights into how the pedagogical issue is seen (as academics would see it) from the other side.

13

On the way to online pedagogy

Martin Good
Cambridge Training and Development Ltd, UK

Editor's introduction

This chapter is written by Martin Good, chief executive of a successful commercial developer of online learning materials. Good argues that educators need expertise in traditional classroom pedagogy and online communication and moderation, but also a high level of technical skills, awareness and competence. Examples are drawn from professional staff development, adult literacy and numeracy.

Background

In the 1990s, Cambridge Training and Development (CTAD) led a European Union (EU) Third Framework project that addressed the issue of Integrating Learning Design in CD ROM and Multimedia (ILDIC). The objectives were to formulate a model of good practice in learning design for multimedia, and identify key roles and competences for educational multimedia development. This chapter briefly describes aspects of ILDIC and extends the model to include e-learning.

E-Learning has crystallized an intractable issue that affected open and distance learning for many years – the question of product versus process. Because of communications technology we now have a much higher level of *process* pedagogy to work alongside and provide a context for learning *materials*. In conventional distance learning, materials and support were separate. The term 'support' now seems inadequate. (It always was.) The skills and processes of face-to-face teaching, extended to include communication technologies, have finally been integrated into open learning in the era of the 'death of distance' (Cairncross, 1987).

Integrating learning design in CD ROM and Multimedia focused on the role of pedagogy in developing multimedia. It identified, but did not resolve, the problem of process. This chapter attempts to combine the application of pedagogy to materials development with the rich processes that e-learning allows.

Learning design and pedagogy

Learning design describes the assumptions and processes that developers use to decide the characteristics of the material they make. You never design learning: a mixture of design disciplines (ILDIC defined eight) all play a role. *Pedagogy* provides the context and the theoretical surround for the activity.

Learning environment

This is how you envisage that the material will be used. It drives many decisions – look and feel, control, assumptions about the level of support. Diverse contexts and varying degrees of support create dilemmas, for example is this for 'average' learners or for the 'lowest common denominator'? The e-learning environment offers far more possibilities and allows many of these problems to be addressed online by skilled tutors.

Instructional position mix

The pedagogic rationale. We used a model developed by the UK's Further Education Unit (FEU, 1981). This proposed 'value sets' that reflect different approaches:

- deficiency model – 'we're here to put something right that went wrong earlier';
- competence model – 'we're here to teach people some specific knowledge and skills';
- socialization model – 'we're here to help our learners fit into society';
- counselling model – 'we're here to help our learners work through the key issues and crises';
- guided discovery – 'we're here to help learners discover things for themselves';

- fostering autonomy – 'we're here to help learners become autonomous and self-sufficient'.

This also works with learners; tensions happen when there is dissonance between the expectations of either party. A 'deficiency model' teacher may show behaviour that is caring, gentle and tender, but if the learner is operating with a competence model, this can seem patronizing. This gets worse when a machine is acting as teacher.

Value-based assumptions drive many decisions: 'we want this product to be idiot-proof' (so the users are mainly idiots?); 'we expect our learners to invest time learning to use the product before they start learning from it' (implies that support will be available).

Learning theory mix

Developers must know the theory behind their learning model. This is especially true of concepts such as 'learning style', which come in many different flavours (perception based, personality based, achievement based and so forth). It is easy to represent behaviourist models on the computer; but it is also possible to take advantage of cognitive models (such as memory, memorization, transfer from short-term to long-term memory), perceptual (visual, auditory and kinaesthetic learning) and constructivist approaches (for example, giving learners the means to work with new thinking structures and frameworks).

Content and coverage

An analysis of (mainly CD ROM) materials showed a tendency to claim comprehensiveness. Does a degree-level CD ROM cover *everything* you need? Clearly not. Developers should see their products as forming part of the corpus of knowledge, rather than replacing it (pace *Encarta*™). Good pedagogical (but not necessarily business) practice involves recommending other publications, including those of competitors, and the encouragement of an eclectic and critical approach to any material.

E-learning seamlessly extends the reach of content, as materials can now include links to relevant Web sites and access to places where you 'meet' other people. The balance shifts from product to process, and interaction becomes as important as content.

Media mix and values

The term 'multimedia' implies plurality, but in many ways it is one medium with some of the characteristics of others. It is dangerous to borrow too heavily from the values associated with, say, broadcast television, when far lower quality is generally considered 'fit for purpose' in a learning resource. The role of each media element, and its relative importance in relation to the rest, needs to be clear.

Machine character

Children ascribe identity to teddy bears. In the same way, the 'character' of a machine is a set of attributes that users ascribe to it. Many people have strong feelings about objects and possessions, such as a car ('my safe place'; 'my power base'). Computers can acquire many 'characters': some find them frightening; some find them exciting; for others they are simply tools.

With learning, a new set of possible characters appears. Is the 'machine' (TV, computer) acting as instructor? Is it a game? A way to communicate with others? A medium for exploration, for 'surfing'? Is it the 'college in your hand'?

E-learning brings us a new set of characters and associated metaphors. Perhaps the most important is the idea that the machine is a 'place' where you find other people doing things – conferences, dialogues, lectures. This range of models forms a 'learning environment' that feels physical even if it is virtual.

Target users, range of uses

It is a cliché to say that courseware needs to target a clear set of learners with known learning needs. This sounds simpler than the reality, however. For example, the range of real learners may be wider than that envisaged in the specified target group; or the material may lend itself to other uses beyond those predicted for the original target group. It may indeed be impossible to know who the learners will be, especially if the aim is to attract a mass audience. The complexity of these truths is hard to model, especially in a behaviourist framework where learning materials are supposed to 'have' objectives, deliver these, assess them and so forth. Zuboff (1984) might have called this 'the automated delivery of knowledge'.

Use can transform content. Think about the jelly question: 'If this packet of jelly was the only material you had, what could you do with it?' Answers can be classified according to different learning models:

- *Use one (behaviourist)*. The packet of jelly is used to teach someone how to make a jelly. Its success is judged by the quality of the jelly and by the extent to which the instructions were correctly followed.
- *Use two (cognitive)*. The packet of jelly is a starting point for other things, like rewriting the instructions to be clearer, or comparing the packet with other forms of packaging.
- *Use three (constructionist)*. The packet of jelly is a stimulus for open-ended debate and creative activity. For example, is it a symbol (how society moulds you), a weapon, a decoration?

E-learning provides greater opportunity to build in uses two and three, as these need more facilitation and support. It provides us with an escape route from the use one straightjacket.

Control/freedom

Your picture of users affects the amount of control you let them have. Some programmes prevent users from doing something new until they have finished something; others assume that everyone can do whatever they like, and at any time.

Including the World Wide Web in a learning system changes the locus of control. E-learning on the Internet allows learners to do what they like and go where they like – and by and large, they do. There is good evidence to suggest that they do not respond to efforts to control too much of the environment: if they want to skip things, they do; if they want greater depth, they expect it to be there.

E-learning pedagogy

E-learning is different from traditional forms, and demands new pedagogical skills *and* a fluency with technology which will be new to many teachers and trainers. Key issues that affect pedagogy and practice include: *weaving in technology* – especially, but not only, the communication opportunities provided by synchronous and asynchronous conferencing, in ways that will add value to the learning. They also include *developing 'technological fearlessness'* – keeping an eye out for new technological developments and for new ways of using the technology, autonomously solving problems and learning.

Weaving in technology

Making technology part of the process of learning is a key issue for pedagogy. How can it be woven in?

The simple fact of asynchronous and synchronous conferencing dramatically changes what matters in the design of distance learning. Every page of text can now generate a conversation, a dialogue, a collaboration, an adventure. It is now standard practice to build an online area in all learning materials. Much of the interactivity that was formerly put into boxes on the page or quizzes on the screen is now located in the online conference. To make that work, teachers need a high level of skill in moderation and virtual classroom management in addition to their subject knowledge.

Pedagogy is now no longer solely about designing distant activities but also about designing virtual and immediate ones. Robin Mason (http://www-iet.open.ac.uk/pp/r.d.mason/main.html) of the Open University proposes three models of online learning:

- *Content + support*: the traditional approach, where course content is separate from support; it is delivered through materials or Web sites, with support provided via e-mail or conferencing as an add-on. Open University students in this model typically spend 20 per cent of their time in online support.
- *Wraparound*: tailor-made study guides to existing materials supported with discussion, application sharing, Web lectures and so forth; this approach leaves students online for about 50 per cent of the time.
- *Integrated*: here the centre of the course is a set of assignments, tasks and collaborative experiences, and students are online for most of the time. This may also include creative online learning such as role-play and simulation (for example, of a trial). This is close to 'pure' e-learning and can become very costly if tutor costs are not controlled.

Examples

Cambridge Training and Development has been developing products that go across Mason's categories and show different aspects of the ILDIC design model (see Table 13.1):

- *The New Reading Disc* is a well-established product, designed several years ago on constructionist lines, which has recently moved from stand-alone to Web functionality. Its principle is that adults learning to read and write

Table 13.1 ILDIC and Mason applied

Title	Mason	ILDIC
The New Reading Disc	Content plus	*Environment*: supported (not online) *Instructional Position*: guided discovery *Learning theory*: constructionist *Content and coverage*: specific, limited *Media mix*: low values *Machine character*: toolset *Users/use*: multiple *Control/freedom*: content freedom; process controlled
Reading and Writing Web	Wraparound (low end)	*Environment*: supported (on and offline) *Instructional position*: guided discovery *Learning theory*: constructionist *Content and coverage*: specific, limited *Media mix*: low to medium values *Machine character*: toolset *Users/use*: as a finished resource, as a development environment *Control/freedom*: content freedom; process controlled
Ufi SDP	Wraparound (high end)	*Environment*: supported (online only) *Instructional position*: self-directed learning *Learning theory*: behaviourist objectives; constructionist process *Content and coverage*: multi-layered using Web links *Media mix*: medium to high values *Machine character*: courseware deliverer; conference communication *Users/use*: Ufi staff induction *Control/freedom*: content controlled; process freedom

need to construct knowledge about the way the experience feels; they use tools to build texts by choosing from existing sentences and compiling a passage, or by adding their own words and voices. All sentences can be heard as well as seen. At the end they print out their work and take it away to read. The new version allows them to publish to a Web site. The pedagogical rationale for this is that the tool may help form communities of newly empowered writers. There is no online interaction yet.

- *Reading and Writing Web* takes the process of *The New Reading Disc* further. Designed for children, it provides a set of tools that allow students to create multimedia Web pages and also offers a Web site where they submit their work for publication and sharing. There is an online facilitator who acts as the magazine editor and promotes and encourages participation.

- *Ufi Staff Development Programme*: 16 Web-based modules supported by local tools and multimedia centred on a conference area. The materials are substantial but contain many Web links to allow users to go further and deeper than the surface texts. Activities include making audiovisual slideshows and using those as evidence of achievement as well as conventional essays and reports. However, the online conference is the central experience in this course and all participants contribute across a number of areas of work.

- *Distance Learning Adviser Programme.* This comes closest to Mason's 'integrated' category. There was online courseware, but it was a stimulus to join the conference and explore key areas. The programme aimed to help people to provide support to learning centre staff and to basic skills learners by e-mail, telephone or online discussion. The course took a group of people whose technological knowledge was low and successfully created a professional community. At first most messages were about perceived failings in technology; it took great effort to get people engaging in professional dialogue. The materials themselves contributed little to this critical change, which happened through moderated communication in the conference areas.

Technical fearlessness

Many teachers steer clear of engaging with technology – they leave it to the technologists and get on with the business of teaching. This is no longer an acceptable position, however. Teachers must reach a point where they are exploiting the full benefits of technology to support their learners. Massy (2000) and Blandin (1997) see four levels of skill:

- Level 1: competent in a few tools that are used in everyday working, for example word processing.
- Level 2: competent in a wider range of everyday tools to a higher level – able to use advanced word processing features to enhance productivity; able to log on to and use a conference area; still a victim of many of the problems that will happen and dependent on others to solve them.
- Level 3: autonomous explorer – engaged with technology and able to solve own problems and look out for new opportunities as things change and develop.
- Level 4: expert.

Many teachers are at levels 1 and 2. They all need to be at level 3 and far more need to combine subject expertise with deep knowledge of the technology to become educational technologists or technological educators.

Gill Salmon (2000) has a diagram showing five stages of e-moderation and the technological skills needed for each one. Stage 1 is about getting started. At stage 2, people start communicating with others online. Stage 3 sees real exchange of information and the start of collaboration. In stage 4, discussions start to take off and things become much more collaborative. At stage 5, people start to be selective and 'look for more benefits from the system to help them achieve personal goals, explore how to integrate Computer Mediated Conferencing (CMC) into other forms of learning and reflect on the learning processes.'

At each stage learners have to master technical skills and e-moderating skills. Interactivity rises with each step up. At stage 1 this tends to be with one or two others. After stage 2, the numbers increase. Interestingly, they seem to reduce at step 5 as people become more selective about what they are doing and why.

For a much fuller account of this model, read the book or go to the Web site (http://oubs.open.ac.uk/e-moderating/fivestep.htm).

The e-learning pedagogue

A problem that predated e-learning is defined by ILDIC. Combined with and enhanced by the ideas of Mason (1998), Salmon (2000), Massy (2000) and Blandin (1997), the same ILDIC model can provide a view of the component parts of e-pedagogy and it suggests that the e-learning pedagogue needs:

- conventional pedagogy – a knowledge of how different people learn, what works in teaching them and why;
- online awareness – how different people learn online, what works in teaching them and why;
- to plan and manage online events and places;
- the ability to explore and extend the potential of technology and solve technical problems without support;
- the ability to interweave technology into the design – learning with rather than from technology.

The e-learning pedagogue is a hybrid creature with multiple skills and a passion for learning!

References

Blandin, B (1997) L'Utilisation des instruments de communication en situation de travail, CESI, France, http://www.cnet.francetelecom.fr/ust/BBlandin.html.
Cairncross, F (1987) *The Death of Distance*, Harvard Business School, Cambridge, MA.
FEU (1981) *Developing Social and Life Skills*, FEU, London.
Mason, R, (1999) *IET's Master's in Open and Distance Education: What have we learned?*, CITE Report No 248, Open University, Milton Keynes, and available at

http://www-iet.open.ac.uk/pp/r.d.mason

Mason, R (1998) Models of online courses, *ALN Magazine*, **2** (2), October, and available at http://www.aln.org/alnweb/magazine/vol2/issue2/Masonfinal.htm

Massy, J, Manager of the CEDEFOP Training Village e-learning sites, http://www.trainingvillage.gr

Salmon, G (2000) *E-Moderating: The key to teaching and learning online*, Kogan Page, London.

Zuboff, S (1984) *In the Age of the Smart Machine: The future of work and power*, Basic Books, New York.

14

Designing online learning opportunities, orchestrating experiences and managing learning

Keith Shaw
Shaw Associates, UK

Editor's introduction

Shaw draws on his experience as an academic and a commercial producer of online materials to take the reader through the issues that have to be addressed when converting raw content into useful online learning and the commercial judgements that have to be made. Open-ended learner managed learning provides richer learning experiences but also raises issues of value for money. By providing a greater choice of learning scenarios, online learning presents more of a challenge to the commercial producer than technological innovations of the recent past.

Context

Over the last 30 years the technology used to deliver learning has developed from Teletype terminals linked to mini computers, through the use of PCs and multimedia, to the current emphasis on online delivery. Whatever the technology, the processes of learning materials development and implementation have been shown to be significantly the same. Surprisingly, therefore, experience gained in previous usage is often overlooked when a new medium emerges. For example, a consistently recurring mistake is to assume that people with excellent subject knowledge will naturally be able to create good learning material. Another is to underestimate the time and resources required. A more recent mistake is to believe that what works well in one medium (as a face-to-face lecture or an open learning text) can be simply and easily transferred to online delivery.

A common factor in the successful exploitation of any technology is the ability to understand how it can be applied to good educational effect. The people with this vision are crucial members of the development team, but they have to be supported by subject matter experts, instructional designers, illustrators, and people with a thorough knowledge of the capabilities and limitations of the respective technology who can construct the software. The members of this team are the creators of the learning experience.

However, with the development of online learning, new features, such as the ability to communicate with tutors and peer groups, and to access other resources, are available and they create the need for new roles within this team. These include supporting learners by facilitating access to learning, helping learners manage and structure their approach to learning, and ensuring that learning outcomes can be consolidated, demonstrated and recognized. If dealt with in a passive manner these activities might be likened to tutoring, whereas a more active approach might result in orchestration of the learning experience.

Learners also have new roles and responsibilities as managers of their own learning. The interplay of the tutor (or orchestrator) and the learner as manager is crucial to the success of an online learning experience.

Matching design to educational need

In some circumstances the design team takes a deliberate decision to exclude the need for tutorial support or for learners to manage their learning. The resulting material is similar in style to computer-based learning delivered on stand-alone PCs. In an online form this can result in a learning experience that is easier to design, develop and deliver, is quicker to complete, and costs less both in development and support. It is a much more easily controlled and directed learning experience, with more predictable outcomes. Typically this approach might be used where mastery of content is the principal outcome, a short period of study is envisaged and a learning approach of sufficiently wide acceptability can be achieved.

Where a deeper, more conceptual, level of understanding is desired a very different design is required: one where the emphasis is on activities and resources, and their use to discover, experience, reflect, practise, discuss and explain. In these circumstances there is the opportunity for learners to exercise choice over the degree of direction they receive, and this can be accessed either from the orchestrator or can be automated through help strategies within the software. The implication is that learners will be more in control of their learning and more responsible for its management. This requires considerably greater sophistication on the part of the learner. Alternatively, there might be a greater contribution by the orchestrator, and herein lies the flexibility that online delivery can offer for those learners who wish to control and manage their own learning.

Designing this type of experience presents new and complex challenges to the creators. They are deciding about more than content. They are designing a complete and integrated experience using a variety of resources and activities. They have to determine which features of online learning to incorporate (synchronous and/or asynchronous communications to tutors and/or peers, applications sharing, virtual classrooms, access to Internet sites and so forth), why and how.

They have to devise the activities, research and review resources, determine appropriate strategies for the use of these resources, anticipate how learners might approach a discovery learning exercise, and ensure that the structure of the experience is sufficiently flexible to accommodate the alternatives. They also have to decide how the learner will be directed and supported, and in what way and to what extent the orchestrator might be in control, and therefore managing, the learning. Too much freedom creates insecurity in the learner and inhibits learning; too little frustrates the learner.

Such heuristic approaches are lengthier and more costly to develop and implement than their more didactic counterparts. They also generate a number of interesting questions for creators and orchestrators. For example, what is meant by 'completion' in such circumstances? How many of the activities must be completed and to what standard? How many and which of the resources should the learner make use of? If the answer is all, to what extent is the learner in control? If learners have the opportunity to achieve satisfactory completion without undertaking all of the activities or using all the resources, does learner managed learning imply the opportunity for some to explore exhaustively and others to complete with less effort? Would exhaustive exploration imply greater interest or an inability to discriminate? Would less effort imply lack of interest or sophistication? How can orchestrators determine which behaviour is being exhibited and counsel learners accordingly?

Determining if one approach is better than another is fraught with difficulty. In trying to decide what approach to adopt, therefore, the following, relatively practical, set of questions can be useful:

- What works?
- In which circumstances?
- Where is the evidence?

- What are the resource, development, validation, implementation and maintenance implications?
- How long will it take?
- How much will it cost?

Some examples

To try to address these questions, five organizations were asked to create an online learning 'experience' on the same subject, but with differing approaches. The target population and the learning outcomes were defined and an outline of the content provided. An existing paper-based document dealing with the same topic was provided to further define the content. A summary of the outcome is given below.

Example one

The first organization created a PDF version of the original paper document. Consequently this was read-only material. A slightly enhanced version with limited interactions was written using HTML and reflected an elementary computer-based learning approach. The study time required to complete the exercise was about one hour.

In evaluation both versions were criticized for failing to generate interest, create motivation, involve the learner, provide opportunities for application of knowledge and so forth. Minimal resources were required for development. The timescale was two elapsed weeks and the cost small (costs are subject to commercial confidence and will be reported in relative terms; this example will be used as the benchmark and denoted as one unit). This outcome was not surprising and supports the view that direct conversion from paper to online is unlikely to yield an acceptable learning experience.

Example two

The second organization developed the content in HTML and displayed pages in conventional browser form. The content was provided as text supported by extensive access to a tutor through e-mail.

This example was relatively simple and straightforward to develop, requiring the skill to create Web pages, an ability to write clearly and concisely, and an understanding of how tutors can support learners. Development time was approximately eight elapsed weeks and the cost two units. Although not making significant use of features available in many managed learning environments, or being exciting or intrinsically interesting, this example provided a simple, straightforward and rapid means of achieving the intended learning outcomes. Its success depends heavily on the availability of tutors, but it was judged to be appropriate in circumstances that are designed for this style of material and type of support.

Example three

The third organization chose a case-study approach in which the learner is free to choose the sequence of activities. Narrative is provided as both text and audio, and attractive cartoon-style graphics are mixed with photographic-quality images for illustration. Minor reference is made to external, Internet-accessed, information and this is more obligatory than optional. Learners review information, draw conclusions, compare these with the opinion of the creators, and thereby determine what approach to adopt when undertaking tasks. Although providing more flexibility of sequence than the previous examples, the conclusions to be drawn by the learner are, in effect, closed, with clearly indicated right and wrong answers. Some leeway is, therefore, provided for learners to determine how they progress but the eventual outcome is carefully directed. There are no opportunities to communicate with other learners or with a tutor to discuss ideas, listen to other viewpoints or obtain more elaborate examination of proposed procedures. The exercise is self-contained and complete, with limited opportunity or need for learners to manage their learning. Study time was one and a half to two hours.

Many learners are likely to be comfortable with this approach; they will gain security from knowing that they have arrived at the 'correct' end point, and have done so in an economic manner (economic as measured by expenditure of time). It was, therefore, considered an appropriate approach where transmission of knowledge was the principal objective.

Resource utilization was more considerable, requiring instructional designers, illustrators, programmers and people with an understanding of the construction of Web sites and the operation of the Internet. There is no requirement for a tutor The elapsed time for development was four months and a realistic cost would be five to six units.

Example four

In the fourth example a similar case-study approach is adopted but with more learner control over the sequence of activities, the information to be accessed and the conclusions drawn. A more heuristic approach is adopted, placing more responsibility on the learner for drawing conclusions and determining appropriate courses of action. This approach requires more reflection and analytical ability and is, therefore, a more challenging learning experience. There are fewer illustrations and no use of sound. Although this does not detract from the challenge, it does make this less entertaining than example three.

As with the preceding example, this material makes little use of features available in many managed learning environments (no communication with other learners or a tutor, and no reference or access to other resources or the Internet for reinforcement and consolidation opportunities). The exercise is again self-contained and complete but, because of its emphasis on reflective learning, is more stimulating and more likely to develop an understanding of why as well as what. Indicators of success are subtler and require more intellectual activity for their interpretation. This adds to the interest of this approach. Study time was about two hours, and again this was considered to be a valid approach to the topic.

This example made considerable use of learning needs analysis and instructional design skills. There was less need for illustrators or Internet expertise. There is no requirement for a tutor. The elapsed development timescale was four months and the cost nine units.

Example five

Organization five adopted an activity-based approach and assembled a range of resources to support this. Many features of an online experience were incorporated: e-mailing tutors and other learners, visiting recommended Web sites, reviewing articles and information held in PDF, compiling notes for later use. Alternative exercises and information are provided for circumstances in which the tutor or other learners are not available for discussion. Learners can explore material in whatever sequence they choose (although there is a recommended route) and can decide which exercises to undertake and how long to spend on them.

More resources were provided than were needed, thus giving the learner the opportunity to exercise judgement about the value of reviewing everything on offer. The learner is also able to exert significant control over the sequencing of activities.

In the simplest way of using this approach, the tutor would take the role of mentor rather than orchestrator of events, although the tutor can take a more active role if this is desired. There is the potential here for learner and tutor to define their respective roles. The experience concludes with an exercise to consolidate and confirm the learning. Total study time is from three to five hours depending on the route taken.

This example exploits a range of features of online learning and learners can be much more in control of their own learning experience. An important consequence is greater emphasis on contact with a tutor, raising availability and cost issues. The creators of this material included an instructional designer who understands the opportunities and constraints of online e-delivery, an illustrator and a software writer. A tutor would be required to support the learner. The development timescale was four months and the cost 10 units.

Only the last example would be considered to have exploited the functionality available in online delivery. All but the first, however, merit the description 'fit for purpose' when deployed in the circumstances envisaged by the developers. The conclusion drawn is that acceptable online learning material can take many manifestations, each with its own degree of opportunity for learners to manage their learning, and costs can vary considerably.

15

Course design for online learning – what's gone wrong?

Quentin Whitlock
Dean Interactive Ltd and Dean Associates, UK

Editor's introduction

Whitlock looks at the issue of online pedagogy from his perspective as a chief executive of a company designing open and distance learning materials for mainly corporate clients, including the UK government's recent initiative, the University for Industry (Ufi). His experience ranges from the early days of programmed learning to current Web-based learning environments. Whitlock argues for more effective training for materials designers and a greater understanding amongst both designers and commissioners of the underlying pedagogy for Web-based instructional materials.

A 50-year quest

The quest for a pedagogy for online learning is the latest stage in an endeavour that goes back more than 50 years. Technology – using the term as it is commonly used today – first made a significant impact on the world of education in the decade following the Second World War with the gradual introduction of equipment such as film, radio, tape recording and copying machines.

For a while these new devices were absorbed into the prevailing model of education – the one-way transmission of information from teachers to pupils – that they suited very well. Towards the end of the 1950s the traditional teacher-centred paradigm began to be called into question. An English visitor to the United States recounts a seminal moment in educational thinking:

I recall listening to Skinner speaking in Washington on education not long after he had published his Harvard review article. The impact was enormous. Here was a cogently reasoned case against educational methods that required an answer; here also was an alternative procedure, powerfully argued and supported apparently by experimental data. It hammered a new empirical philosophy into teaching.

(Kay, 1979)

Skinner's theory and the models derived from it eventually failed to gain acceptance 'because they could not predict different results in the macro-situations with which they had to contend' (Kay, 1979).

Learners come first

Despite its failure, the remarkable teaching machine experiment has a number of lessons for those engaged in the current debate on online learning. First, the learner was brought to the centre of the stage. Skinner himself drew attention to the potential of the new technologies 'to threaten the individual student... the danger is that mass techniques will make students all alike'. And, again, 'failure to provide for differences among students is perhaps the greatest single source of inefficiency in education' (Skinner, 1968). Most of Skinner's contemporaries, thinkers about education taking part in the quest for a new pedagogy, would have shared this view regardless of their theoretical stance. Forty years later the same sentiments continue to be repeated. Last year Charles Reigeluth stressed 'the need for a paradigm of training and education in which the learner is at the top of the organizational chart rather than the bottom' (Reigeluth, 1999).

Two approaches to innovation

Skinner's theories and the teaching machines that they inspired illustrate another point relevant to our current enquiry. There are two different approaches to innovation in education as in many other fields of human interest. One approach is driven by a new idea or theory that suggests a course of action. The necessary tools to achieve the desired results may not exist and thus will need to be created. The other approach is to explore ways in which a new tool or technology may be adapted to applications that are totally different from those for which it was originally designed. Lasers in the 1970s and more recently Smart-cards are an example of this. The early days of programmed learning illustrated the former approach. Teaching machines represented an attempt to create a new pedagogy that was learner-centred – a goal that was driven by ideas. Many current strategies for online learning represent the second approach – an attempt to discover new applications for tools that were created for another purpose. One interesting model of a learning system that could take us well beyond the confines of the e-classroom is the personalized portal described by Dickinson and Stewart elsewhere in this volume.

Online is OK – or is it?

The focus on learner-centred instruction has generated a steadily, but until recently rather slowly, increasing interest in alternatives to the classroom as the place where learning occurs. I say 'until recently' because the tremendous surge of interest in online approaches gives the impression that the traditional classroom's days are numbered. But is this the case? Certainly there are already entire institutions in North America offering exclusively Web-based learning opportunities. And let us not forget that the Open University signed up its first students over 30 years ago. However, there is still great reluctance among many educational practitioners to take new approaches seriously. The director of a higher education (HE) institution in England once told me that he did not regard the development of open and distance learning materials as an equivalent competence to lecturing when considering academic staff for advancement. This, apparently, is still a commonly held view among further education (FE) and HE professionals.

Nevertheless we must be wary of the attitude that 'online means OK'. Indeed another uncanny echo of experience half a century ago is the recent awareness that our capability to produce open and distance learning materials is limited whether in the education or corporate sector and many of the materials that we do manage to develop are sadly lacking in quality. In a paper given at the 1959 meeting of the American Psychological Association the authors commented:

the reason that most teachers will not be using or trying out automated teaching is that their courses are not programmed (ie authored for open learning). How did we get into this ridiculous situation in which machines outnumber (learning) programmes? We do not have to search hard for the reasons. Programming (authoring) is an aversive task because it is time-consuming and difficult. At least part of the trouble lies in the fact that there are no rules for programming of sufficient precision to be helpful.

(Homme *et al*, 1959)

An endangered species

These are precisely the sentiments of the authors of a research report published earlier this year by the DfEE and called *Authoring for CBT and Interactive Multimedia.* It is a kind of snapshot of the situation in which those whose current responsibility is the development of learning programmes currently find themselves. The findings are depressing, not to say shocking. They support an impression that many experienced practitioners have had for some years: good authors are few and far between.

There is a crisis of supply. The DfEE research demonstrates that most authors of electronic learning materials employed in corporate development teams have little or no training in any aspects of courseware development. Only one-third of the 125 designers who took part in a survey associated with the research had received training in the use of authoring tools. Worse, only one-fifth received training in the design of technology-based training (TBT), and this training merely comprised a one- to three-day workshop. Incredibly, less than 3 per cent said that they have received any training in instructional design or questioning techniques. Not a single respondent had been trained in developmental testing of draft courseware.

Respondents to the questionnaire were also asked to identify those areas of their personal skill repertoire that, in their opinion, needed improving. The three highest scoring improvement areas were: understanding how people learn, writing aims and objectives and English-language skills.

Taking a slightly different tack, the researchers went on to investigate skills in short supply. Again 'understanding how people learn' headed the list. This is depressing. As Reigeluth points out 'a good instructional designer knows theories of learning and human development' (Reigeluth, 1999).

The Arenicola report (2000, *Authoring for CBT and Interactive Multimedia* DfEE, Sheffield) reveals that the majority of course designers and developers in the corporate sector lack the skills that are fundamental to the successful production of learning materials, in whatever medium they are working. This is particularly damaging when the materials are intended to stand alone. The situation is an indictment of those responsible for managing the process of learning materials development.

The Arenicola findings are supported by a totally different source. At the same time as they were being compiled, the University for Industry was evaluating bids from prospective materials providers seeking UfI accreditation. Approximately 700 institutions ranging from multinationals to FE/HE institutions and individuals submitted samples for inspection. Of these, no more than one quarter were deemed by a panel of experts to have achieved UfI standards at the first assessment. The quality of submissions was comparable across the spectrum of education and training.

An unrecognized profession

The reasons for this depressing state of affairs have yet to be thoroughly investigated. My own view is that there are several deep-seated forces inhibiting the development of skilled designers.

There is generally a lack of awareness and acceptance in both the education and training sectors that learning materials development is a worthwhile career path. The HE director I cited earlier typifies this attitude. Few, if any, HE institutions in the United Kingdom offer a qualification in learning materials design. This contrasts sharply with North America and Australia where qualifications in instructional design are widely obtainable. A variety of printed and electronic journals dealing with learning technology are published in these countries and they commonly publish job advertisements for learning materials designers.

The idea that learning design could be a career hardly exists in the United Kingdom. We have seen that materials designers have a low status in education and this is generally matched in the corporate environment. Typically they have what one might call non-commissioned officer rank in the company hierarchy. They are often seconded to the training function from a line job for no more than two years. They take no part in decisions about project selection or design strategy. There is no nationally recognized accreditation to which they can aspire.

Getting priorities right

There is a general tendency to emphasize the technology-related aspects of course production at the expense of the learning-design process. Too many college and university programmes with titles such as *multimedia design* focus largely on the use of software tools for generating graphics and audio-visual presentations. The Arenicola report records the comment of one TBT consultant: 'TBT and multimedia is technology led at present, which is the wrong way round. It is like saying classroom teaching is flip-chart led'.

Designers should be seeking to adapt the technology to their goals but lack the know how and decision-making responsibility to do so. Thus they allow their courseware to be moulded by technology specialists for whom the learner's interests are secondary. It is disappointing to note that the designers surveyed in the Arenicola report themselves rated computer programming as more important than writing aims and objectives.

I referred earlier to the recent upsurge in interest in Web-delivery of learning courseware. Earlier this year the director of the Open University's Institute of Educational Technology described a significant new arrival:

One of the key points about the launch of the University for Industry two years ago was the emphasis on 'open learning and new technology' generally as a key means of bringing lifelong learning to all. Under the name Learndirect, UfI has forged ahead with online provision as the key to its operations. We shall see even more publicity for the computer as an all-purpose gateway for all kinds of learning beyond schooling as well as at school.

(Thorpe, 2000)

Thorpe concludes: 'the future really is online'.

This innovation in delivery mode has, if anything, aggravated the problem of course design. A college or university lecturer who uses the terms 'online learning' or 'e-learning' has in mind a particular model of distance learning that may well be quite different from the model that a corporate trainer has in mind.

Three models of online learning

There are at least three prevailing models of online learning, each of which has hybrids and derivatives. The first model is what one might call CBT on the Web or Web-based training. Some people felt that this form of self-contained training would disappear with the advent of the Internet; that it belonged to the bygone era of the CD ROM. This has not proved to be the case. It has continued to be popular particularly, though not exclusively, for occupational training applications.

The second model entails using technology – for example video-conferencing – to transmit a classroom experience in real time to distant learners in different locations. This model, known as synchronous learning, is a form of class training at a distance. It is particularly popular in the United States. A variation is to use the Internet to transmit the tutor's voice in combination with electronic documents.

The third model, sometimes known as the electronic classroom, entails engaging learners in a (largely) planned series of activities via the Internet. Typically the learners will be individuals sometimes subdivided into small groups so as to promote discussion and participation. Some activities will be undertaken individually, some in pairs or by the group working as a whole. Feedback on activities is given by a tutor and (sometimes) by other learners. All communication is by Internet using e-mail or more sophisticated conferencing systems.

Course designers working on the development of any of these models need to acquire a new range of skills. The skills required to perform as a virtuoso in the classroom or lecture theatre are in many cases irrelevant to success in developing distance learning materials. This is particularly the case with Web-based training and the asynchronous electronic classroom. The former can easily degenerate into a form of electronic page turning. The latter is often little more than the tutor's lecture notes 'on the Web'. These debased forms of distance learning demonstrate a lack of understanding of what is needed to help learning to occur.

Criteria for good course design

David Merrill has observed, *a propos* the use of the Internet for teaching, 'there seems to be an assumption that if we have sufficient information then people will learn. The Internet is a wonderful new medium for the exchange of information. However information is not instruction' (Merrill, 1997). Merrill suggests three key principles that course designers should bear in mind:

- there are different kinds of knowledge and skill;
- the different kinds of knowledge and skill each require different learning strategies;
- if an instructional strategy does not include presentation, practice and learning guidance consistent with the knowledge or skill to be taught then it will not teach.

How do we recognize an online course of learning that is well designed? Over the past 20 years or so I have put this question to participants in courses on the design of open and distance learning. Over the years the same items occur regularly. These are the top 10:

- clearly specified *objectives*;
- attractive *presentation*;
- clear *signposting*;
- ease of *use*;
- appropriate *language*;
- modular *structure*;
- variety of *questions and problems*;
- *feedback* on progress;
- *testing* (diagnostic and achievement);
- *logical sequence*.

The ability to generate courses that meet these criteria is not acquired at a three-day workshop. James Leach, who has researched how classroom trainers develop their professional skills, suggests that the novice trainer progresses to competence over an average of four years and may take a further five years to achieve expert status (Leach, 1996; Goodyear and Steeples, 2000). An instructional designer's skills are significantly different from those of a class teacher but they are no less complex and a similar timescale of progression from novice to expert may be expected.

Key design skills

The 40 skills identified by Arenicola Designs are shown in Figure 15.1. There is an element of redundancy about some of these items and there are some missing skills such as giving feedback and briefing a tutor.

Nevertheless they represent a formidable repertoire of competences. In practice, course development is done by a team who, between them, should possess most, if not all, of these attributes. Generally they subdivide into four groups (management, instructional design, programming and audio-visual skills) plus one skill that is in a category of its own – English language skill.

Those skills that most clearly relate to instructional design are numbers 7, 9, 10, 11, 16, 17, 18, 22, 23, 27 and 28. We need to ensure that authors acquire and develop these skills and are given early and continuing opportunities to apply them.

Figure 15.1 Course design skills

1. Project management	21. Assessment techniques
2. Client management	22. Questioning techniques
3. Planning	23. Answer analysis
4. Costing & budgeting	24. Management system design
5. Training needs analysis	25. Courseware monitoring techniques
6. Performance analysis	26. Evaluation techniques
7. Task analysis	27. Validation techniques
8. Training techniques	28. Storyboarding
9. Understanding how people learn	29. Audio/video scriptwriting
10. Instructional design	30. Graphics design
11. Writing aims and objectives	31. Animation software
12. English language skills	32. Stills and video production
13. Word processing	33. Audio production
14. Desk top publishing	34. Computer data control
15. Implementation techniques	35. PC programming
16. Media selection	36. Web programming
17. Subject matter research	37. Authoring software
18. Self study design	38. Bandwidth awareness
19. Simulation design	39. Materials production
20. Interactive screen design	40. Delivery platform development

The need for a model

Course-design skills for online and other forms of open and distance learning will be brought to bear more effectively when applied within a model and based on a workable theory of instructional design. In the 20 years between 1970 and 1990 the predominant model for open and distance learning designers (at least in the field of occupational training) was instructional systems design (ISD), which originated in the United States. In the United Kingdom this was adapted under such guises as the Sheffield system and the models applied in the various branches of the Armed Forces.

In the past decade or so such models have tended to wither away. What remains is a random set of skills with little if any theoretical basis. In North America ISD has been superseded or enhanced by newer paradigms such as component display theory and, more recently, instructional transaction theory. These have tended to be described in rather esoteric terms and publications that the average trainer is unlikely to encounter.

One of the critical advances that needs to be made in both North America and the UK is to reformulate such a model of course design with a coherent theoretical background. It is interesting to recall the finding of the Arenicola report that designers believe that they need to enhance their understanding of how people learn. Such an understanding is an essential prerequisite for the evolution of a theory of instructional design. As Reigeluth (1999) observes, such a theory 'offers explicit guidance on how to better help people learn and develop'. He goes on to describe the key attributes of an instructional design theory: it is goal directed, it identifies methods of instruction (ways to support learning) and can be broken down into more detailed component methods.

As I have already suggested, one of the factors that inhibits the development of a model for instructional design that practitioners can readily apply is that much of the work on new models has been carried out by what has been called the REAR (Research Academic Reform) community. The REAR community has tended to focus on general descriptive theoretical models rather than the goal-directed models that are more likely to be of immediate use to practitioners. Moreover they tend to communicate in terminology unfamiliar to the corporate course designer. Good examples of this are the two volumes of Reigeluth's instructional design papers and the ongoing discussions on international standards for learning technology involving experts on learning object metadata.

What is required is the development of a plain-language designers' practicum using an up-to-date model of instructional design on which to base a development programme for practising course designers. This could be applied within the context of an intensive development programme. Such a programme existed in this country some 15–20 years ago in the form of the Project Author programme. A similar development opportunity linked to an acceptable professional accreditation would be one step towards improving the poor standards of course design that are so widespread throughout adult education and occupational training.

References

Arenicola Designs (2000) *Authoring for CBT and Interactive Multimedia*, DfEE, Sheffield.

Goodyear, P and Steeples, C (2000) *The Role of the Tutor in Corporate CBT*, DfEE, Sheffield.

Homme, L E and Glaser, R (1959) *Problems in Programming Verbal Learning Sequences*, paper read at the Symposium on Research Issues into the Study of Human Learning, American Psychological Association.

Kay, H (1979) *Aspects of Educational Technology XIII*, Kogan Page, London.

Leach, J (1996) Distinguishing characteristics among exemplary trainers in business and industry, *Journal of Vocational and Technical Education*, **12** (2).

Merrill, M D (1997) Instructional strategies that teach, *CBT Solutions*, November/December, pp 1–5.

Reigeluth, C M (1999) *Instructional Design Theories and Methods*, Lawrence Erlbaum, Mahwah, NJ.

Skinner, B F (1968) *The Technology of Teaching*, Appleton Century Croft, New York.

Thorpe, Mary (2000) Online learning – not just an eUniversity idea, *Adults Learning*, April, **11** (8), pp 10–12.

Part 6

The vanguard

Part 6 moves outside the immediate world of education to show what other players are doing. The conversion of television to a digital format is opening up some exciting prospects, not least through integration with Web technology. Archives of major television companies contain substantial quantities of educational materials and Web technology is making individualized programming and personal access to materials a real possibility. Steve Pollock and David Squire (Chapter 17) describe some of the experience at the BBC, including the emergence of 'edutainment'. David Dickinson and Valerie Stewart (Chapter 16) anticipate the impact of three major trends outside formal education: the growth of knowledge management as a major concern of employers, the granularization of learning materials and the development of intelligent software and smart cards. It is certain that online learning still has some way to develop and will drive education towards a more learner-managed culture.

16

Towards an androgogy for living in an information society

David Dickinson and Valerie Stewart
Consultant, UK and Industrial Psychologist, UK

Editor's introduction

In this chapter, Dickinson and Stewart take a look at trends in online learning in the wider context of the information society and continuing technological development to give us a view of the future. The fragmentation of information into granular components linked to new systems of organizing and accessing that information will have a dramatic impact on how people engage with learning. Smart cards, personal portals and intelligent software will give learners greater control over their own learning, prompting the authors to explore what they describe as a parallel track – an androgogical rather than a pedagogical approach to online learning.

A student who can weave his technology into the fabric of society can claim to have a liberal education; a student who cannot weave his technology into the fabric of society cannot claim even to be a good technologist.

(Eric Ashby, *Technology and the Academics*, 1958)

The impact of technological change

In the past, a teacher's scheme of work, with its lesson plans and activities, were of necessity linear, synchronous and designed for the classroom. The paper-based format – with its screeds of text, its lists, its indexes – makes for an ungainly transliteration to the world of e-learning, but it is nonetheless the most common by far. We believe that this is symptomatic of the desire to continue using familiar procedures, referencing, and signposting, although in an online world they may be counterproductive and miss important opportunities. Not that we are pointing the finger of blame specifically at the teaching profession or the software designers – everyone uses past experience as the first step in problem solving.

Relying on yesterday's methods can be effective in a climate of incremental change, where adaptation can also be incremental and feedback is usually rich and easy to recognize. But the online world constitutes a qualitative change in the way we manage our interactions. The education system is struggling to optimize its limited resources and inherited skill sets to respond to technological change. Barker (1993) perceptively offers the 'back to zero rule' arguing that in any paradigm shift, if people continue with traditional working methods, they find themselves less effective than they were prior to the arrival of the technology. Some of the effects of new technology fall into the category of 'things we don't know we don't know', which is very uncomfortable. Arthur Clarke said that any sufficiently advanced technology is indistinguishable from magic. Magic is fine as entertainment, but frightening if it is an inescapable and growing influence on life (Handy, 1987; Drucker, 1999).

The teaching profession has been subjected to repeated changes to its goals, curriculum, processes, structure, funding and stakeholders. Some of these changes have been badly planned and the burden of adapting has fallen on the teachers. Some of them have been presented as helpful but are perceived as punitive. Between us, we have been a departmental head, adviser, researcher, consultant and psychologist, and we have direct experience of trying to introduce change into the teaching profession. Frankly, almost all teachers are suffering from 'change burnout'.

Personalized services and social inclusion

The purpose of this chapter is not to add to the debate about pedagogy. We want to suggest that the most appropriate and cost-effective solutions might be found by taking a parallel tack: a structured androgogical approach, more related to active citizenship and modern government yet supportive of the pedagogy relevant to the institution attended. The term 'androgogy' is often used with respect to adult education only (Knowles, 1973). But we are drawn to broader definitions which focus on the shift in the locus of control, the learner knowing that he or she is at the centre of learning, with the teacher as one facilitator of that process.

Politically, socially, logistically, tactically and, importantly for this chapter, technologically, the environment exists or could be created to promote and develop learner-centred learning and other interactions. So the purpose of this chapter is to indicate a variety of initiatives and strategies that have the opportunity to gather their own momentum and become dominant where it matters – in the lives and minds of young people and the adults with whom they come into contact. The very word *education*, coming as it does from the Latin *educare* (to lead out) suggests a relationship between the leader and the led. Learning, on the other hand, is an individual activity; one in which the incentives and the processes are intra-personal. This is an important point because, *inter alia*, there is much research to show that people who describe themselves as happy, effective and self-confident have an internal locus of control (Cattell, 1970). The concept of 'locus of control' is best explained by asking 'who's in charge of your life?' If the answer is, broadly, 'I am', there is a basis for planning and enjoying your own life and probably having the time and energy to give to others. If the answer amounts to 'not me but them', you cannot trust yourself and you almost certainly cannot trust 'them'. That way lies social exclusion.

The economist Galbraith (1992) draws a number of sobering conclusions from one simple proposition: in times past, the discontented in society outnumbered the contented and so it was in the collective interests of the contented classes to throw the discontented ones a bone or two: the right to organize trade unions; a minimum wage; health and safety legislation, and so forth. The contented classes would rather do this than contemplate being dragged through the streets on the tumbrels.

However, says Galbraith, in recent years the balance has tipped, so that now the contented effectively outnumber the discontented. This is partly due to increased earning power for the middle classes and partly due to the effective disenfranchisement of the poor, who can see no point in putting their energies into participation in democracy. The result is that the contented have much less incentive to placate the discontented, although Galbraith points out that this is a rather short-sighted view: there are a great many of them and they will not go away. One small indicator of things to come was the arrest in the Philippines of the person suspected of creating and distributing the ILOVEYOU virus. *Vox pop* interviews with Philippinos could be summed up as 'we may be a third world country, but we have muscle and can exercise it'. We believe that there is a moral, as well as an economic, argument for developing online technologies that engage as many citizens as possible.

Within the global economy, each country is trying to identify the macro-economic edge, and the strategies to achieve it, which will make them more competitive. The common theme is the creation of a knowledge economy. This of course necessitates a foundation of knowledge management. Taking the UK as an example, let us first examine the developing environment that, we believe, is conducive to the encouragement of constructivism, the personal management of learning and androgogy. Secondly, we will outline the programmes and strategies already in progress that could be built on in order to achieve our goals. Next, we will explore the technological advances that now make true learner-managed learning feasible. Finally, we will share some of the work that we are doing to contribute to the development of online environments for learner-managed learning. To achieve a knowledge economy, the UK government has determined that it must first address the 'three wicked issues' – so called because of their importance and complexity. They are: transition to a networked economy; transition to a citizen-centred government and transition to inclusive lifelong learning. The second in the list is a hugely complicated task. It is not simply a problem of restructuring; the unspoken social contract between the parties must also change. For example, one identified strategy, getting citizens to carry and use citizen smart cards (Kabledirect, 2000), implies that they must trust the government of the day, and 'government' in general, not to misuse the data. Without such trust, the citizen may choose to detach himself or herself (for example, see the shrinking of the electoral rolls when the Thatcher government introduced the poll tax). In an inclusive learning society, service providers, including government, must ensure that demand and not supply dominates the process. (The subtleties of supply and demand and their application to learning are key themes of this chapter and will be drawn out later.)

For example, anyone taking even a perfunctory interest in the UK's Department for Education and Employment (DfEE) would have noticed a remarkable transition within the last 12 months. It has become the delivery arm for major social inclusion and regeneration initiatives – for example the National Strategy for Neighbourhood Renewal (Cabinet Office, 2000), individualized learning accounts (DfEE, 2000a), progress file (DfEE, 2000b) and education maintenance awards (DfEE, 1999). All these initiatives send a strong signal to those who can listen that the government intends to make the higher and further education sectors demand responsive.

An even more striking example is the Connexions strategy (DfEE, 2000c) currently being put into place. This includes a smart card (DfEE, 2000d) by which means young people can collect reward points and gain retail discounts for good performance in school and the community and exchange points for a series of benefits, enablers, and discounts. The strategy will be supported by personal advisers, each helping the young people in their care to manage their relationships with educational, social, health and legal services – a comprehensive professional service, delivered by one agency, for all our young people. The contrast with what went before, dealing with young people when they got into trouble, and then through an often-bewildering variety of agencies, should be stunning. The common factor in these initiatives is the demonstrable political will to make learning more pragmatic, relevant to the needs of the individual, and to affirm that all people have the need and the right to be included in our society.

Add to the above initiatives recent increases in funding for improved infrastructure and hardware for schools and colleges, and most of the bricks seem to be in place. What we now need is the mortar to bind them together so that we can learn and communicate in an online world. We believe this could be informed by genuine androgogical values. We need to affirm that, just as people will differ in the way they use real house bricks, they will differ in the way they use these metaphorical bricks. Unless all these initiatives are bound together in a way that is perceived as being personally appropriate, realistic and relevant, none of the services will encourage personal engagement.

The Internet: opportunities and pitfalls

The marketing profession has been quick to see the opportunities in personalization. Internet-based retailers greet you with a selection of choices based on analysis of your recent buying patterns. Although we could live satisfactory lives without engaging with e-retailing or being aware that we are part of a seller's database, we cannot live without the skills of learning and communicating with oneself and others. But in this field little is done, in terms of the software, the content and the human-computer interface, to accommodate the individual, his/her preferences, needs and changing circumstances. No wonder so small a percentage of the population engages, and fall-out rates for e-learning of over 50 per cent are not uncommon. Even in the field of customer relationship management there is a tendency for its acolytes to speak of the demand side but in words and phrases more appropriate to the supply side. They tend to refer to server capacity and technical issues rather than the capability of each individual to access the information and make sense of it within his or her frame of reference. Seely Brown and Duguid (2000) indicate another difficulty with which we can readily identify:

> … some of the people driving us all hard into the future on the back of new technologies, appear to assume that if we all focus hard enough on information, then we will get where we want to go most directly. This central focus inevitably pushes aside all the fuzzy stuff that lies around the edges – context, background, history, common knowledge, social resources. But the stuff around the edges is not as irrelevant as it may seem. It provides valuable balance and perspective. It holds alternatives, offers breadth of vision, and indicates choices. It helps clarify purpose and support meaning. Indeed, ultimately it is only with the help of what lies beyond it that any sense can be made of the information that absorbs so much attention.

(Seely Brown and Duguid, 2000)

This problem, which has the potential to be very serious if it continues to evade resolution, was described by Borges (1989) in his short story *The Library of Babel*. The library is a series of hexagons containing books, and nothing but books. And – here's the catch – between them, the books consist of every possible combination of the letters of the alphabet, plus the space, the comma and the full stop. So it contains:

> all that it is given to express, in all languages. Everything: the minutely detailed history of the future, the archangels' autobiographies, the faithful catalogue of the Library, thousands and thousands of false catalogues, the demonstration of the fallacy of the true catalogue…

The initial reaction was one of 'extravagant happiness' that answers to all the world's problems were stored in some great library. But of course this hope was quickly dashed because the books were inaccessible. Some argued in response that 'men should juggle letters and symbols until they constructed, by an improbable gift of chance, these canonical books' whereas others 'believed that it was fundamental to eliminate useless works' a futile task since 'the Library is so enormous that any reduction of human origin is infinitesimal' and 'every copy is unique, irreplaceable' (Borges, 1989).

We feel this is the way the Internet is heading. Cognitive overload is driving out cognitive complexity, not merely because there is so much information out there but also that, increasingly, we lack the means to differentiate it. Her concern is that, as it becomes easier for a student to download a paragraph, or a whole essay, he or she will lose the ability to think conceptually: to form and test hypotheses; to set personal cognitive challenges and to respond to those from others.

The model of a global information network is now being designed; in the United States it is in the early process of construction. It will grow to interconnect with other information networks, in much the same way as the Internet has grown. But this need not be a Library of Babel; and here is the opportunity for those who are committed to personalization in online learning; this model of information handling will support the concept of granularity. Granularity is the means by which production engineers rationalize the number of components by redesigning to reduce the number of specialist components. Usually this is done by encouraging the use of smaller components that can be used as frequently as possible across a variety of lines. Extend the analogy from engineering components to the global network: think of tiny elements of digital information such as single images, sound files, a sentence or phrase of text. The smaller these elements are, the more flexible will be the way in which they can be used, allowing Web environments to be far more responsive to user context, to localization and ultimately to personalization.

But this is still applying traditional thinking to the possibilities of new technology. Let us apply the granularity of information to the process of accreditation. When Jessup (1991) first proposed the national framework for National Vocational Qualifications, he was frustrated by the size of the units of study and their lack of flexibility. In higher-level technology-based courses where the half life of information is decreasing almost exponentially, by the time some elements of a course have been approved they are outdated. Imagine the concept of granularity being applied to accreditation. A person could demonstrate their competence in a whole range of areas: academic; interpersonal and intrapersonal and also involvement in the community. But each competence would be automatically disaggregated into a series of granular elements that would sit in a dynamic database until needed. For example, in the 1970s the Industrial Society ran courses to encourage women to return to management after they had had their families. The course director said that the first obstacle she had to overcome was to convince the women that they already had a range of management skills – planning, budgeting, crisis management, negotiation and so forth. All they had to do was to learn to apply them in a different context. In the world we have in mind, if an individual wanted to demonstrate their suitability for a job, or further education, and so forth, he or she would be able to use the data-mining technology to fulfil the request. Project Theseus (Harnden, 1994; Harnden and Stringer, 1993) generated some of the most exciting thinking in this field. What began life as a university project to help their own lecturers manage lecture media led to a whole new way of thinking about multimedia architecture, essentially exploring the 'memory' of each multimedia element, its capacity for knowing where it had been used previously and the other elements with which it had been combined.

Of course, these granular elements need to form a coherent whole: each person needs to process them into his or her own gestalt. The point we are making is that the gestalt will be shaped by individuals and their particular circumstances rather than being specified externally by, for instance, an examination board. It is a shift from inputs to outputs and outcomes: a difficult shift for any self-referencing bureaucracy to make, but those who cannot make it will be left behind.

We believe each of these issues, coupled with a fundamental incapacity or unwillingness of service providers, (in the public and private sectors) to come to terms with the notion of personalization, is due in part to an outdated notion of supply and demand.

In trying to come to terms with this, we have rejected the traditional, linear construct of supply at one end of a continuum and demand at the other, for a dynamic model (Figure 16.1) in which supply and demand are represented as two planets around which the user makes a figure-8 orbit. This illustrates the possibility that there must be something beyond the commonly held notions of demand and indeed of supply. As the point on the line (represented by the arrow head on the right of the diagram) passes around the demand planet, the concept of 'supplying in the demand zone' emerges. As the other arrow head (shown on the left of the diagram) passes around the supply planet, so too does the concept of 'demanding in the supply zone'. Either way, the real value to the end-user is right in the centre, where the degree of personalization is at its greatest.

Figure 16.1 An alternative model of supply and demand

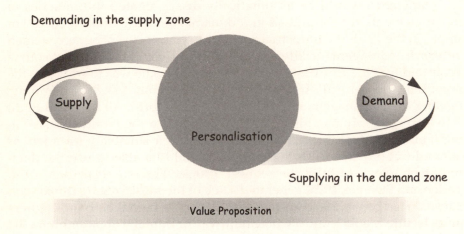

In terms of what this might mean for the learner, imagine a textbook or software package where every illustration is familiar to the learner, where every new competence builds absolutely on the last one gained, where every aspect of the curriculum is relevant to the learner's experience and aspirations and where no element, however small, is in any way incommensurate with that learner's personal profile. Clearly the epicentre of the personalization sphere in the diagram is out of reach at the moment, but for the organizations attempting to get close to it, the rewards will be considerable.

Another way of representing this concept is to think of the e-user inhabiting a force field. At any time three types of forces will be operating: the information utility (the Web and all the information contained in digital form thereon); the access utility (the rapidly growing number of media through which the information utility can be accessed); and the user's life episodes. A change in the user's life – major, such as redundancy, or minor, such as planning a new garden – implies a change in what the user needs to know and to learn. Understanding life episode management and the burden that failure to do this places on young people is one of the battery of tactics presently being explored by the Cabinet Office as a part of its strategy to modernize government.

The access utility facilitates the link between the information available on the information utility and the immediate needs of the user. It therefore plays a key role in personalizing and contextualizing the information the user needs to fully participate in a knowledge society. Four key elements comprise the technology behind the access utility:

- access hardware;
- network access; the Internet service package and the value-added services provided by it;
- a portal or gateway;
- some form of access key, most likely a smart card holding metadata such as name, address, unique identifier, similar to that envisaged for the Connexions card, as well as the capability to be read by a wide variety of access devices.

At the moment, for many people their access utility is in a fixed place and may be controlled by someone else – most likely their employer. However, if the access utility were on a smart card in their own possession they would be able to realign it as they feel the need to do so in line with their circumstances. Because the engine behind the portal uses dynamic, database-driven environments, the next time they log on to the system using their smart card, the information utility recognizes that the environment is changed and so are the information needs. Whether driven by iteration or by major change, the access utility becomes a mirror of the self, and also an intelligent agent that interrogates the information utility for and on behalf of the self it mirrors.

That this level of sophistication would be valuable when applied to online learning is an understatement. Each student would interact with the information utility on his or her own terms. Take, for example, the film *The Full Monty*. There is a point where the would-be dancers are learning the choreography and keep getting it wrong, earning the wrath of their instructor, until one of them says 'it's the Arsenal offside trap innit?' Immediately they get it right and another comments 'why didn't you say so?' The access utility would reflect not just what the student needed to learn but how best to learn it. This would not only make learning more cost effective, by giving each student a personalized learning plan; it would make a qualitative difference to the tasks of learning and teaching.

We have tried to avoid technical issues, regarding them as secondary to the subject matter although we do know what we suggest is technologically possible. However, we now need to include a little technology in order to ensure the reader has the same frame of reference. Most computer learning uses *pull* technology – the user either searching through directories or employing search engines to find the information required. Within certain sectors of the industry, in particular customer relationships management and online shopping, *push* technology is employed. In this way users can be targeted with advertising relating to previous purchases, can be sent details of commodities in which assumptions about lifestyle are based upon postal codes, and so forth. The technology to achieve this is simple using a cookie (a small piece of computer code automatically saved on the user's hard drive) to call up the relevant information.

Let us assume, however, that the cookie sits not on a particular hard drive but on the user's smart card or other input device. When the smart card is inserted into any access device on the user's available network it takes the user straight to a personal portal. The smart card has the capacity to become the ultimate *thin client* – a viable and socially inclusive means of accessing information technology entitlement without needing to own the hardware. Once the portal is accessed, so too can be any *pushed* information, for example e-mail, information that the smart card has gleaned from its neighbourhood: colleges, vocational and personal interest groups, the government's own portals, and so forth. As online languages develop, supporting increasingly flexible application management, and applets covering common application packages (for word processing, spreadsheeting and so on) we would expect these, too, to be rationalized into this portal environment. To make this personal portal successful, for it to be the only natural starting place for an online user wishing to learn or communicate, it needs to be androgogically sophisticated. This is what we shall address next.

Most learner management and active citizenship roles are presently being fulfilled by paper-based solutions. The result is that whereas there is an intention for these strategies to be joined up and interrelated, the means for so doing is far from clear. A particular example of this is Progress File. In England, Progress File is still in the pilot phase. However, its advocates are fighting with the fact that it was produced for paper rather than the computer, in linear and synchronous worksheet form rather than with the flexibility of dynamic database-driven Web environments. If the functionality of Progress File were to be combined with a smart card such as we have described, the result would be closer to an androgogically sound learning and communicating environment capable of responding to the changing needs of a learner in an information society.

However, we have introduced another element into the picture – a personalized decision-making engine. The technology for this has existed for over 60 years, although it requires the e-world to show its full potential. The technique, known as the repertory grid, was devised by George Kelly, a US engineer turned clinical psychologist. He wished to develop a means by which an individual person's view of his or her world could be mapped accurately and non-judgementally. He could then measure how the person's construction of his or her world changed, compare one person's construction compared with another's, and so on. Unlike many psychologists of his time, Kelly was no self-publicist and so his theories and techniques remained the province of a small number of committed professionals; moreover, his contribution could not be fully exploited until the necessary data-crunching power had been developed.

With her colleague John Mayes, Valerie Stewart has put the repertory grid onto an interactive computer platform, Enquire Within™. This software guides users into revealing and then developing their mental map of their chosen topic; it is a value free, pure process, and employs nothing but the user's own words and perceptions. It is the ultimate in personalization. With Enquire Within on their smart card, people making a career change would be able to explore their career choices, discover their training needs and evaluate the usefulness of any training undertaken, explore what their key motivational drivers are, explore the circumstances that facilitate their learning and use these discoveries to 'pull' the appropriate information to them. Enquire Within can be used to explore the user's professional knowledge and interests, and will 'pull' only the information needed to extend his or her range. Managers can use it to review their past decisions and plan future strategy. In fact, wherever you need to understand more about how you personally have constructed your world, Enquire Within will not only do this but it will lead you to greater understanding. (Enquire Within also teaches generic thinking skills by stealth, because it behaves rather like a good Socratic teacher does. And it will relieve teachers of the burden of producing 'one size fits all' linear lesson plans and give them the space to respond to students' individual needs.)

So we already have the technology to make e-learning 'just for me, just in time'. It applies to many other fields besides e-learning, of course. A personalized access utility, shaped by and for the individual user, will undertake an informed interaction with the information utility, congruent with the challenges, opportunities, hopes, fears and interests in the user's life. That is the vision, and it can be achieved. It is a technical challenge with a social and ethical goal: to make the e-world available to all, to embrace those who would have been excluded and to enhance the skills of everyone in our society.

References

Barker, J (1993) *Paradigms: The business of discovering the future*, HarperCollins, London.

Borges, J L (1989) *The Library of Babel in Labyrinths*, Penguin, London.

Cabinet Office (2000) *National Strategy for Neighbourhood Renewal*, HMSO, London.

Cattell, R (1970) *Handbook for the 16 Personality Factor Questionnaire*, Institute of Personality, Assessment and Testing, Champaign, IL.

DfEE (1999) *Educational Maintenance Awards*, DfEE Publications, London.

DfEE (2000a) *Individual Learning Account*, HMSO, London.

DfEE (2000b) *Progress File*, Progress File Publications, Nottingham.

DfEE (2000c) *Connexions: The best start in life for every young person*, DfEE Publications, Nottingham.

DfEE (2000d) *The Connexions Card: Proposal for a public private partnership*, DfEE, Sheffield.

Drucker, P F (1999) *Management Challenges for the 21st Century*, Butterworth-Heinemann, London.

Galbraith, J K (1992) *The Culture of Contentment*, Sinclair-Stevenson, London.

Handy, C (1987) By Way of Encouragement: the path to a better society, *RSA Journal*, December, pp 6–12.

Harnden, R (1994) Theseus: a way of doing, *Kybernetes*, **23** (3), pp 49–58.

Harnden, R and Stringer, R (1993) Theseus: evolution of a hypermedium, *Cybernetes and Systems*, **24**, pp 255–80.

Jessup G (1991) *Outcomes: NVQs and the emerging model of education and training*, Falmer, Brighton.

Kabledirect (2000) *Computer Weekly*, 6 June 2000.

Kelly, G A (1963) *Theory of Personality: The psychology of personal constructs*, WW Norton & Company, New York.

Knowles, M S (1973) *The Adult Learner: A neglected species*, Gulf, Houston.

Seely Brown, J and Duguid, P (2000) *The Social Life of Information*, Harvard Business School Press, Cambridge, MA.

17

Television and learning: ways of connecting media and learning

Steve Pollock and David Squire
BBC, UK

Editor's introduction

Pollock and Squire look at the current and potential use of broadcast media for education and learning. They show how, in the rapid shift from analogue to digital, the UK television industry is making tentative steps to combine television broadcasts with learning content, mixing the benefits of old and new technologies to face the challenge of learning in a digital era. The authors pose questions for broadcasters and educators alike on the impact of broadcasting on learning with a range of new media, and give their hints, tips and reservations for the future. Emerging digital broadcasting technology may turn out to be a powerful force for effective learner-managed learning.

Lesson planning

Any media studies undergraduate knows that the media, and in particular television, can captivate and exert an influence on its audience. According to Broadcasters' Audience Research Board Ltd (BARB) research, over 24.3 million UK households had a television set in 1998. According to the same source, nearly 14.5 of the 58.8 million UK population million switch on *Eastenders* every week. It's mass audience, mass consumption, mass entertainment, and some might argue mass persuasion.

Television has established itself as an intrinsic part of British culture; it informs opinions, stimulates debate and controversy, it distributes information, news and current affairs. It is a powerful force for gelling an often disparate, disconnected society into one nation at times of cultural or political crisis. In the case of the televising of the funeral of Diana, Princess of Wales, it was estimated that 31 million people in Britain and 2.5 billion people around the world watched the funeral on television.

Television asserts itself way beyond the living room where it resides. 'The television is often the centre of collective attention in the living room of a household... families and households are drawn together, and sometimes divided in argument, by this shared experience' (Gauntlett and Hill, 1999). Its influence carries over the garden fence, to the pub and into the workplace or school playground. 'The social activity which derives from watching television [is] an important aspect of television's place in everyday life' (Gauntlett and Hill, 1999).

Television does not only entertain; it can affect people's attitudes and behaviour. Programmes that demonstrate how to do something, such as cookery or gardening, lead audiences to consume, whether it is information, skills or goods, above and beyond the broadcast. The cookery book accompanying the second BBC television series of Delia Smith's *How to Cook* sold 200,000 copies in the first two weeks of print (BBC, 1999). In one episode Smith extolled the virtues of a small frying pan, creating a sales bonanza for the small catering equipment manufacturer, which was previously selling 200 of the pans per year, to orders in excess of 90,000 in a four-month period.

So, if Delia can do it with a frying pan, can television and its associated range of digital media engage, stimulate and educate its audiences, turning them into potential learners at a distance?

This chapter looks at this question from both the broadcasters' and educators' perspectives and comments on the current practice of UK broadcast led education campaigns. It also examines the transfer of media content firstly to the Web, then to other digital platforms like interactive digital television, and is intended as food for thought for the impending digital entertainment and learning age.

Current practice

Let's start with the television itself and how the educational use of television is currently structured. The UK government sets requirements for public service broadcasting for the BBC as well as commercial channels. The BBC, as a publicly funded broadcaster, is statutorily required to provide sound and television programmes to inform, educate and entertain.

The BBC does this primarily in two ways: broadcasting to those who want to participate in some kind of behaviour or social change such as losing weight or giving up smoking, or by helping viewers become more skilled in a particular area, such as learning how to use a computer, or improving their numeracy. This approach enables the audience to either directly or indirectly change attitudes or behaviour, or develop skills. Secondly by providing learning resources with structured content and a clear educational focus, which enables the audience to enhance their learning. All this we are loosely bracketing as 'educational broadcasting'.

Beyond educational television there is perhaps a more subtle and pervasive strand of television production and broadcasting, something we call *edutainment broadcasting*, which is often ignored or unacknowledged as a learning device. (This is a term that these authors are using for the purposes of categorizing a range of programme genres. It is not a term agreed within the broadcasting industry itself.)

Education programmes have traditionally been perceived by the television industry as marginal rather than mainstream; but as 'how to' formats have migrated more towards the entertainment genre, the potential for stimulating more learners has increased. The huge potential of *Walking with Dinosaurs* or *The Human Body* to encourage enquiry has been increasingly recognized. As more and more mainstream programmes include some kind of learning outcomes in their content and yet can be entertaining too, the lines between education and entertainment blur, creating the notion of 'edutainment'.

Each of these uses of television for learning is as important as the other, but they target two categories of audience/learner. We will refer to them as 'browser learners' and 'learner browsers'. The former group comes to the programme with a degree of serendipity, perhaps not even thinking about learning; the latter are people who are already actively searching for learning or participating in it, and therefore are seeking learning content to support them.

Educational broadcasting

Educational programmes are led by clear educational objectives and a learning purpose, where programme structure is intended to reflect specific learning outcomes – whether these are formal, course-related or informal. Educational objectives create the structure and narrative of the programmes, informing the making of the programme and its structure. Educational broadcasting is designed for a specialized, sometimes minority audience. In simple terms the broadcasts become tools for learning used for supporting learners' needs and are constructed accordingly.

One successful example of this broadcasting strand is the BBC's *Learning*

Zone – a separate channel or strand on BBC Two, broadcasting programmes at night for learners with particular needs and interests. Programmes are constructed with the learner in mind, and therefore can be instructional, curriculum led and focused, with clearly defined learning outcomes. Unlike mainstream programmes the *Learning Zone* programmes have elements such as signposting, repetition of ideas, summaries and other educational tools to support the learner or mediator. Effectively, many *Learning Zone* programmes become videos for learning.

Educational television has its place in serving the needs of specific captive audiences that are already in the education system. It creates focused learning resources. You never hear the conversation opener 'did you see that Open University programme on telly last night?' unless it is a tutorial group. Such programmes are unlikely to engage new learners or motivate people to start learning, but that's not what they are there to do.

Edutainment broadcasting

Borrowing the term 'edutainment' from the video games industry helps to corral television programmes with a looser educational content. 'Edutainment' programming is a term that can be used to encompass television formats like natural history, documentaries and some 'doc-soaps'. When this kind of television receives good audience ratings it is often allocated a mainstream, or even peak, viewing slot.

In such programmes the narrative and format of the programme comes first and the educational value comes an implicit second, if stated as present at all. The programme has to actively attract the audience. There are greater expectations on achieving high audience viewing figures: the audience is wider, the purpose of the programme broader and the educational potential does not necessarily appear in the programme maker's brief.

'Edutainment' – the combination of education and entertainment – tells a story; it uses the power of narrative to encourage understanding in ways that a formal approach to education cannot. It can emotionally engage so that the potential learner can construct his or her own way of responding to the story being told.

This is not to say that combining learning and entertainment is easy; there's an art in making programmes that are both engaging as well as educational. Moreover, those who produce curriculum programmes have a different perception of education and learning, different objectives and reasons for making television programmes to those producing 'mainstream' programmes; the notion of learning and entertainment combined within the same programme are culturally inconsistent with mainstream broadcasting.

'Edutainment' helps motivate and stimulate learning (the process of engaging the 'browser learner' back into learning) but the problem is that, all too often, factual and documentary programme makers fail to see the connection between their television output and potential and actual links to learning. Narrative comes first; education connections come a low second – despite the remit to educate as well as entertain, edutainment often leaves the viewer with questions unanswered. The 'Delia dimension' discussed earlier is ignored; there is often nowhere to go, no 'next step'.

Take the Channel 4 series *1900 House* (produced by Wall to Wall Television). The *1900 House* series was innovative, mixing documentary with soap, placing a family into a refurbished replica Victorian home and filming their lives over three months.

A thoroughly modern 1999 family was transported back to 1900 to live in a house restored to the exact specifications of the late Victorian era. They lived there for three months with no central heating, no refrigeration, no detergent and no penicillin, exposed to every detail of turn-of-the-century living from cleaning the cutlery with brick dust to shaving with a cut-throat razor (Channel 4/Wall to Wall, 1999).

Packed with background information and historical facts and statistics, it brought to life the social aspects of the Victorian era, referring to modern day and comparing the turn-of-the-century lower middle-class family with the experiences of modern-day family and social life. The level of historical detail and in-depth research, and how the series placed Victorian life into an understandable context, made the series captive viewing.

Despite the depth of content, context and engaging narrative, there were missed opportunities for educational extension, for a 'next step'. Seven- to eleven-year-old children in primary schools in England study Victorian Britain as part of a history study unit in the National Curriculum at Key Stage 2 (DfEE, 1995), looking at the lives of the Victorians at work, at home, at leisure and at school – all aspects covered in the *1900 House* series. Couple this Key Stage 2 educational objective with the informal hobby interests of many adults in Victoriana, furniture restoration, antiques, and social, political and family history and the programme screams for more detailed information and follow-up resources.

With factually rich television the viewer may want something more, during and immediately after the programme has finished. The audience is stimulated, its curiosity is aroused, but there is nowhere to move on to, no way of accessing more information or focused content, or to follow a line of personal inquiry. The missing link in edutainment programming is where to go next from the point of interest inspired by the television. So how might this next step be facilitated, to make the transition from passive viewing to active learning smooth and seamless?

From television to the Web

One emerging way of bridging the gap between this point of interest – the 'television moment' – and the next step is by leading viewers to associated Web sites. This is by no means a revolutionary concept and is being used across the board by most UK television channels. Television channels like the BBC and Channel 4 create Web sites that provide additional content in an attempt to engage viewers with more interactive services.

These television-related portals can provide a real opportunity for more focused study, whether formal or informal. They are a good starting point in the use of, and transfer to, the growing array of digital media formats and their pedagogical use. The BBC's 'Education Site' and Channel 4's 'Next Step' site are current examples of this emerging practice (for details, see: www.bbc.co.uk/education and www.channel4.com/nextstep).

Broadcasters are integrating this next step with education campaigns, supplying materials and resources on a range of digital media platforms, often linked to local events, in partnership with schools, colleges, libraries and museums. One example of a multi-platform educational campaign is BBC WebWise.

BBC WebWise (see www.bbc.co.uk/webwise) is a BBC campaign giving those who have little experience of the Web their first opportunity to try exploring what the Internet could do for them. In 1999, over 5,000 centres across the United Kingdom, including colleges, libraries and company work-places, provided the computer resources to enable 284,000 members of the audience to attend 'taster' sessions, using a BBC WebWise CD ROM. During the television campaign period, 2.5 million hits were recorded on the associated WebWise Web site, with its Internet basics guide, features and discussion forums.

This was achieved by showing trails for the campaign on television, with 85 per cent of the UK population seeing a trail at least once. In addition 17 million people watched the associated television programmes.

WebWise and other BBC campaigns like *Computers Don't Bite* demonstrate the unique opportunity to capitalize on the television's power to reach the majority of homes in the United Kingdom, promoting skills and knowledge of direct value to the audience. All this interaction and educational extension hinges on the familiarity of the television format, and the power of the 'television moment' to instigate this process. The television and online advertising world grapples with how to bridge the gap between the point of stimulation (watching an advert) to the transaction, buying the product (see Broadcast Bonus, in *Create Online*, Issue 2, August 2000). The same transitional problem can be applied to television and learning. Moving from one media platform (television) to another (Web) is a difficult transition to make, without losing the impetus of the 'television moment' in the exchange.

Educational campaigns like the BBC's and television branded and promoted Web sites go some way in providing the viewer/learner with something more than a solitary, passive television experience. They also point to the potential future direction of television and learning in a digital cross-platform age. Digital technology platforms have the potential to provide much more and more immediately.

But why does a transition from the 'television moment' to the next step not happen more often? Why is there not more cross-fertilization between broadcasters and educators, extending the use of television for learning? The following are some pointers, comments and observations for the future.

Future scenarios

Television versus education

There is a problem of perception, both in the way in which the media views education and the way in which education views the media, which creates a head-on collision of views and conflicts of interest. Television attempts to make sense of things: to engage, to simplify and edit often complex information, to make programmes that are accessible to large audiences. The education world tends to disapprove of this approach, believing that, in the process of making something simpler and more accessible, values and meaning get watered down, giving a false impression of a subject. Television, in the minds of many academics (Gauntlett, 1995) distorts perception and values, oversimplifies and generates passivity and desensitization in its viewers.

From the point of view of broadcasters and programme makers, education fundamentally does not make 'good television'. Education creates too many structures and parameters to work in, leaves too many of the threads undone and does not complete the story being told. Educational content is seen as 'dry' and laborious and doesn't fit within the engaging narrative framework of programme making.

You are left with a situation where the media arouses interest and stimulates viewers with information-rich content but does not take them any further or provide more structured content. Moreover, the education world is often reluctant to use or engage with the power of the medium, believing the premise that 'content is king' will lead learners to see media assets as the be all and end all of the learning process; a quick-fix approach to learning: watch the television programme, follow the online content and pass the course.

Teachers and television

A secondary school Religious Education teacher was heard to say he didn't know what to do with a schools programme that covered Hinduism in 10 minutes, when he had to plan lessons to cover the subject for a whole term. Getting his pupils to watch the 10-minute programme would not help his lesson planning, yet he wanted to engage them in as many different ways as he could. He realized the potential of the medium to draw his pupils into the subject and bring his lessons to life, but the available programme was not in the correct format to help him teach.

Teachers and educators realize the potential of the medium but may not always know how to harness its power or not know what to do with the media they have available, or how to integrate different media in lesson delivery. Furthermore, the medium itself is not always teacher/learner friendly. Teachers and educators do not have the time or the know-how to truly integrate media with learning.

Media to new media

For broadcasters, the transition from linear narrative television to lateral digital media is problematic and somewhat of a paradigm shift for the television industry. It has its benefits, however. The integration of multi-platform delivery into television production extends and enhances programme shelf life, beyond the broadcast – beyond the 'television moment'. It provides media companies with an opportunity to interact more closely with their viewers; it enables more personalized marketing, and extends the audience's interest in the programme. The resources used to make a single programme or series (the out takes, the research and so forth) can be re-used and re-presented on a digital platform like the Web, CD, DVD or interactive digital television (iDTV) channel.

But in terms of merging output with learning, the media industry needs to engage their narrative skills, editorial abilities and research capabilities with the process of learning. It needs not only to supply and re-version its output, but to understand how media assets need to be presented and structured, to enable their extended use in the classroom or virtual learning environment. The television world needs to understand learning design and learning styles.

There are some examples, early days though it is, in engaging browser-learners beyond the broadcast. The BBC's *GCSE Bitesize*, Channel 4's *Homework High*, and Sky's *Reach for the Sky* are setting the standards for (online) production and raising expectations as to television's role in education.

The media and the education 'market'

Media companies are converging and expanding their services and remits. Media giants and conglomerates are entering learning material production and related support services. They have a desire to enter the 'education market' and, for them, this makes commercial sense. There is a captive audience of 565,600 pupils in UK schools (www.dfee.gov.uk/statistics) with direct access to parents and carers, with worries and desires for their child's education. There are 3.8 million students enrolled at colleges in the further education sector in England in 1998–9 (www.fefc.ac.uk), and there were 1.2 million students enrolled on full-time higher education courses in 1997–8 (www.statsbase.gov.uk). The learner browser market is there. The browser learner market is waiting in the wings, potentially limitless.

There seem, in these authors' minds, to be two schools of thought and two needs that require satisfying. If the databanks and archives of the media are to be successfully opened up for learning, one is off the peg, the other bespoke. The first is pre-prepared, packaged educational content, to satisfy the high demand for instant learning materials, made and approved for educational use. The second is an opening of the archives for a more free-form tagging and searching of materials, with teachers, lecturers and curriculum advisers constructing their own route through the content available to them. We are not proposing one approach above the other, rather an opening of minds from both sides of the learning and media fence to facilitate learning in the best way possible.

Online, online, online

No new delivery platform has ever revolutionized education. The original all-pervasive vision for the Open University as the 'university of the air' never actually threatened traditional university courses, but did provide opportunities for those who wanted to learn in their own time, in their own way and at their own convenience. But new technology platforms for learning are not as revolutionary as they might at first appear to be.

The Internet has its limitations. It is not the be-all and end-all; it is often sluggish and cumbersome; it has a tendency to create too many options (the shift from linear to lateral is a long and fraught one) – after all, all play and no structure makes a Web surfer switch off.

Current educational use of the Internet tends to strip out the charisma of presenters/tutors (the 'personality of the cult' extends far beyond the confines of the media). E-learning takes personality and humanity away, under a false illusion that offering learning any time anywhere means that people lose the need for human contact. Tutorial support, guidance, conversation, discussion and immediate feedback are key elements in successful (traditional) learning delivery. So often, and despite the Internet's ability to enable it, communication is lost in a sea of hyperlinks.

A general principle must be to use a media format to its full potential. The right platform used for the right audience, for the right reason. The Web provides great opportunities for communication and debate, the ability to make links (as long as they are guided), to interconnect content and provide user and group interactivity. But, in its current form and by its access via PCs, the Web tends to diffuse the 'television moment' by forcing audiences to move from the couch/remote to the desk/mouse to continue a train of thought.

Digital television habits

Interactive digital television (iDTV) is likely to enhance the next step process beyond recognition, but there are complex cultural shifts in the perception and use of television to deal with first.

The simple four or five channels to choose from and the 'there's nothing on the box tonight' mantra may well be relegated to the twentieth century. Diverse, multi-channel television will undoubtedly embed itself into contemporary culture, after a transitional period, when analogue television is switched off and replaced entirely by digital television transmission. How we perceive television, how we watch television, how we learn to 'graze' and to interact with this medium and other more lateral new media will change and impact on the way it can be used for learning. But for this to be successful in educational terms means that those who are creating the materials need to understand the way in which this new medium can enable learning to take place and can produce the high quality and production standards set by 75 years of analogue broadcasting.

Programme scheduling in an era where repeats and replays are instant and where viewers can personalize their channel viewing to their own interests is upon us (see www.bbc.co.uk/info/revolution/index.shtml). Television production and scheduling will alter to reflect the new digital transmission technology. This should mean more space in the system to accommodate interactive learning services at times when users want it.

But it may also mean educational programmes slipping back into a ghetto, the only consolation being that many of the other channels may well become ghettoized because of the tyranny of the electronic programming guide (EPG), used to navigate digital television channels. The EPG is already being harnessed by children, flicking through digital channels to find cartoons. According to a study by the cable/satellite channel Nickelodeon, children are learning to 'graze': 'If they want Rugrats they want Rugrats now, and they will scroll down the EPG until they find it... They develop their own tricks to memorise the time, date and location of favourite channels and bypass menus' (Brown, 2000). Bespoke digital channels, marketed and targeted at specific sectors, will inevitably segment the audience and could potentially transform the viewer into a more active learner via a targeted education channel.

In the maze of new ways of accessing learning, there is a fundamental requirement to learn how to learn. There's an art in navigating resources and materials (call it what you will – browsing, skimming, grazing) and learners are going to be increasingly reliant on their ability to search, decipher and dissect content from a variety of sources and media. New media learners need to have sophisticated skills to transfer their minds from linear, narrative media to more laterally based media. Perhaps ironically, the best people to do this may well be the 'playstation generation' – those who have honed their lateral thinking abilities on video games, newsgroups, chat rooms and the EPG.

And finally...

Maybe there is no single way forward? Maybe a 'multiple media' approach, combining the best uses of different digital platforms (games console, mobile, PC, DTV) for many users (the viewer/audience, the browser, the learner) and with many uses (from entertainment to edutainment to education) is the route into engaging television and learning.

Pitfalls abound. There are dangers of marginalizing learning in a multi-channel world, dangers of splintering services. Our hope is that learning does not become ghettoized further in the age of multiple, specialized digital television channels, and that teachers and educators embrace new media as a learning tool. There is potential for true convergence, interaction and mass access by the remote control.

Content, materials, resources and sources of information should relate to and inter-work with learning objectives. They are an asset, a tool and a stimulus, but taken out of context and without necessary guidance and learning moderation, they are useless. The pertinent issue is: who controls, monitors and validates this process and who decides what content is suitable for what learning? Will media companies and the originators of 'content out of context' assign themselves with the task of tagging their content to learning objectives?

The experience of creating analogue learning resources has created a concept of understanding how to communicate with learners, and a set of skills, which will need to be applied to the new digital technologies for learning. Ensuring that those who are expert in the media and those who can construct the pedagogy work together is a good way to address the new multiple media nature of digital. Multiple media is exactly that and in the process of transformation will take on its own disciplines, as it becomes a universal tool for learning.

But only when the production values of multimedia learning content reach a really high standard will users increasingly commit to multiple-media learning. We are not at that point yet and have to go a long way before the benefits of 75 years of broadcasting can be fully integrated into new media and before both broadcasters and educators are to seduce learners completely into the delights of multiple media learning.

References

BBC (1999) *Second helpings for Delia fans*, online news feature, 23 December, www.bbc.co.uk/news

Brown, M (2000) Kids stuff, *The Guardian*, 20 March, pp 8–9.

DfEE (1995) *The National Curriculum*, HMSO, London.

Gauntlett, D (1995) *Moving Experiences, Understanding Television's Influences and Effects*, John Libbey, London.

Gauntlett, D and Hill, A (1999) *TV Living, Television Culture and Everyday Life*, Routledge, London.

Learner-managed learning – an emerging pedagogy for learning online

John Stephenson
Middlesex University, UK

So what does it all add up to? Do the reports in this book tell us whether a new pedagogy for online learning is emerging? At first sight the evidence suggests that it is not. Many of the authors argue that online learning is simply another, albeit sophisticated, medium for doing what we have always done. Rather than look for something new, it is argued, we should first concentrate on using the right methodology for the educational purposes we have in mind, and then look at ways in which online learning can be structured to ensure effective learning takes place. However, there are a number of pointers within the chapters that suggest that a re-balancing of the range of pedagogies in use is slowly taking place as more people begin to exploit the full range of facilities that the medium can offer. The re-balancing being stimulated by online learning is towards giving learners greater responsibility for managing their own learning.

Features of online learning

At the simplest level, online learning offers alternative ways of delivering materials previously delivered in print form or in lectures or classes, often appearing to the learner as 'electronic page turning'. In such cases, learners can simply print out the texts and use them as hard-copy handouts. Student assignment reports based on that material make the return trip, posted to teachers as attachments to e-mails for printing out by the teacher. Such usage replicates the pedagogical practice of many lecture theatres and classrooms – content delivery, follow-up activity, materials submitted for assessment, albeit with considerable savings in time and distribution costs.

Online learning, however, has much more to offer than easier text exchange between student and teacher. On the basis of the material in this book the following *features of online learning* should be of particular interest to teachers and learners:

- easy access to and interrogation of high volumes of diverse learning resources, including texts, pictures, library materials, learning tools and other aids to learning assembled by the teacher and institution;
- ease of access to other materials from other sources, including non-educational sources;
- ease of access to experts, inside and external to the institution;
- dialogue: teacher–student, student–student, specialist closed groups, open groups, in real time (synchronous) or over a period (asynchronous), one-to-one, one-to-many, many-to-many;
- routine recording of all transactions in an accessible form capable of adaptation and access as lessons from other students' experience and concerns, threads of discussions and development of argument, frequently asked questions, and for quality assurance and accessible archives;
- access to a range of personal support by e-mail with tutor and mentors, or through specialist or peer discussion groups;
- ease of navigation to sources and persons – within and outside the package of materials – according to the interests and needs of the learner;
- logging or tracking of activities for personal records or sharing;
- multiple levels of engagement via navigation buttons – to different depths of understanding, different volumes of data, difficulty of learning activities – according to the interest or capacity of the learner;
- feedback loops, either from teachers, peers and others or from within the materials themselves through progress checking, quizzes and online assessment;
- linkages to other media, such as sound, video and TV;
- ease of access to simulations of dangerous or complex activities for learning purposes;
- choice of learning styles within the same package according to needs of the learner;
- opportunities for working 'live' in collaboration with others from anywhere in the world.

The overriding feature of online learning is that it has the potential to allow each of the above features to be controlled by learners – at the same time if necessary – in their own learning station, home or place of work. Moreover, online learners are not confined to the materials, services and activities provided by the instructor. If all of the features of online learning are to be exploited to best effect there need to be significant changes in the roles of the teacher and the development of the skills to carry out those roles. We will need to rethink the idea of the course as the main organizing structure for learning.

As many of our authors report, not all of the features of online learning described above are exploited. Even when they are, they are not necessarily taken up by learners without considerable effort by tutors and programme designers to ensure that they are fully used. Many students, it seems, respond to the notion of a course in a traditional manner, seeing the experience as being just another course delivered online rather than an online experience from which considerable learning can take place. As an illustration, the Global Campus programme at Middlesex University (Chapter 12) shows how considerable investment in high-quality software and materials can sustain a traditional instructional mode of delivery – constrained by institutional regulations and student scepticism. In contrast, the Global View programme at Chico, California (Chapter 9) shows how a more adventurous approach by staff in a less constraining institutional environment (they control it themselves) has facilitated a learner-managed international collaboration programme that takes learners beyond the expertise of their professors. The Chico collaborative project makes use of most of the online features and is significantly managed by the learners themselves. Comparison of these two examples suggests that much depends on how the managers of online learning choose to manage (or constrain) the potential within its features. The same online features, it seems, can be used to support either traditional instruction or a fully learner managed approach.

The medium is still evolving

Whether or not online learning encourages learners to become more responsible for more aspects of their learning, external trends are strongly running in that direction. Young people are already adept at surfing according to their own developing interests and companies are pressing for more expertise in knowledge management and knowledge sharing amongst their employees. The hardware and software necessary to take advantage of online learning are increasingly available outside the formal educational system, beyond the control of teachers. Many homes have one of the most powerful learning tools ever invented controlled by potential learners. The tide of 'online anything' is still running strong. Commercial companies, including major publishers, broadcasters and film companies are moving in.

This cultural trend is being matched by technical innovations. Publishers and designers of materials are beginning to *dis-aggregate* their archived materials, broadcast clips and so forth, into bite-sized learning objects capable of being stored and easily retrieved in any order or combination appropriate to the user's needs. This is being matched by developments in electronic *meta-tagging*, whereby each dis-aggregated learning object can be tagged with details of its characteristics, to facilitate high-speed retrieval and re-assembly according to individual learners' needs. New software tools, or 'agents' are being developed that will further reduce learners' dependence upon tutors to mediate what they learn. Intuitive or 'intelligent' agents can give access to complex and multi-level data sources and present material in a format appropriate to the learner's requirements. Some agents can learn about their users' learning styles, interests and intentions intuitively *from the learners themselves*, and automatically gather information, monitor the learner's progress and assist in the planning of further learning.

The way it might be

On the evidence of the chapters in this book, existing pedagogies will continue to flourish online. External pressures and technical innovations, however, are likely to push the next generation of online teaching and learning more towards learner-managed learning. Any new pedagogy that fully embraces online learning is likely to embrace some or all of the following:

- Learning will be substantially learner managed, and not just in terms of location, timing and lack of direct supervision. Learner responsibility will extend to the relevance of their learning to the learner's longer term development and its applicability to and opportunities for involvement in their current interests and activities.

- There will be a major switch in emphasis from the selection, processing and packaging of content *by the teacher* to the selection, processing and adaptation of materials *by the learner*, drawing on multitudinous sources – much of which will be beyond the control or expertise of the teacher.

- Interactions between learners and learners, learners and experts, and learners and non-experts will be a major source of information, advice, reassurance and monitoring of progress, requiring the teacher to ensure that such interactions are encouraged and operate effectively both technically and educationally.

- Networking and collaboration between individuals or groups of learners will be a key learning activity, and will extend globally.

- The educational roles of the teacher will expand beyond pedagogical, subject or age-group expertise to include systems management, technical support, specification of new materials and systems, orchestrator of collaborative learning, advisor on quality and provider of support.

- A new role of educational producer will appear, linking the educational aspirations of teachers and learners with the expertise of material designers.
- The design and delivery of online learning materials will become a major educational activity in its own right, with clear signposting for learners, bite-sized learning objects, multiple levels of engagement, built-in formative assessments, internal and external linkages, connectivity with progress tracking and learning support systems.
- Assessment will accommodate a wide range of learning outcomes, judged as comparable to, though different from, those specified.

Courses, as organizing structures for learning – with fixed syllabi, predetermined outcomes and assessments, and strictly timetabled activities imposed by programme managers – will give way to frameworks or shells of support materials surrounding loosely defined fields of study, generalized outcomes and activities pursued by the learners. Such a framework would embrace:

- clear statements of levels or non-negotiable content for any qualifications involved;
- varied examples of other learners' activities and achievements, frequently asked questions, helpful hints and help pages;
- guidance on accessing and judging the merit of different sources of materials;
- materials and activities to assist with self-diagnosis, prior knowledge and starting levels relevant to the intended area and level of study;
- learning tools and materials to prepare action plans that embrace intended learning outcomes, sources of information, planned activities and linkages, networks, milestones and rationales for what is planned;
- procedures for engaging in debate about the appropriateness, feasibility, level and, where appropriate, formal recognition of the plan;
- materials and support for the review of the programme and reflection on progress;
- assistance with the preparation and marshalling of evidence to demonstrate achievements;
- a learning support environment, integrated with the programme framework or shell, which provides easy access to online support for

tutors, mentors or external specialists, open chat facilities, special interest groups, one-to-one exchanges with a personal supervisor, tracking and personal log services and links other frameworks and activities.

The above scenario is fully learner managed, exploits the features of online learning and is consistent with current trends and developments. It may not happen exactly that way – there are always surprises and disappointments in learning technology. But one thing does appear to be certain: the challenge facing teachers is not *whether* to give their online students responsibility for their own learning, but *how much* responsibility they are going to *deny* or *facilitate*, and *how* they are going to do it.

Index

NB: numbers in *italics* indicate drawings, figures, graphs or tables

WITHDRAWN